PITT SERIES IN RUSSIAN AND EAST EUROPEAN STUDIES ·

JONATHAN HARRIS, EDITOR

BREZHNEV'S FOLLY

THE BUILDING

OF BAM

AND LATE

SOVIET

SOCIALISM

CHRISTOPHER J. WARD

UNIVERSITY OF PITTSBURGH PRESS

Published by the University of Pittsburgh Press, Pittsburgh, Pa., 15260

Copyright © 2009, University of Pittsburgh Press

All rights reserved

Manufactured in the United States of America

Printed on acid-free paper

10 9 8 7 6 5 4 3 2 1

Library of Congress Cataloging-in-Publication Data

Ward, Christopher John.

  Brezhnev's folly : the building of BAM and late Soviet socialism / Christopher John Ward.

     p. cm. — (Pitt series in Russian and East European studies)

  Includes bibliographical references and index.

  ISBN-13: 978-0-8229-4372-3 (cloth : alk. paper)

  ISBN-10: 0-8229-4372-7 (cloth : alk. paper)

  1. Baikalo-Amurskaia magistral—History—20th century. 2. Communism—Soviet Union—History—20th century. 3. Brezhnev, Leonid Ilich, 1906–1982. I. Title.

  HE3138.W37 2009

  385.0957'5—dc22

                         2009000822

CONTENTS

Illustrations follow page 68

PREFACE

MY INTEREST IN the Baikal-Amur Mainline Railway (BAM) dates back to 1988, when I by chance encountered a videocassette copy of director Mikhail Pavlov's 1987 documentary film *The BAM Zone: Permanent Residents* at the Cumberland County Public Library in my then hometown of Fayetteville, North Carolina. Intrigued, I viewed the film and became interested in the railway and its history. The film tells the compelling story of thousands of former BAM builders who, having nowhere to go after the project's fall from grace, eked out an existence along the railway in the hope that one day their lives would improve along what had been known in its halcyon days as "The Path to the Future." I hope that this book will increase the public's awareness of the human and environmental tragedy of the railway's construction. Whatever its future, BAM will always be a part of the lives of hundreds of thousands of people in the former Soviet Union, as it has become part of mine.

I would like to especially thank Donald J. Raleigh of the University of North Carolina at Chapel Hill. His tireless dedication to and passion for the history of the Soviet Union have inspired me to demand more from myself both as a scholar and a person. For their support of my work and for providing me with the opportunity to publish this book, I am grateful to Editorial Director Peter Kracht and Russian and East European Studies Series Editor Jonathan Harris, as well as David Bauman, Lowell Britson, Deborah Meade, Ann Walston, and Alex Wolfe of the University of Pittsburgh Press. My thanks also go to Amy Smith Bell for her editing assistance and to Bill Nelson for creating the maps that appear in this book. I am pleased to recognize the financial support that I received from a Foreign Language Area Study (FLAS) Fellowship, an American Council of Teachers of Russian (ACTR) Advanced Russian Language and Area Studies Scholarship, a United States Department of State Program for Research and Training on Eastern Europe and the Independent States of the Former Soviet Union Advanced Research Fellowship, and the history department of the University of North Carolina at Chapel Hill. The support of Oleg Akimov and Marisa Fushille at the Moscow ACTR office and Graham Hettlinger in ACTR's Washington, D.C., headquarters was particularly beneficial.

Many friends and colleagues assisted me in this endeavor. For their assistance in reading and commenting on various aspects of this book, I am grateful to Robert Argenbright, Roza Bazyleva, E. Willis Brooks, Vladimir Buldakov, Martha Cooley, John Farrell, W. Miles Fletcher, Juliane Fürst, David Griffiths, Sharon Kowalsky, Steven Harris, Viacheslav Isakov, Tatiana Isakova-Bettelyoun, Jeffrey Jones, Aleksandr Karpikov, Eric Kasischke, Lawrence Kessler, Vladimir Kozlov, Thomas Lahusen, Oleg Lebedev, Ilia Levitine, David MacKenzie, Eleonora Magomedova, Shuo Masutani, Kimitaka Matsuzato, Paula Michaels, Galina Mironova, Edward Mozejko, Jacqueline Olich, Gust Olson, William Pomeranz, Kristofer Ray, Donald Reid, Kristin Roth-Ey, Kelly Smith, Lidiia Sholokhova, Valentin Sushchevich, Michael Waganda, Jon Wallace, Katherine Weaver, Christopher White, Micah Williams, Athol Yates, Anthony Young, and Nicholas Zvegintzov. I am especially thankful for the assistance of Galina Tokareva, head of the reading room at the former Komsomol archive in Moscow. Without her encouragement and insistence on detail, my foray through the alphabet soup of the BAM project would have been far more difficult. Finally, I wish to thank my wife Heidi, my son Neil, my mother Carol, and my father Jim for their unwavering support during this project's lengthy development. I could not have accomplished this without each of you.

A note on translations and transliterations: I have used the Library of Congress system of transliteration throughout this work, with the exception that I have omitted the Russian soft sign from proper and place names. I have not used the Library of Congress system, however, for well-known terms (for example, *glasnost*). Commonplace English spellings of well-known individuals have also been used throughout the book (for example, Yeltsin). All translations are my own unless otherwise indicated.

Portions of this work appeared previously in *Acta Slavica Iaponica, Canadian Slavonic Papers, Global Crime,* and *Problemy slavianovedeniia.*

LIST OF ACRONYMS AND TERMS

bamovets / bamovtsy	BAMer (male BAM worker, singular / plural)
bamovka / bamovki	BAMer (female BAM worker, singular / plural)
BMMT	*Biuro mezhdunarodnogo molodezhnogo Turizma* (Bureau of International Youth Tourism)
CMEA	Council for Mutual Economic Assistance
CPSU	Communist Party of the Soviet Union
DOSAAF	Voluntary Society for Collaboration with the Army, Air Force, and Navy
EPG	environmental protection group
GAI	*Gosudarstvennaia avtomobilnaia inspektsiia* (State Motor Vehicles Inspectorate)
GES	hydroelectric station
GlavBAMstroi	main BAM construction directorate
GOREM	*Golovnoi remontno-vosstanovitel'nyi poezd* (chief repair and restoration train)
GTO	Ready for Labor and Defense!
KMK	Komsomol Youth Collective
Komsomol	All-Union Leninist Communist Youth League
LOVD	Line Division of Internal Affairs
MK	*Mekhanizirovannaia kolonna* (mechanized column)
MMD	International Youth Camp
MO	bridge-building detachment
MVD	*Ministerstvo vnutrennikh del* (Ministry of Internal Affairs)
MZhK	*Molodezhnie zhilie kompleksy* (youth housing complex)
NKVD	People's Commissariat of Internal Affairs (subsequently renamed the KGB)
NOT	*Nauchnaia organizatsiia truda* (scientific organization of labor)
OBKhSS	Department for Combating Theft of Socialist Property
OKOD	*Operativnye komsomolskie otriady druzhinnikov* (Operational Komsomol Peoples' Militia Detachment)

ORS	workers' supply department
RSFSR	Russian Soviet Federated Socialist Republic
SKTB	*Spetsializirovannoe konstruktorsko-tekhnicheskoe biuro* (specialized design-technical bureau)
SMP	*Stroitelno-montazhnoe podrazdelenie* (building and erection subdivision)
SMU	building and erection directorate
SSMP	*Spetsializirovannoe stroitelno-montazhnoe podrazdelenie* (specialized building and erection subdivision)
SSO	student construction brigade
SU	*Spetsializirovannoe upravlenie* (specialized directorate)
TO	*Tonnelnyi otriad* (tunneling brigade)
TPK	*Territorialnyi proizvodstvennyi kompleks* (territorial production complex)
US	construction directorate
VODREM	water supply maintenance
VOOP	*Vserossiiskoe obshchestvo okhrany prirody* (All-Russian Society for the Protection of Nature)
VTsSPS	All-Union Central Committee of Professional Trade Unions
VUKO	All-Union Pace-Setting Komsomol Detachment
VUZ	institution of higher education
ZSSO	Zonal Student Construction Brigade

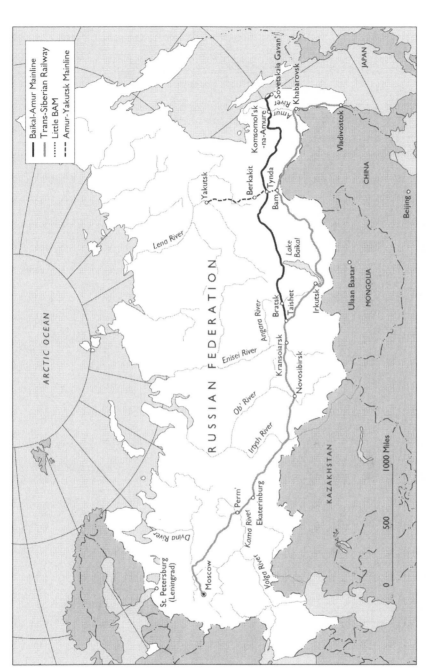

Map 1. BAM, the Trans-Siberian Railway, Little BAM, and the Amur-Yakutsk Mainline Railway.

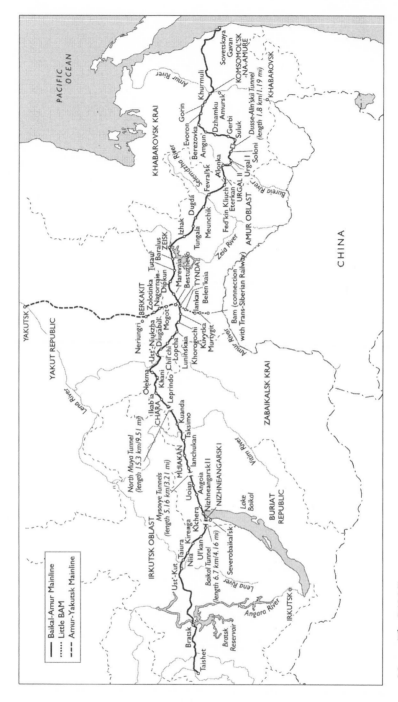

Map 2. The BAM Zone.

BREZHNEV'S FOLLY

1 // Introduction

The Project of the Century

WITHIN ONLY TWO DECADES, the assessment of the Baikal-Amur Mainline Railway (BAM) and its effects on the Soviet Union transformed radically. In 1974, Leonid Brezhnev addressed the Seventeenth Komsomol Congress: "The Baikal-Amur Railway will transform the cities and settlements of Siberia, the North, and the Far East into high-culture centers while exploiting the rich natural resources of those regions!"[1] By 1993, however, the *Moscow News* told a different story: "What is the railway like today? It is in a state of ruin and desolation. Rarely does a train whistle disturb the surrounding silence. The stations are deserted. The passenger terminals, beautiful structures built from individual designs that were chosen in competitions, are neglected. The settlements built by envoys from various republics of the former USSR have fallen into decay. Each year the number of residents dwindles—they keep scattering in all directions."[2]

The chasm of social and political change that these assessments bracket proved more vast than even the four thousand kilometers of harsh Siberian terrain traversed by one of the most ambitious public works projects ever conceived. The BAM was so important to the entire leadership of the Soviet

Union that it tirelessly poured massive resources into a project doomed to crumble almost immediately upon completion.[3] The Soviet Union used the railway to bolster collective faith in the command-administrative system as well as to improve the economy. The personal influence of Brezhnev represented a strong force in the push to popularize the project. In its heyday, BAM represented the quintessential Soviet big engineering project, as the nation's scientists, journalists, academics, and propagandists extolled the railway's virtue as the USSR's first step toward realizing a utopian society. BAM was the last example of Soviet "gigantomania". Like its many predecessors it shared a massive allocation of human and material resources, a highly inefficient utilization of them, and a general disregard for any impact on the environment. The project represented the government's attempt to exploit the USSR's vast natural resources for propagandistic and economic reasons.[4] As one in a long progression of Soviet colossal schemes that the party used to herald the accomplishments of state socialism, BAM was the final expression of post-Stalin Prometheanism, in which the conquest of nature through technology was seen as a panacea for various political, social, and economic problems.[5]

Although the project achieved little in terms of tangible accomplishments, the propaganda effort created by the Soviet state to cast BAM in a favorable light was one of the most significant, if not the greatest, achievement of the eighteen-year Brezhnev period.[6] The resources employed to portray BAM as an epic victory of humankind over nature, a forum for ethnic cooperation, and a catalyst for the economic development of the USSR's eastern reaches equaled and occasionally surpassed those used to build the railway itself. In fact, the propaganda system created to promote BAM touched the lives of more Soviet citizens than its actual construction. Interviews with BAM participants stress the propagandistic nature of BAM rather than its concrete accomplishments.

Interestingly, although never publicly conceived as such by the state, the railway served as a place where Soviet youth could express themselves with relative freedom. This situation was the product of a number of factors. One was that the project's great distance from the centers of state power in the European part of the Soviet Union and Moscow in particular allowed the BAM labor population the space to voice a number of taboo ideas. They could engage in behaviors that were antithetical to official Soviet notions of civil obedience. These behaviors included, but were not limited to, expressions of national identity from a variety of non-Russian ethnic groups that resided both inside and outside the Soviet Union, a voicing of environmentalist and ecological tendencies that in some cases exceeded the scope of what the state allowed, philosophies of women's liberation and expressions of gender equality, and even widespread participation in criminal activity ranging from petty theft to rape and murder.

One of the most intriguing aspects of BAM is the stark contrast between the project's public portrayal in official media outlets and the private impressions of the railway held by those who worked it. Among other things, this disparity reveals the regime's fundamental lack of understanding of one of its most important constituencies—the next generation of Soviet youth, which the project was intended to motivate. Exploring the disparity between BAM propaganda and BAM reality deepens understanding of the social dynamics of the Brezhnev era and beyond. BAM was not simply a microcosm of the Soviet Union during this period; rather, it provided a venue in which behaviors and attitudes that defined public and private discourse throughout the Brezhnevian USSR were magnified to a considerable degree. As such, the history of the Brezhnev years generally and BAM specifically cannot be defined solely as products of an era of stagnation (*zastoi*), as some Gorbachev-era, post-Soviet, and Western observers have characterized it.[7] The BAM project illustrates a multiplicity of dynamic tendencies that shaped this critical period in Soviet history.

After the Bolshevik Revolution of 1917 and subsequent Russian Civil War, the newly created Soviet Union maintained the imperial-era emphasis on railway construction and added a new push to mobilize the populace toward achieving a common goal of constructing socialism.[8] A series of ambitious undertakings drew international attention to the Soviet Union's program of rapid industrialization. This was particularly true in the case of Magnitogorsk, a steel-making complex that was built in the southern Ural mountains from the late 1920s to the mid-1930s.[9] Describing Magnitogorsk, American socialist and Magnitogorsk welder John Scott remarked that "in Russia . . . the world's most gigantic social experiment is being made—amidst a galaxy of picturesque nationalities, wondrous scenery, splendid architecture, and exotic civilizations."[10] The construction of Magnitogorsk provided the Soviet Union with a steel-producing capacity that soon rivaled those of the United States and Western Europe. An integral part of the authorized propaganda campaign behind the Magnitogorsk and other contemporary efforts was the official apotheosis of Stalin himself, in which the mass media portrayed the Soviet dictator as a modern-day Prometheus who successfully harnessed the power of nature for the good of all Soviet people.[11]

During the Stalin years, such construction schemes as the Turkestano-Siberian Railway (commonly known as Turksib), the Moscow metro system, and the Belomor (White Sea) Canal in the northwestern part of the USSR closely integrated the country's rail and water transport networks, albeit with substantial human and material costs that the Soviet government had no qualms in accepting.[12] Also during this period, the Dneprostroi dam and hydroelectric project brought flood control and cheap power while fostering a sense of inclusion among the thousands of young Soviet citizens who had tamed the wild Dnepr River with tractors and "socialist fire."[13] Each of these efforts helped to augment the Soviet Union's industrial capacity and advance the careers of those Communist Party of the Soviet Union (CPSU) members who managed to avoid the Great Purges of the 1930s and emerge as the country's new leadership.[14] Two of these surviving managers were young CPSU members Nikita Khrushchev and Leonid Brezhnev.

The Khrushchev-era Virgin Lands Campaign, which sent young Soviet men and women to introduce mechanized agriculture to the republic of Kazakhstan and other areas of the USSR, pointed to the state's sustained interest in extending its control over nature but represented a distinctly different type of mass mobilization project than the costly and ultimately successful endeavors of the Stalin era.[15] Although Turksib had successfully connected the burning deserts of Soviet Central Asia and the frozen tundra of Siberia, the Virgin Lands Campaign ran into difficulties after initially delivering bumper harvests from the steppe soils of Kazakhstan. In the mid-1960s, the state promoted Sibaral, a plan to redirect the paths of several major Siberian rivers to control flooding and provide water for the parched cotton fields of Soviet Central Asia. A number of fantastic schemes were proposed, including the use of nuclear weapons to reverse the flow of the Irtysh and Ob rivers in an effort to bolster the flow of the Amu Darya River, which leads to the Aral Sea.[16] The government's primary motivation for such a radical plan as Sibaral was that it could provide an economic stimulus for the USSR's impoverished Central Asian republics. By the mid-1980s, however, a series of technical glitches and environmental concerns doomed the project, and the state officially abandoned Sibaral during the late Gorbachev years.[17]

Long before BAM came to be known as the "Project of the Century," earlier projects of Russia's imperial and Soviet eras laid the groundwork for

Brezhnev's folly. BAM's legacy begins with the construction of the tsarist Trans-Siberian Railway in the late nineteenth century. Begun in 1891, the original route of what would eventually become the 5,772-mile Trans-Siberian Railway was completed in 1905 during the Russo-Japanese War.[18] With the outbreak of World War I in 1914, the tsarist government relocated the railroad around the southern shore of Lake Baikal beginning in 1916 as a replacement for the Trans-Siberian Railway's original and vulnerable course through northwestern Manchuria. That area had been held by Japan during a war with Russia in 1904 and 1905 and would again fall under Japanese control in 1932 as a part of the Japanese imperial protectorate of Manchukuo. Part of this original section of the Trans-Siberian is now known as the Trans-Manchurian Railway, which splits from the Trans-Siberian Railway at the city of Taishet in Irkutsk Oblast (region) and ends at the Chinese capital of Beijing, nearly six thousand miles from Moscow. Another section, known today as the Trans-Mongolian Railway, begins at Ulan-Ude, the capital of the Russian Federation's Buriat Autonomous Region, and runs to the Mongolian capital city of Ulaan Baatar.

The BAM of the 1970s and 1980s was not the first undertaking to carry the name Baikal-Amur Mainline Railway. In fact, it was the third such project. Built between 1932 and 1941 and 1943 and 1953, respectively, these endeavors stretched from Komsomolsk-na-Amure in Khabarovsk Krai (region) to Sovetskaia (also known as Imperatorskaia) Gavan, also in Khabarovsk Krai.[19] These railroads were built by labor camp inmates, military personnel, and in the case of the 1943–1953 project by thousands of German and Japanese prisoners of war.[20] It is estimated that perhaps 150,000 of these forced laborers died during construction of the railway, which was abandoned after Stalin's death in March 1953. The idea of restarting the BAM project would not again gain official favor until the Brezhnev era.

In contemplating a third BAM attempt in the late 1960s, the state hoped that a completed BAM would serve as the prototype for further conquests of the Soviet Union's vast and resource-rich northeastern frontier in the twenty-first century.[21] The project's boosters within the upper echelons of the CPSU, who were in their forties and fifties at the outset of BAM, came of age during the so-called Stalin Revolution. Spurred by the "great purges" of the Stalin period, this was a period of sweeping economic, social, and cultural changes in which a new and younger cohort of Soviet citizens, many of whom had little or no direct experience in the Bolshevik Revolution, were molded into the nation's elite administrators, academics, and military officers.[22] As a product of that era, BAM's advocates sought to organize and motivate a new generation of young people to serve as the labor force for this fresh attempt to open Siberia's vast natural resources to exploitation. The railway's planners were also eager to establish a secondary lifeline between the European USSR and the nation's eastern reaches in the event that the Trans-Siberian Railway fell into the hands of the Chinese or another rapacious enemy of the Soviet Union.

After several years of planning within official circles, the Komsomol (the Party's youth organization) and the USSR Academy of Sciences announced plans to begin construction of a new BAM in the early 1970s.[23] As opposed to previous undertakings, this incarnation of the railway would be the responsibility of and under the direct supervision of the Komsomol, rather than the Party itself. With the beginning of construction in March 1974, the Soviet Union witnessed a mobilization of the nation's youth in a colossal struggle between humans and nature in a distant sector of the country that had not been seen since the Virgin Lands Campaign some twenty years before. With BAM, the state asked the youth for self-sacrifice and "fraternal cooperation" to achieve a common goal of the Soviet people—the economic and social strengthening (*ukreplenie*) of the Soviet Union. By constructing a "Second Trans-Siberian Railway" (Vtoroi Transsib) between Eastern Siberia and the Far East, BAM's supporters intended to exploit the vast natural resources of Siberia and the Soviet Far East and also to bring "civilization" to some of the USSR's most desolate regions.[24] Soviet citizens would hear these proclamations repeated numerous times between 1974 and 1984 as the state lionized BAM as "the project of the century" (Stroika veka) and "the path to the future" (*Put k budushchemu*).[25]

BAM Basics

The Brezhnev-era BAM railway eventually stretched some 2,305 miles (4,234 kilometers) and was built on some of the planet's most inhospitable terrain. It runs some 380 to 480 miles (610 to 770 kilometers) north of and parallel to the Trans-Siberian Railway. During the period under examination in this book, the region crossed by the railway's tracks was referred to as the "BAM Zone" (Zona BAMa). This region includes those areas within the watersheds of Lake Baikal and the Amur River, the latter of which forms a major part of the contemporary Russian border with China.[26]

Approximately 1.2 million square miles in area, the BAM Zone is crisscrossed by a number of formidable Siberian and Far Eastern rivers, including the Amgun, Bureia, Kirenga, Lena, Olekma, Selemdzha, Vitim, and Zeia. The area presented geologic, seismic, climatic, and epidemiological challenges to its would-be conquerors, as much of the region is composed of taiga.[27] Within this area, BAM begins at the Eastern Siberian city of Taishet, located to the northwest of Lake Baikal, and moves east across the Angara River at the city of Bratsk, whose hydroelectric station was made famous by the poet Yevgeny Yevtushenko in the his 1967 work *Bratsk Station*. The railway then crosses the Lena River on its way to the city of Severobaikalsk, at the northern edge of Lake Baikal. BAM then crosses the Amur River at the city of Komsomolsk-na-Amure, and it terminates at the Far Eastern port town of Sovetskaia (Imperatorskaia) Gavan on the Pacific Ocean. Today, the railway includes 21 tunnels totaling 29 miles (47 kilometers) as well as more than 4,200 bridges totaling approximately 260 miles (approximately 400 kilometers). Of the railway's total length, some 913 miles (1,469 kilometers) of its track was electrified as of 2007.

In its heyday, BAM represented the quintessential Soviet "big science project," as the nation's scientists, journalists, and academics produced a volume of scholarly literature extolling the railway's virtue: it would be the USSR's first step toward realizing a utopian society in the early twenty-first century.[28] During the Tenth Five-Year Plan (1976–1980) and beyond, BAM's proponents boasted that the railway would open the entire eastern third of the Russian republic to economic development. BAM was one in a long progression of Soviet colossal schemes, most notably the Virgin Lands Campaign and the Soviet space program, which the party used to herald the accomplishments of state socialism.[29] The Soviet Union employed BAM to improve the economy as well as to bolster collective faith in the command-administrative system. The personal influence of Brezhnev, who was a keen supporter of the project, represented a strong force in the push to popularize BAM. Although no definitive figure of BAM's cost exists, the general consensus in the scholarly community is that the Soviet Union built the railway for between fifteen and twenty billion U.S. dollars (in 1980 money) and that approximately one percent of the USSR's annual gross national product was devoted yearly to its construction from 1974 to 1984. The expenses associated with moving approximately 300 million cubic meters of earth, as well as building thousands of bridges and nearly two dozen tunnels, contributed greatly to the railway's high price tag.[30]

More than any other factor, BAM's large construction force (known collectively in Russian as *bamovtsy*, best rendered in English as "BAMers") was defined by its youthful composition. Between 1974 and 1984, BAM construction involved more than five hundred thousand people, approximately two-thirds of whom were members of the Komsomol. Soon after it began, the Communist Party designated the endeavor as an "All-Union Komsomol Pacesetting Project" (Vsesoiuznaia Komsomolskaia udarnaia stroika). This appellation meant that from an organizational standpoint, the Komsomol was responsible for organizing both the labor and the political activities of those Soviet youth deemed worthy of membership in the young people's organization. In addition, the youth league was charged by the Party to oversee all BAM construction and place its own administrators and members in prominent positions throughout the project's bureaucracy. The burden of staffing and running BAM ultimately proved too onerous for the Komsomol to handle successfully.

This BAM labor pool also included some professional railway workers and soldiers in the Soviet armed forces. Although military personnel were employed in the construction effort and by some post-Soviet newspaper reports accounted for around 25 percent of the railway's labor force, the exact numbers and activities of draftees on BAM have been difficult to document.[31] In contrast to the projects of the Stalin era, in which forced labor was used frequently, no prison labor was used in the construction of the third BAM. This fact was revealed in a remarkably candid statement from Brezhnev, who stated that "BAM will be constructed with clean hands only!" (of course, this meant that the BAM construction force would not include coerced labor). Research indicates that Brezhnev's categorical statement remained true throughout the construction process.[32]

From an ethnic standpoint, the majority of BAM workers were Russian, as the proportion of ethnic Russians remained at around 60 percent throughout the decade.[33] While many of these individuals hailed from the USSR's Russian Republic (RSFSR), a number of ethnic Russians who worked on BAM came from a number of the other fourteen Soviet republics, most notably Belorussia, Kazakhstan, and Ukraine. As for the non-Russian BAMer population, it was highly diverse. Youth from such far-flung areas of the Soviet Union as Estonia, Kyrgyzstan, Latvia, and Uzbekistan came to work on the railway along with thousands of young people from a number of nations in the Soviet Union's global spheres of interest. These included representatives from the Warsaw Pact nations (particularly Czechoslovakia, East Germany, and Poland), as well as other such Soviet client states as Angola, Cuba, Mozambique, and a number of nonaligned nations like India. Women represented some 40 percent of the BAMer population, nearly half of whom were under twenty.[34]

Why would anyone want to work on such a difficult and poorly managed project? There were a multitude of reasons, which in some cases included a genuine desire by BAMers to advance the state by participating in the signature endeavor of their generation. This motivation was more common than some Westerners might expect, as the Soviet Union had always possessed individuals who expressed true faith in the state, at least in public. However, interviews with a number of BAM participants reveal that although many of them initially possessed genuine enthusiasm for building BAM, they soon lost that sentiment after seeing the project in the flesh.[35] But there were other reasons a person might want to work on BAM, including a desire for financial gain. Those who completed a tour on the railway received triple pay and were promised future vouchers for new apartments and automobiles, which were almost never received, however. Finally, in many cases, some young bamovtsy had a burning desire to leave their homes and seek out adventure (and often trouble) in a place far from the strictures of the nation's more established communities.

Promoting BAM's Construction

In the mind of Soviet officialdom, BAM would restore national pride and prove to the world that the USSR was still capable of completing a large-scale public works campaign through a massive mobilization of human and technical might. Unlike its predecessor, the tsarist-era Trans-Siberian Railway, BAM would be laid down with "Leninist enthusiasm" through the barren taiga toward the promised land of Communism.[36] Indeed, both economic and strategic concerns pushed the Soviet leadership to promote BAM. Brezhnev conceived of the railway as *the* project of the era of "developed socialism." What was "developed socialism" and why did Brezhnev link himself so closely with this concept? After the 1936 Soviet constitution declared that socialism had already been achieved, Stalin's successors (including Brezhnev) coined this term. The notion was created to explain the Soviet Union's development after Khrushchev's proclamation that the USSR would reach Communism by 1980, which of course it did not. Rather than repudiate Khrushchev completely, Brezhnev and his cadres used developed socialism to indicate that the USSR was still on the path toward Communism, despite Khrushchev's unattainable deadline. Such unattainable deadlines came to characterize BAM—the project was plagued with a series of embarrassing missed deadlines.

Brezhnev, who was now the primus inter pares within the Soviet government, adopted the railway as his pet project. In his mind, the undertaking served several purposes. Past experience showed that involvement in a major project of this sort could help to legitimate the regime in the eyes of a new generation. The railway had the added benefit of deflecting attention away from the government's crushing of the so-called Prague Spring in Czechoslovakia and its ongoing attempts to silence dissent. For Brezhnev, the technical and social exigencies of building the "path to the future" (*Put k budushemu*) were problems to be solved as BAM construction began, not before.

Armed with the general secretary's personal seal of approval, the Komsomol (with the support of the USSR Ministry of Transportation) began mustering and dispatching groups of inexperienced and untrained youth to the distant BAM Zone without having carried out sufficient geologic and topographic surveys of this rugged area of North Asia. The necessity of providing such critical information to those who actually built the railway was only an afterthought in the rush to complete BAM by 1984, a promise that Brezhnev repeated several times before his death in November 1982. In the aftermath of Khrushchev's declaration that the Soviet Union would achieve communism by 1980, Brezhnev could not afford for BAM, one of the most prominent symbols of his "scientific-technical revolution" (which had actually begun during the Stalin years) to be behind schedule. This movement, a common propaganda theme throughout the Brezhnev years, stressed technological upgrading and increased scientific education among managers and workers to overcome shortcomings in planning and production.

Party and state economic officials in both Moscow and the BAM Zone viewed the railway as an economic panacea that would convert the Soviet Union into a transport conduit for goods traveling between its Eastern European allies and the burgeoning Pacific Rim economies, thus making the USSR an indispensable link in the movement of raw materials and finished goods across Eurasia. BAM representatives hoped that the railway would allow vast quantities of Soviet petroleum and timber to be shipped to the energy-hungry and resource-poor Pacific economies, while providing the USSR with high-quality consumer products, especially electronics, from East Asia. Many journalists and Communist Party officials based both in the European USSR and in the BAM Zone itself viewed technology in general and the railway specifically as part of the officially promoted scientific-technical revolution. Proponents of the project boasted that the railway would allow Soviet citizens to exploit the riches of Eastern Siberia and the USSR's Far East. In addition, *bamovtsy* would also be molded into model Soviet citizens in the process of building the railway.[37]

The regime undertook BAM to ease tensions among a number of potentially disaffected groups, including youth, members of minority ethnic populations, and women. BAM was to be the thread that would bind these loose elements of Soviet society into a tightly knit cloth that would ensure the Soviet Union's long-term survival. That this grandiose undertaking ultimately failed in this ambition is by now self-evident. But that failure is far from the most interesting aspect of the story of BAM. Rather, the compelling aspect of BAM is found in those who labored to blaze its path across the subarctic taiga and to a future Russia that they could not begin to imagine.

2// Prometheanism versus Conservationism on the Railway

The Baikal-Amur Railway crosses all of Eastern Siberia and the Far East. The construction of this railroad will cut through the expanse of Siberia and open that region's inestimable natural wealth to industrial development—towns and cities will emerge alongside factories and mines on the face of this new land.

Leonid Brezhnev to the Seventeenth Komsomol Congress, 1974

A N ELABORATE, officially generated propaganda apparatus heralded the construction of the BAM Railway as the vanguard of Soviet Prometheanism. This ideology promoted the notion that humankind would conquer nature by using technology to push BAM through Siberia and the Soviet Far East. But within the railway's large construction force (known collectively in Russian as *bamovtsy*, best rendered in English as "BAMers"), some workers espoused a conservationist consciousness in the struggle to determine the fate of the BAM Zone's ecology. These BAMers' experiences mirrored a larger trend felt throughout the Soviet Union during the Brezhnev years. By the early 1970s, some Soviet citizens had begun to publicly express concern over the widespread damage that centrally planned industry was causing in their country.[1]

Soon after the massive project's inception, a small but influential group of administrators—based primarily within the All-Union Leninist Communist Youth League (the Komsomol) and the USSR Ministry of Transport Construction—voiced their concerns. With the central bureaucracy urging completion of the railway on schedule, these administrators questioned the impact of the railway's construction on the ecology of Eastern Siberia and the Soviet Far East. BAMers themselves engaged in a debate over whether to actively protect the local environment. This debate originated within a framework that was both created and administered by the twin pillars of official Soviet society—the government and the Communist Party of the Soviet Union (CPSU). Although the discussion was at times dynamic and even divisive, those BAM bureaucrats who attempted to inculcate a sense of environmental consciousness to their subordinates never directly challenged the Party's authority to dictate environmental policy. Nevertheless, the disagreement among BAMers and others outside the BAM Zone over what degree of attention should be given to the fate of flora and fauna along the railway's route did not cease after BAM's announced completion in 1984. Instead, the discussion expanded in scope and boiled over during the Gorbachev years, eventually contributing to the demise of the entire Soviet experiment in 1991.

On one side of this environmental debate were journalists and high-level administrators based outside the region (mainly in Moscow) who promoted the BAM project's Promethean qualities. These developers maintained that any obstacle put forward by nature could be conquered by humankind through the use of technology. Showing little regard for environmental concerns, these individuals served as the mouthpiece of one perspective of the official rhetoric. They characterized the BAM Zone as a "virgin territory" with abundant resources ripe for immediate and complete exploitation. Representing another view were the BAM "environmentalists"—namely, a group of locally based scientists and higher CPSU, Komsomol, and government officials in Moscow who rejected Prometheanism as a problematic philosophy. If left unchallenged, they felt, the project would ravage the delicate ecological balance of the BAM Zone's permafrost and forests. These individuals struggled to instill environmental awareness in the larger public, but their message was only moderately successful because of their small numbers and near total lack of support from the center.

In addition, this effort to bolster environmental consciousness was likely ignored by many of the half-million *bamovtsy* who actually built the railway. The majority, many of whom were under twenty-five, lacked adequate knowledge of railway construction and sought merely to complete the project on schedule to receive lucrative bonuses (some of which equaled a worker's entire annual salary) from such agencies as the Ministry of Transport Construction and the Ministry of Railways. In a quest for financial remuneration and career advancement that rewarded meeting deadlines and building quotas on time or ahead of schedule, many young BAMers ultimately ignored the conservationist message espoused by those in the scientific and governmental communities.

Nevertheless, the self-styled BAM conservationists used the local press to heighten BAMer awareness about the environmental damage caused by railway construction. Local editors and journalists were more sympathetic to the cause than most national publications because of their firsthand knowledge of the dire ecological situation in the BAM Zone. Many local journalists, scientists, and administrators examined and exposed the ecological damage caused by those who laid track carelessly or clumsily employed high explosives to build the railway's thousands of bridges and tunnels in early 1974.[2] Although some local groups attempted to increase environmental consciousness throughout the railway's decade of prominence, they depended on state support and approval for both their livelihood and social standing, thus limiting the parameters and the intensity of environmental activism in the BAM Zone. An important qualification, however, must be made. The very existence of an embryonic and often quiescent BAM conservation movement during the Brezhnev years represented a sprout of civil society *within an official context,* defined as much by the periphery as by the center, that flourished after the removal of state strictures.

Beginning with the Dneprostroi electrification project and continuing with the Belomor, Volga-Don, and Volga-Moskva canals as well as the Virgin Lands Campaign, scholars have examined the subservient role nature protection has played to the expediencies of state economic development in the Soviet era. From once modest origins in the late 1980s, scholarship on the Soviet environmental movement has grown steadily in recent times. Douglas Weiner, the foremost environmental historian of the Soviet era, has noted that the state employed mammoth development projects both to augment its legitimacy in the public eye and to deflect attention from other problems in society.[3] His scholarship reveals that environmentalists and their causes served state interests but nonetheless retained a modicum of independence. The BAM project was no exception. The state used Prometheanism as a recurrent legitimization theme in such national publications as the Communist Party newspaper *Pravda* (Truth) and the government daily *Izvestiia* (News), while ecoconscious coteries of BAM Zone activists voiced their concerns in a far more muted fashion.

The historian Paul R. Josephson has remarked that during the Gorbachev era, many scientists and others noted with alarm the environmental damage done in the name of BAM construction.[4] This expression of concern contributed to a loss of faith in "big science" among the Soviet populace as a whole. But this process actually began among concerned BAMers during the Brezhnev era. These individuals did not espouse sentiments that were antithetical to the state, as did the members of the dissident movement at that time. Rather, the BAM environmentalists firmly believed that the solutions to the ecological woes in the BAM Zone lay within a number of preexisting state institutions.

Among scholars working in the former Soviet Union, Oleg N. Ianitskii has produced a number of monographs that trace the growth of the environmental movement beginning in the late 1980s. Ianitskii focuses on student groups that awakened the public to such misguided plans as the proposed Siberian rivers diversion project and environmental problem areas including the Aral Sea with its increasing salinity. Although Ianitskii does not look closely at BAM or at the years before Gorbachev's ascension in 1985, he observes that individual concerns over the destruction of nature, which were sparked by but not nourished by officialdom, motivated some BAMers to pick up the banner of conservation even before the profession of environmental crusader became popular in Gorbachev's time. Ianitskii concurs with Weiner that most students did not conceive of environmental activism on their own; instead, they joined state-sponsored environmental clubs whose members only later became more strident in their criticism of official environmental policy.[5] The scholar Peter Kenez has focused on the development of Soviet propaganda during the decade after the Bolshevik revolution. He defines the "Soviet concept of propaganda," in which the purpose of propaganda is to convince and inculcate official doctrine through education rather than brainwashing. Kenez sees "one voice" running through Soviet journalism between 1917 and 1929. Articles on the BAM railway written in the center from 1974 to 1984 show a similar monolithic perspective in their adherence to Prometheanism.[6]

Journalists Build a Promethean Language

With few exceptions, journalists and administrators based outside of the BAM project created a rich but unchanging Promethean language to describe it. They urged those living in the BAM Zone to use the region's natural riches without hesitation. The use of a Promethean lexicon represented a critical component of the so-called BAM myth that emerged after the project's beginning in 1974. The officially sanctioned representation of nature as a treasure trove of endless resources can be gleaned from numerous journalists' characterizations of the BAMers as "trailblazers" (*pervoprokhodtsy*), whose eagerness to conquer nature equaled their dedication to finish the railway 1984. In an archetypal example of this rhetoric, *Izvestiia* correspondent Leonid Shinkarev proclaimed "glory to the pioneers!" soon after the project's inception.[7] BAM hagiographer S. Vtorushin touched on a commonly used Promethean chord when he stated that "BAM is the key to the riches . . . of Eastern Siberia and the Trans-Baikal region" and boasted that the BAMers' labor would produce "millions of tons of South Iakutiian coal" for the Soviet economy.[8] Furthermore, many other accounts predicted that the BAM Zone would eventually serve as a rich source of hydroelectric energy. The Zeia River, for example, was estimated to be able to provide 300,000 kilowatt-hours of electricity.[9]

Journalists Sergei Bogatko of *Pravda* and B. Prokhorov of *Izvestiia* related in great detail the BAMers' first fearless foray into the depths of the BAM Zone. Prokhorov conjured stirring images of the utopian days that BAM would usher in with the use of words like "dawn" and "morning."[10] Bogatko went as far as to proclaim the railway to be "the light in the darkness" of remote Chita Oblast (district).[11] Finally, contributors A. Suturin and N. Petrov of *Gudok*, the daily newspaper of the Union of Professional Railway Workers, agreed with Bogatko that as "seekers" (*podymakhiny*) and the "trailblazers of tomorrow," the BAM workers were taming nature successfully, despite earthquakes, extreme temperatures, and an ever-present threat of disease.[12]

The All-Union Komsomol Shock Construction Brigade, which early on prepared the way for the arrival of the main labor force by dropping thousands of "first wavers" into the BAM Zone by helicopter, was of particular interest to BAM propagandists.[13] In 1974, A. Iankovskii of *Gudok* noted that these individuals had come en masse directly from the Seventeenth Komsomol Congress in Moscow with an insatiable urge to confront wild nature.[14] Iankovskii remarked that although bitter cold and mountains of snow presented tough natural obstacles to socialist progress, these realities were not insuperable because of the superiority of Soviet technology over the taiga. In another variant, a *Pravda* editorial team dispatched to the region in 1981 marveled at the size and power of the construction equipment, which in their words demonstrated "*Russian* might" (*rossiiskoe mogushchestvo*) in Siberia.[15] Their use of the word "Russian" rather than "Soviet" indicated that, at least for these writers, the glory of mechanization was a distinctly Russian, and therefore non-Soviet, attribute.

Other writers employed martial analogies familiar to most Soviet citizens by portraying the BAMers as a military vanguard engaged in an epic battle against nature amid the permafrost. Several reporters used the trope of "shock-brigade effort" and reveled in descriptions of the workers as "warriors" in an effort to induce more workers to come to the area.[16] In 1974, *Gudok* correspondent B. Prokhorov embraced a military vocabulary in his profile of "shock" (*udarnye*) railroaders. In his interviews with those living in the tent city of Zvezdnyi, he described the first BAMers as the "vanguard of the nation."[17] Another *Pravda* team looked at the battle to build BAM at the "front" as well as the "rear," where "all the power of socialist industry" was clearly visible.[18] Two Moscow-based journalists riding along a remote stretch of track in the Buriat Autonomous Soviet Socialist Republic (ASSR) described the railway as a "line of courage" and declared certain victory over the region's harsh topography.[19] For *Izvestiia*'s A. Kleva, the never-ending push of "assault-work" (*shturmovshchina*) in Chita Oblast ensured that BAM would be completed on time.[20] (In fact, however, BAM was not even three-quarters' complete by its intended finish date of October 1984; it would not be truly finished for another fifteen years.) The use of familiar military terminology, which Soviet propagandists had employed since the civil war, served as another means of transmitting the Promethean language promoting BAM to the entire nation.[21]

A rare expression of an anti-Promethean message that originated from the central bureaucracy came in 1978 from Zeev Wolfson, a Moscow-based and union-level ministry official. Under the pseudonym Boris Komarov, a last name that can be translated as "of the mosquito," he wrote *Unichtozhenie prirody: Obostrenie ekologicheskogo krizisa v SSSR* (The destruction of nature: The exacerbation of the ecological crisis in the USSR). The work was published in West Germany as *tamizdat* (that is, literature published outside the Soviet Union).[22] Wolfson noted that some BAMers pursued an active program of environmental protection, while others blatantly refused to acknowledge that the "scale of the destruction of nature around the railway exceed[ed] anything previously known."[23] Wolfson, whose true identity was not revealed until the Gorbachev era, could not express his views publicly during the Brezhnev years because of the anti-Soviet nature of his comments. Despite the book's general unavailability within the USSR, it was circulated within the dissident community as an unpublished manuscript. Geologist Aleksandr V. Karpikov of Irkutsk State Technical University, who in the late 1970s was a graduate student working on his degree in petroleum geology, "read Wolfson's work as *tamizdat*."[24]

The fact that the state blocked the publication of Wolfson's blatant attack on official environmental policy revealed the degree to which it felt threatened by any criticism of officialdom's ecological irresponsibility. Nevertheless, Wolfson's work was known to many BAMers. According to interviews with BAM "veterans," *The Destruction of Nature* gave hope to those individuals willing to lambaste the fiction of BAM Zone environmental protection, if not the viability of Soviet "big science" as a whole. Interviews with former BAMers Nikolai V. Nikitin, who worked on the railway after studying physics at Tomsk Polytechnic Institute in Western Siberia, and Nikolai N. Shtikov, who went to BAM after studying in Irkutsk, strengthen this assertion. Nikitin and his classmates regarded the environmental protection movement associated with the project as "a joke," and Shtikov recalled that "no one believed in any of that [official] environmental shit."[25]

The Alternative Voice of the Conservationists

In contrast to the Promethean notions of BAM generated by the center, some members of the BAM Zone Party and Komsomol organizations conceptualized the project in measured conservationist and environmentalist terms. Their proximity to the realities of the railway was a primary reason for this. BAM administrators and journalists and even some builders, in contrast to their colleagues based in the European USSR, witnessed the environmental destruction caused by the railway's construction on a daily basis. They could not help but notice the danger posed by irresponsible construction techniques not only to local flora and fauna, but also to themselves and their families. Admittedly, some BAM administrators entertained "careerist" notions (to use a popular Soviet-era label) and hoped their proactive stances would be noticed by their Moscow superiors and result in professional and

Party advancement. However, ecologically conscious individuals like Wolfson who voiced concern over environmental degradation along the railway's route risked demotion and criticism from the same upper-level officials in the capital.

One of the endeavor's most serious environmental problems was an omnipresent danger of forest fires in the heavily treed BAM Zone. BAM conservationists such as B. A. Turkin, the chief of the RSFSR Ministry of Forestry, addressed the lack of forest fire prevention throughout the zone, which for administrative purposes was divided into four semiautonomous segments under the control of GlavBAMstroi. Based in the city of Tynda, GlavBAMstroi was responsible for overseeing and completing all BAM-related rail and building construction. In turn, the directorate functioned under the auspices of the USSR Ministry of Transport Construction. The BAM divisions included the Western BAM Segment (headquartered in Irkutsk), the Eastern Segment (in Khabarovsk), the Buriat Segment (in Ulan-Ude), and the Central Segment (in Tynda). A 1975 report by a Tynda-based official within the RSFSR Ministry of Forestry commented on the agency's inability to protect the BAM Zone from forest fires because of an insufficient amount of fire-fighting equipment.[26] Eric Kasischke, a researcher with the Environmental Research Institute of Michigan and an associate professor of geography at the University of Maryland in College Park, conducted a project for NASA that examined the patterns of forest cover change along BAM's path. He looked at the impact of BAM construction on the amount of forest cover in Eastern Siberia and the now Russian Far East through the use of satellite imagery. The data indicated a 40 percent loss of trees in the BAM Zone from 1960 to 2000, which in Kasischke's opinion was due primarily to heavy timbering and railway construction.[27]

A joint CPSU Central Committee (a titular legislative body of some three hundred Party functionaries that approved policies and made recommendations to the Politburo, the nation's supreme policy-making body) and USSR Council of Ministers commission met in 1978 to examine the problem of forest fires in the BAM Zone based on recommendations made to it by members of the RSFSR Ministry of Forestry. Ostensibly, the impetus behind this gathering was the 1974 resolution known as "The Construction of the Baikal-Amur Railway" of the USSR Council of Ministers, the CPSU Central Committee, and the RSFSR Council of Ministers. A coterie of high-ranking officials, including the RSFSR minister of transportation, V. Filippov, listened to the staff of the Komsomol BAM construction headquarters in Tynda and played a critical role in organizing the meeting.[28]

The Tynda settlement served a major role in BAM construction and propaganda efforts. Located at the geographic center of the BAM Zone, Tynda grew from little more than a hamlet of a few hundred residents in 1974 to a thriving city of five hundred thousand by 1984. It was also home of the regional offices of the USSR Ministries of Transport Construction and Railways. The commission drew on a 1978 report written by Chief Turkin of the RSFSR Ministry of Forestry, who noted with alarm that his organization had assigned only sixty individuals to forest fire prevention duty for all of Irkutsk Oblast, one of the largest districts in the BAM Zone. Turkin predicted that some two hundred forest fires would occur in that area in 1979 as a result of severe understaffing of forest rangers and a lack of fire-fighting equipment.[29] Unfortunately, his prediction proved to be a conservative one. According to former BAMer Nikitin, "over four hundred blazes broke out in Irkutsk Oblast during 1979."[30] As the frequency of forest fires increased throughout the 1980s, a growing number of local-level functionaries with no direct connection to the RSFSR Ministry of Forestry began to voice concern over the highly destructive yet preventable nature of the region's infernos. Along with an officially sanctioned movement to protect Lake Baikal, the forest fire prevention effort represented one of the most cohesive outlets of BAMer environmental consciousness between 1974 and 1984.

In 1979, a special gathering composed of members of the CPSU Central Committee, known as the Lake Baikal Environmental Committee, summoned high-level representatives of various national industries to report on the ecological footprint of their respective enterprises. The session was marked by the committee members' harsh criticism of the industries' pollution of the Baikal region.[31] The impetus for this organization's creation came from a small but influential collection of environmentally conscious officials who sought to expose the wastefulness and incompetence of ministry officials associated with the project. The committee members were not solely motivated by a concern for the environment, however, as some sought to improve their chances at Politburo membership by making a name for themselves in a high-profile forum. Nevertheless, some members recognized the gravity of the region's ecological situation based on personal visits to the BAM project itself. This explosion of popular interest in the Baikal's ecology that was sparked by BAM construction was foretold by geographer Craig ZumBrunnen some five years earlier.[32] ZumBrunnen correctly predicted that the plight of Lake Baikal would become one of great popular interest by the 1980s.

Charged with upholding a pair of resolutions from the CPSU Central Committee and the USSR Council of Ministers, the Lake Baikal Environmental Committee castigated the heads of the nation's chemical, paper, energy, and fishing industries for failing to protect the Baikal watershed from "numerous ecological threats."[33] The watershed included the geographic territory of Lake Baikal itself as well as the numerous rivers, most notably the Angara River. The resolutions included two measures: "On the Additional Merits of the Rational Use and Conservation of the Natural Riches of the Lake Baikal Basin" (dated June 16, 1971—before the beginning of BAM construction) and "On the Merits of the Further Protection and Rational Use of the Natural Resources of Lake Baikal" (dated July 21, 1977).[34] Foremost among this group were those ministers whose organizations had polluted Baikal's water and air along the lake's northern shore. The committee reserved particular disdain for the Buriat ASSR Council of Ministers, whose members had "not taken the proper steps to ensure the environmental protection of Lake Baikal."[35]

Although widespread interest in the health of the Baikal ecosystem emerged somewhat later than in the Soviet Union, the lake's plight has not gone unnoticed in the West. Several international efforts have focused on the issue. Baikal's fragile limnetic environment was the subject of a September 1994 NATO Advanced Workshop, which was the first joint Russian-Western effort to address issues of rational use and conservation regarding the source of one-third of the planet's surface fresh water.[36] Western interest in Lake Baikal's delicate ecosystem remains keen to this day, especially among environmental activists.

The Lake Baikal Environmental Committee

In 1979, the Lake Baikal Environmental Committee charged two BAM-affiliated operations—the Buriat Locomotive Factory and Aviation Factory R-6759—with polluting the Uda River, a Baikal tributary, with oil and heavy metals. As a result of the activities of these two plants and other "dirty" BAM Zone industries, the committee reported, Lake Baikal oil pollution stood at 112 times the acceptable limit, copper at 215 times, and zinc at 27 times.[37] In addition, beginning with the BAM project's inception in 1974, effluence from water transport craft added more than 10,000 cubic meters of chemical- and oil-contaminated waste water into the lake annually. Committee members representing the USSR Ministry of Waterways also noted that the sewage system of the newly constructed city of Severobaikalsk and runoff from the North Muisk BAM Tunnel near the city was fouling the lake's once pristine waters.[38] Incomplete until the late 1990s, the North Muisk BAM Tunnel cuts through the seismically unstable North Muisk mountain range. After a number of fatalities occurred that were connected with the tunnel's construction, the government of the Russian Federation temporarily terminated funding for the project during the early 1990s.[39] The tunnel now functions as part of the operational BAM.

The Lake Baikal Environmental Committee placed direct blame for the deplorable condition of Baikal's limnetic environment on the Buriat ASSR authorities, who repeatedly failed to implement environmental protection directives from the center. Other administrators, most notably Buriat Segment staffers working at the Ministry of Transportation office in Ulan-Ude, complied with only five of twenty-one such orders from Moscow. For example, of some 8.8 million rubles allocated to the Selengorsk paper mill to improve its pollution control systems, only 5.4 million rubles had been spent by 1979, with no appreciable reduction in waste water toxicity or volume. The committee also remarked that the entire Baikal paper industry had failed to meet clear water and air standards as mandated by the center in 1978 and instead had exacerbated fishkills and other environmental problems on the lake.[40]

Although the influence of public opinion on the Lake Baikal Environmental Committee's decision to investigate the lake's pollution is difficult to assess, awareness of its critical ecological condition was widespread at least within the BAM Zone population. According to geologist Karpikov, this group was bombarded by alternately Promethean and conservationist "environmental propaganda" from media outlets based in both the center and the BAM Zone.[41] Nevertheless, the fact that the committee did not address the issue of the lake's pollution until two years after the meeting of the joint CPSU Central Committee and USSR Council of Ministers plenum revealed its sluggishness in implementing environmental protection legislation.[42]

In addition, the mere existence of the Lake Baikal Environmental Committee, let alone its activities, was not made public until the government of the Russian Federation outlawed the Communist Party in 1991, resulting in the publication of the Party's records. Although the committee announced its intention to issue a progress report in 1981, no record of any such activity is present in the archives of the former CPSU Central Committee or of any of the criticized ministries.[43] Based on the lack of evidence of further activity by the committee after 1979, it appears that it never met again after its initial gathering. Nonetheless, the group represented an important effort to address the environmental impact of BAM construction on Lake Baikal and the wider BAM Zone. This Moscow-generated organization had deep roots within the BAM bureaucracy, and a significant number of committee members had traveled personally to the BAM Zone. Valentin A. Sushchevich, the former head of the Komsomol BAM headquarters at the Russian Youth Organizations headquarters in Moscow, stated that "the Lake Baikal Committee was ours [*nash*]," meaning that BAM's managers had a strong influence over the membership and agenda of the committee.[44]

The activities of the Lake Baikal Environmental Committee notwithstanding, many ministers and bureaucrats in Moscow and elsewhere outside the BAM Zone generally ignored the cause of environmental protection along the railway's route. In contrast, the interest in ecological issues among many local journalists, scientists, and Party bureaucrats was piqued not only by the activities of the environmental committee, but also by the personal experience of witnessing environmental destruction on a daily basis. Former BAMer Nikitin recalled: "I saw tremendous environmental destruction very consistently. There were areas I saw that will never recover from what they [the railway builders] had done there."[45] Such expressions of cautious environmentalism ran counter to Moscow's Promethean rhetoric and relegation of BAM's ecological problems to locally based institutions.

An array of BAM Zone journalists served as a catalyst in the effort to increase local environmental consciousness. In 1981, journalist L. Maksimova writing in *Amurskii komsomolets* (Amur komsomoler) reported that a law enacted by the USSR Supreme Soviet called "On the Protection and Utilization of the Animal World" was the "first such law in the history of mankind" to ensure the protection of animal life "on land, in the water, in the atmosphere, and in the soil" from destruction by industrial and agricultural enterprises. Maksimova proclaimed that this new law, which received little publicity in national publications with larger circulations, "defends all the nation's fauna." In addition, she urged her fellow Amur region comrades to honor the law by taking an "active initiative" as conservationists and serve as "champions" for otherwise defenseless animal species.[46] Within one mechanized column (*mekhanizirovannaia kolonna*, or MK), Komsomol members of the All-Russian Society for the Protection of Nature (*Vserossiiskoe obshchestvo okhrany prirody*, or VOOP) acted upon a RSFSR Council of Ministers' resolution that authorized them to enforce Soviet environmental protection law among all citizens regardless of age or party affiliation.[47]

One of the largest nonconstruction organizations in the BAM Zone, the youth-dominated VOOP enjoyed a membership of 60,845 in 1974 in the Iakutsk ASSR and a whopping 288,698 individuals by 1977 in Khabarovsk Krai, of whom 12,000 were under twenty-five.[48] The Amur Oblast VOOP trumpeted its nearly nine hundred showings of films commemorating the organization's fiftieth anniversary, and in 1974 the group claimed that more than one hundred thousand BAMers had seen these presentations. This statement ignores the fact that the grand total of those working on the BAM project did not reach such a large figure until later years. Regarding VOOP's apparent popularity, Weiner has asserted that many young Soviet citizens joined VOOP out of a desire to fraternize and make new friends rather than a heartfelt desire to protect the environment. Other Komsomol members became involved with VOOP in the hope that their participation in this voluntary organization would boost their chances for party membership and consequently social advancement. In addition, locally produced reports on VOOP formations throughout the BAM Zone revealed that many BAMers cared little for their ostensible roles as "environmental warriors." VOOP leaders in Moscow often boasted of their "army of thousands" engaged in the struggle to defend nature in a classic statement of Promethean language.[49]

Nevertheless, some VOOP members throughout the BAM Zone were genuinely concerned with environmental protection. An anonymous letter sent in 1977 to the Komsomol Central Committee by a "concerned student" stated that "environmental protection cannot be ignored by the Komsomol" and that the realization of this process had been "far from the ideal up to this point."[50] Dozens of similar anonymous reports exist in the archives from Komsomol members who were uneasy with criticizing the project publicly but nonetheless commented on the woeful level of environmental awareness and education among the BAMer population.[51] The fact that no response from the Komsomol headquarters in Moscow to this or other such letters can be found in the archives points to the central bureaucracy's lack of concern with the negative attention elicited by BAM's wanton push across the USSR's eastern reaches. Other criticisms of official efforts at environmental protection were not anonymous. Early in the project's history, N. N. Boronov, the second secretary of the Irkutsk Oblast Komsomol organization, attacked unnamed individuals in Moscow and elsewhere for "want[ing] to exploit every hectare of land" in the BAM Zone. Boronov termed such people "wolves" for their rapacious attitude toward the region's resources, but he was unwilling to risk his own position by making any personal accusations. Other representatives of the youth organization demanded that local officials work harder to educate the central bureaucracy about the precarious environmental situation in the area.[52]

In a 1975 statement, the Komsomol BAM construction headquarters declared that selected BAMers who served as participants in a "Protection of Nature and the Environment Campaign . . . ignored the preservation of living things in construction areas" and demonstrated a "careless attitude toward flora and fauna." At a 1980 conference, delegates criticized their comrades for "poorly employing construction machinery and other technology" as well as "rarely implementing the ecological protection initiatives of the 'Twenty-Thousanders' [*dvadtsatitysiachniki*] of BAMstroimekhanizatsiia."[53] A construction trust headquartered in Tynda and part of GlavBAMstroi, BAMstroimekhanizatsiia was a locally initiated and tightly knit group of so-called pacesetters who introduced environmentally friendly earthmoving techniques to the project's workforce. According to Twentieth Centurion (special, hand-selected members of the Komsomol BAM construction brigade) delegates to the Tynda conference, most BAMer cadres viewed them as outsiders who were slowing the pace of construction and had no understanding of the difficulties of maintaining the unrealistic rail-laying tempo as dictated by BAM construction headquarters.[54] A partial explanation for this problem may have been the youthful composition of the BAMer population. By early 1977, of the some sixty thousand individuals currently involved in BAM construction, some 70 percent were under twenty-eight.[55]

Officials at the headquarters were fully aware of the failure of their top-down approach to environmental protection and education. In a 1982 letter, Z. Apresian, editor in chief of the Moscow-based Komsomol journal *Molodoi kommunist* (Young Communist), asked BAM chief Iurii Verbitskii to comment on an article published in an earlier issue of Apresian's journal that chastised the BAM administration for its lack of attention to environmental issues.[56] In his response to Apresian, Verbitskii admitted to some shortcomings, but in defense of his organization's policies, he cited Lenin's statement that the Soviet population must not be "slaves of blind necessity" or sacrifice nature for the sake of progress.[57] After characterizing Lenin as a defender of nature and Leninism as a pro-environmental philosophy, however, Verbitskii went on to note with alarm that large-scale mechanized excavation and railway construction had inflicted severe damage on the BAM Zone's delicate permafrost and fauna in a reckless effort to complete the railway quickly. He also related that during the construction of a bridge across the Upper Angara River, an important Baikal tributary that flows into the Lower Angara through the eastern Siberian city of Irkutsk, two bridge-building brigades deliberately permitted electric power generators used at the construction site to leak diesel fuel into the river. The result of this and other instances of water pollution, Verbitskii said, was a marked decrease in the population of the *omul*, a species of fish indigenous only to Lake Baikal. During the 1940s, the species numbered more than one million, but by the early 1980s the number had decreased by over 80 percent.[58]

Verbitskii pointed to the activities of the VOOP organizations throughout the BAM Zone as evidence that a "rational view of the environment" had begun to permeate the BAMer consciousness. He also confirmed journalist Iamil Mustafin's impression that "those BAMers located far from Tynda and the other BAM Zone centers have yet to learn from their mistakes" by noting the "lack of control" within the water-protection campaigns of the Tyndatransstroi and TsentroBAMstroi construction trusts that had "dirtied the shores of the Getkan and Tynda rivers with [their] petroleum wastes."[59] Like BAMstroimekhanizatsiia, Tyndatransstroi and TsentroBAMstroi were construction trusts headquartered in Tynda and subordinate to GlavBAMstroi. Each detachment was responsible for completing a segment of track within one of the four semiautonomous segments. Verbitskii revealed his lack of confidence in the average BAMer's desire and ability to protect the environment by stating that "it is possible to mention a number of examples in which a typical BAMer, having worked on the railway five or more years, has not thought to notice the environmental damage inflicted by his work."[60] Verbitskii thus identified himself as one of the rather small yet vocal minority of upper-level BAM administrators who took "environmental propaganda" and nature protection seriously, despite their understanding of the general failure of such policies.

In 1980, a number of Tynda-based BAM authorities, including Verbitskii, designed the "For the Cleanliness and Preservation of Taiga Rivers" campaign to encourage a heightening of environmental awareness among BAMers by awarding emblems, medals, and even cash prizes to those workers voted by their peers as the best "Defender of the Environment" in his or her respective brigade.[61] According to its creators, the competition acknowledged those who demonstrated "the spirit of a Leninist relationship with nature and an especially careful attitude toward the water resources [*vodnoe bogatstvo*] of the Motherland."[62] These officially proclaimed "defenders" worked to protect fisheries, particularly spawning grounds of endangered species, in accordance with powers granted to them by the USSR Fisheries and Regulation of Water Law. Victors in the campaign received the privilege of coordinating the activities of the "green and blue patrols" of local schoolchildren.[63]

Other environmental protection movements under the auspices of the Komsomol Central Committee BAM construction headquarters included the "Save the Birch" forestry awareness drive as well as the "BAM Nature— Our Common Concern" and "My Project—My Pride!" campaigns, which included BAMers from building and erection subdivision 571 (*stroitelno-montazhnoe podrazdelenie,* or SMP), MK-94, and tunneling brigade 12 (*tonnelnyi otriad,* or TO) at Ulkan in the Western BAM Segment of the Buriat ASSR.[64] These activities composed a part of the "My Contribution to the Five-Year Plan" movement, which the Komsomol BAM construction headquarters designed to instill a sense of personal responsibility among participants. A December 1977 statement of environmental awareness by the members of SMP-571 revealed the level to which the environmental protection message had reached some BAM cadres, although the penetration of such conservationist sentiments among the BAMers is difficult to gauge: "In the struggle to be recognized as a 'Settlement of Communist Order and Daily Life,' and in conjunction with the effort to defend nature and the environment, [we] are working at Ulkan under the slogan of 'Save the Birch.' We are employing concrete measures in the struggle against those who display an immoral [and] rapacious attitude toward nature."[65]

Somewhat bland proclamations of environmental activism emanated not only from BAM headquarters in Tynda, but also from the individual segment headquarters. Despite the concerns Verbitskii and others voiced, some BAM leaders confidently proclaimed that "people working on the 'Project of the Century' correctly understand environmental protection issues." Indeed,

the segment's bosses declared that Eastern Segment BAMers "live alongside
. . . 'Comrade Taiga' as a 'superintendent' of nature" and maintained the pu-
rity of the Chemchuko and Urgal rivers.[66]

The Komsomol Spotlight

An array of small groups, known collectively as the Komsomol Spotlight,
also served as watchdogs for environmental protection compliance throughout the decade of BAM construction. This tightly knit but underequipped
and overworked group of Komsomol members, most of whom were between the ages of seventeen and twenty-five, voluntarily traveled throughout
the BAM Zone to confirm observance of "Communist morality" and Soviet
law, with an emphasis on environmental law compliance, among the half-
million-strong BAMer population. As early as 1974, the Komsomol Spotlight
established "control posts" throughout the region, verified the implementation of official environmental protection directives, and levied fines against
polluters. In particular, the Spotlight identified those who carelessly started
forest fires that, in the words of one anonymous Spotlighter, threatened to
destroy the "unique landscapes" of the BAM region.[67]

Perhaps the best expression of the Spotlight's professed mission can be
found in a broadside published in 1975 which, among other items, discussed
the notion of "green zones." These referred to a territory of variable dimen-
sions surrounding construction sites, generally residential, in which no heavy
equipment could be operated or stored and where no earthmoving of any
kind could take place. Although nearly every non–rail-laying project was
supposed to be surrounded by a so-called green zone, in reality most construction detachments failed to heed the activity restrictions within their
zones, created an area that was far too small to adequately protect the adja-
cent flora and fauna, or never established a green zone at all. The broadside
commented: "While building [the BAM railway] quickly and efficiently, we
must not forget that we are constructing not only a railway, but the future as
well—we are laying down the railway to Communism. Therefore, we must
always remember our daily duty. We will make our settlements beautiful and
comfortable . . . and we will work under the slogan of 'Save the Birch.' Of
course, it would be easier to build without 'green zones,' but we *will* undertake the additional effort to preserve the greenery of our settlement. This
work continues today and will continue tomorrow."[68]

The Komsomol Spotlighters often defined themselves and their mission in martial terms. One 1976 "raid" on a BAMstroiput (another division of GlavBAMstroi that was responsible for coordinating rail-laying and siding construction activities in Amur Oblast) automotive repair base revealed that mechanics stored equipment and machinery improperly, thus allowing automotive oil and gasoline to run off and contaminate the surrounding soil and water. This bulletin, along with other highly critical dispatches, was published in such local newspapers as *Avangard* (Vanguard), the Amur Oblast CPSU organ. Although it accurately reported the environmental carelessness of the BAMstroiput workers, this Spotlight statement falsely noted that the BAMstroiput administration had "corrected" all the problems discovered by the Spotlighters.[69] But materials in the Komsomol archive subsequently show that those fined by the Komsomol Spotlight, including the BAMstroiput administrators, typically chose to pay a modest penalty rather than devote any financial or material resources to correct the problem.[70]

Indeed, reports by Komsomol Spotlighters who participated in other raids, such as those at Kuvykta and Ust-Niukzha, indicated that the young Spotlighters charged the directors of MK-148 and MK-149 with failing to maintain a green zone around their construction site, allowing loose dirt to dissolve in a primary tributary of the Tynda River, and failing to clean up spilled oil and gasoline. In addition, return visits by the Spotlighters demonstrated that these BAM construction trusts blatantly continued to ignore environmental protection statutes.[71] One indicative example was that of the Komsomol Spotlight division that conducted a number of raids on SMP-572 throughout 1977 but that admitted to failing to achieve its goal of compelling the construction subdivision to build sewage treatment facilities within its Buriat ASSR territory.[72]

Despite the Komsomol Spotlight's activities and well-publicized reports, many violating brigades went unpunished. The pollution of the BAM environment continued unabated due to a combination of factors: Spotlight understaffing, the organization's lack of financial and material resources, and an institutional culture that rewarded those BAMer detachments who reached their construction quotas the quickest by ignoring the environmental impact of their activities. Although the dedicated members of the Komsomol Spotlight played an active role in defending the BAM ecosystem, their numbers proved far too few to patrol adequately the entire half-million square miles of BAM Zone territory. The membership of the Komsomol Spotlight ranged from fewer than a hundred to more than two thousand during BAM's decade of prominence.

Under Verbitskii's influence, the Komsomol BAM construction headquarters in Tynda began to voice environmentalist sentiments, a process that continued with his successor, Valentin A. Sushchevich. In a 1977 report, the new BAM chief noted that members of SMP-266 working at the Zvezdnyi settlement had delivered more than three thousand cubic meters of black earth (humus-rich, fertile soil known as *chernozem* in Russian) to assist in the planting of two thousand trees, while its members paid "special attention" to keeping their new homes free of construction trash and remnants.[73] In interviews with Sushchevich, he failed to mention these "new homes" were composed almost exclusively of old railway cars and used shipping containers. Sushchevich added that "such attentiveness was necessary in order to protect the environment as well as to prepare the track in the Zvezdnyi and other BAM Zone areas for permanent use."[74]

In the same report, Sushchevich described a joint program involving his Komsomol BAM construction headquarters, the governmental North Baikal People's Control Committee, and the Komsomol Spotlight organization, which combined forces to organize nature protection work "in the spirit of a Leninist relationship to nature" among the members of MK-138. This detachment was designated by Sushchevich as a "special environmental protection column," worked under its own slogan ("Little Rivers—Deep and Clean"), and included a program of financial and promotional incentives.[75] Specifically, selected participants from the MK-138 fueling detachment—a group that the Komsomol Spotlight had cited for pollution in the past and that was now the focus of official attention—were responsible for overseeing "the protection and rational use of water and forest resources" by the approximately fifty members of the mechanized column.[76]

After the project's inception, BAM headquarters developed a broad-based motivational campaign to instill a sense of personal responsibility in each BAMer. By proclaiming that each builder played a critical role in ensuring the project's ultimate success, the BAM bureaucracy hoped to increase both the pace of construction and the quality of work. The first motivational effort concerned the granting of the title "environmental protection group" (EPG) to certain worker brigades that had followed specific construction guidelines and left a minimal ecological footprint. The impetus to have one's detachment labeled as an EPG was not purely conservationist, however.

Members of EPGs received additional pay, known as "environmental consciousness bonuses," and were also allowed the first choice of any new BAM Zone housing that became available each year.[77]

Other high-level BAM officials noticed Verbitskii's and Sushchevich's environmental activism and asserted their own previously muted opinions on the critical need to encourage a sense of ecological awareness in BAMers of all ranks. In a 1977 essay entitled "The Protection of Nature and the Environment—the Duty of the Komsomol Spotlight," Iurii V. Galmakov, Sushchevich's deputy and head of the Buriat BAM Segment Komsomol headquarters, boldly summarized the importance of his organization: "The taiga has an enormous influence in the water and air ecosystems of the entire Earth."[78] Galmakov warned that forest fires threatened to turn the taiga into a "lunar landscape," and he presented a particular danger to local forests because of the slow rate of tree regrowth after a fire. He noted with some sadness that soil erosion caused by BAM construction had begun to "alter the hydrological function" of the region.[79] In warning against the danger of avalanche-causing demolition work, Galmakov remarked that "any violation of the laws of nature involves far-reaching environmental consequences."[80] In particular, he cited the overfishing of the Buriat ASSR's major rivers by dozens of BAMer and native poachers, only twenty of whom were ultimately arrested. In a bold assertion of ecoactivism, Galmakov vowed to "fight a war" with those who continued to hunt and fish local species to extinction. Finally, the Buriat BAM chief soberly commented that although the impetus for the "Save the Birch" and other conservation campaigns originated from the upper echelons of the BAM bureaucracy, the onus of taking a proactive attitude and implementing BAM headquarters' environmental directives fell upon those young people who were actually constructing the railway in the Buriat ASSR and elsewhere.[81]

Aside from the forty- and fifty-year-olds who inhabited the upper reaches of the Komsomol-controlled bureaucracy, others assumed roles as self-proclaimed environmental defenders. For example, VOOP official A. Grigorev revealed that in 1975, some six thousand young members of so-called green patrols protected the environment in his region. Also known as "blue patrols," these VOOP-sponsored and -controlled organizations consisted of elementary schoolchildren (between the ages of five and ten years old) and were designed to provide youth with a physical and moral outlet for their energies (conceivably keeping them out of trouble). Membership in a green patrol required that a prospective patroller be of "good moral and socialist character," and to take an oath to devote all of his or her emotional and physical resources to defending the environment, seeking out and punishing those who violated Soviet environmental law, and assisting local party, Communist Party, and particularly Komsomol organizations in upholding "environmental discipline" on the railway. In 1975 alone, Grigorev's charges planted ten hectares of trees and forty-five-hundred square meters of gardens in Ulan-Ude; they also prepared a calendar with nature photographs that was distributed to schoolchildren throughout the region.[82] The VOOP apparatus in Grigorev's Buriat ASSR sponsored the "Your Green Friend" project in an effort to educate local schoolchildren through a number of "environmental protection weeks" during which nature conservation lessons were taught by classroom instructors and occasionally by VOOP members themselves.

Buriat VOOP members also inculcated their environmental protection message in the wider population in the monthly, locally broadcast television program *Chelovek i priroda* (Man and Nature). They further publicized their activities by contributing articles to and being interviewed in such local newspapers as *Pravda Buriatii* (Buriat truth), *Molodezh Buriatii* (Buriat youth), and the Buriat-language *Buriad Unen* (Buriat youth). Finally, Buriat ASSR members of the All-Union Knowledge Society (or Znanie, a state-sponsored and center-controlled knowledge dissemination organization that enjoyed a membership of thousands of academics, specialists, and laypeople) delivered thousands of lectures a year on a variety of topics throughout the USSR. In 1974 alone, their presentations included more than a thousand talks on "V. I. Lenin and Issues of Environmental Protection" to local workers' councils. By all accounts, this process continued until BAM's announced completion in 1984.[83]

Other VOOP activists were instrumental in increasing environmental awareness in the Tynda region as well. In 1977, L. Khromchenko of Komsomol BAM headquarters reported that some five thousand young men and women joined the Tynda VOOP, and that in 1976 these and other members gave a number of presentations on "BAM and its Leninist relationship to nature" to the people of the BAM capital.[84] Khromchenko added that some 345 young *druzhiny* (volunteer patrollers) served as "volunteer green patrollers" and "protectors of public order and safety" under the auspices of the USSR Interior Ministry and BAM Zone police departments. The green patrollers engaged in such environmental protection activities as litter control and agitational billboard making.[85] In 1981, the head of Tynda's VOOP organization noted that his charges established special green zones around the city where they confirmed that construction was prohibited. The children of the "BAM capital" planted more than five thousand trees and bushes as well as some fifteen thousand flowers under VOOP supervision. Tynda VOOP members also cataloged seventeen endangered bird and animal species into a special "Red Book," which resembled a Western-style endangered species list, to assure their protection.[86] The impetus for the green zone movement appears to have come from Iurii Valkov of the RSFSR Ministry of Forestry, who proposed the idea at a 1977 conference on environmental protection and the rational use of natural resources.[87]

A 1984 article in the newspaper *BAM* (published in Tynda twice weekly by GlavBAMstroi) by I. Tkach of the Amur Oblast VOOP provided some interesting detail about the composition and activities of this branch of the Soviet environmental protection society. In Amur Oblast alone, more than two thousand VOOP cells promoted environmental awareness among some thirty-five thousand local schoolchildren, many of whom were members of VOOP-led green and blue patrols who were "compelled to defend nature and preserve natural wealth." To bolster his statement, Tkach cited Article 67 of the Constitution of the Soviet Union, which decreed that "necessary measures must be taken for the protection and scientifically grounded rational use of natural riches in the interests of present and future generations in the USSR." Tkach went even further by saying: "The protection of the environment is the constitutional obligation of all Soviet peoples."[88]

Not all environmentally conscious BAMers echoed the sentiment that the region's VOOP organizations successfully stimulated environmental awareness among the BAMer population. In another *BAM* article entitled "Nature Is Our Home," N. Morozov of VOOP noted that the "powerful words of the North Baikal CPSU Executive Committee" should evoke concern for the BAM ecosystem among the populace, but that members of the local Party executive committee and the Council of Peoples' Deputies "often overlooked questions of environmental protection."[89] Morozov charged the North Baikal Party officials with failing to enact environmental defense legislation in a report called "On the Unsatisfactory Conditions of the Construction of Environmental Protection Objectives along the BAM." The North Baikal VOOP chief excoriated his region's Party apparatus for failing to heed the aforementioned CPSU Central Committee's and USSR Council of Ministers' statements regarding the need to protect Lake Baikal from industrial pollution. Finally, Morozov maligned the RSFSR Ministries of Forestry and Fisheries for their lax enforcement of environmental protection law.[90]

Undeterred by the BAM bureaucracy's lack of progress in enforcing environmental protection law, Morozov followed his condemnation with a summary of his own organization's productivity, including the activities of VOOP chapters in other North Baikal construction settlements. Morozov's VOOP members organized and participated in lectures, meetings, and speeches in addition to writing articles that "educate[d] the workers en masse about the daily events of the VOOP's work for the environment through the formation of 'nature corners.'"[91] Here Morozov carefully differentiated his VOOP cadres from the general BAMer population. Although he claimed that the deeds of his local VOOP members were inspired by the nature protection declarations of the delegates to the Twenty-fifth CPSU Congress in 1976, Morozov nevertheless took credit for the 354 hectares of land in the North Baikal area that his VOOP members designated as nature preserves that then became off-limits to future logging. To Morozov's credit, the demarcation of a "tree protection zone" was a singular accomplishment within the BAM Zone in that no records exist detailing such resourcefulness elsewhere along the railway.

Regarding "environmental propaganda," Morozov theorized that it is "one of the most important forms of natural protection work." He remarked that the USSR Council of Ministers' directive (known as "On the Measures of the Further Exploitation of the Natural Resources of the Baikal Basin") had fallen largely on deaf ears among BAM officials. The North Baikal VOOP leader again pointed to his own organization as an example of effective local environmental activism. He declared that not only did his charges plant twelve thousand trees in several BAM Zone settlements, but they also energized their fellow BAMers with "environmental propaganda" in the form of lectures, meetings, and speeches, which the local media outlets publicized extensively.[92] In a martial conceptualization of his group's mission, Morozov heralded his environmentalist "soldiers," who fought and won the battle to convince the population of the North Baikal region of the need, both as individuals and as model Soviet citizens, to facilitate the "rational use of the Baikal basin's natural resources."[93]

Locally generated and officially sponsored environmental activism did not stop with Morozov and the North Baikal VOOP, however. In August 1981, the BAM Zone division of the USSR Ministry of Transportation's Railway Construction Directorate announced a railway workers' environmental protection essay contest that awarded cash prizes to those individuals who submitted the best written answers to the problem of how to reduce the discharge of wastewater from railway and bridge construction operations and exhaust emissions from earthmovers and other heavy equipment. The first prize was 500 rubles, a good deal more than the average railway worker's monthly salary of approximately 150 rubles.[94] In addition to receiving monetary compensation for their winning essays, successful railroaders were given the possibly distasteful "opportunity" to deliver a series of lectures on their environmentally friendly construction strategies. Although the effectiveness and popularity of this competition varied from region to region, reports found in the archives of the Union of Railway Transport Workers reveal that most BAM cadres participated because of monetary, not environmentalist, motivations.[95] Another essay contest was developed by students working with SMPs and specialized directorates (*spetsializirovannoe upravlenie*, or SUs) in a number of North Baikal workers' settlements.[96] Aside from reading their essays on the significance of environmental protection, the participants noted that many workers had received no environmental education and training and that this deficiency had led to a number of violations of environmental statutes due to simple ignorance and, in some cases, a lack of interest in non-Komsomol BAMers.[97]

Other BAMers criticized the railway's bureaucracy for its lack of compliance with national environmental protection law. In a 1975 declaration, Party members P. Ermolaev and Z. Gaeva chastised BAMstroiput for doing a poor job in complying with the resolution of the CPSU Central Committee and the USSR Council of Ministers (the resolution was known as "On the Strengthening of Environmental Protection and Improvement in the Use of Natural Resources").[98] Specifically, Ermolaev and Gaeva took BAMstroiput to task for ignoring the increasingly severe problem of used construction materials, such as timber and loose earth, that were choking roads and waterways. Voices from within BAM officialdom that criticized environmental protection campaigns continued to be heard throughout the railway's decade of prominence. Verbitskii and others began to note the critical damage inflicted by the many careless BAMers on the fragile permafrost, limnetic environment, and fauna after their arrival in 1974. Specifically, the Komsomol Central Committee pointed to the example at the South Tynda railway station, where absentminded and indifferent builders allowed the soil to become contaminated with petroleum distillates, machine oil, and other caustics, leading to massive fishkills in the Getkan and Tynda rivers.[99] Despite this sobering report on the conditions in South Tynda, no records that any official action was taken to remedy this situation could be found in the Komsomol archives.

Criticism of many BAMers' carelessness regarding the environment was not limited to Komsomol-affiliated administrators. In a scathing March 1981 letter addressed "to the Young Builders of the Central BAM Segment," V. Stebelkov, chief inspector of Tynda region fisheries, castigated several mechanized columns for their destruction of fish habitats. Rather than "demonstrating a Leninist, Communist attitude toward their duties," he wrote, the members of these brigades "destroyed the riches . . . of our rivers and lakes."[100] Stebelkov noted with alarm the dramatic decline in the region's populations of salmon since the project's inception. He warned that building brigades in Tynda had dumped enough fuel and waste oil into the Olekma and Niukzha rivers to "nearly sterilize them." Although he stopped short of calling for the punishment of any particular brigade or individual, Stebelkov stated that such violations of the country's clean water laws were not only illegal, they also contravened Leninist teachings on the absolute necessity to cherish nature.

Environmental Discussions within the Academic Community

Early in BAM's construction, the scientific and academic communities within the Akademgorodok (Academic Village) at Novosibirsk, in addition to the BAM bureaucracy, attempted to increase awareness about the vulnerable BAM ecosystem.[101] In September 1975, academics from Novosibirsk, Irkutsk, and other Siberian cities joined railway construction specialists to convene a conference in Chita on "problems of the economic development of the BAM Zone." Regarding the impact of BAM construction on the "social development of the small peoples of the North," conference participants agreed that the region's native population must "adapt" to the changing economic and environmental realities that the railway's construction had brought to their land.[102] In a somewhat paradoxical declaration, conference members also proclaimed that the native people's environmental awareness and personal relationship with nature should be emulated by the area's new (that is, non-indigenous) residents. (Clearly, however, this was not an endorsement of animism or shamanism.)[103]

Regarding the Buriat, the Evenk, and the Iakut, who were the BAM Zone's original inhabitants, local administrators and journalists generally ignored the impact of BAM construction on these major indigenous groups.[104] Sources on the relationship between the project and the native population display a naïve assumption that although all of the area's aboriginals may not have supported the changes wrought by BAM, they did not actively oppose the demographic and environmental transformations introduced by the railway's construction. At a conference on "issues of economic development in the BAM Zone" held in Chita in September 1975, a concerned participant broached the subject of the effect hundreds of thousands of non-natives would have on the local ecology and the social development of the "small peoples of the North." This anonymous conference member remarked that the only attention these people received was their relation to the project as heavy equipment operators; the participant wondered openly if the BAM Zone's aboriginals could contribute to the undertaking in other ways. After a short discussion, the membership echoed the sentiments of previous meetings and declared that the region's indigenous peoples "must adapt to the changing conditions caused by BAM construction."[105] The forms and methods that this adaptation would entail, however, were left unanswered, and the question of whether to provide the indigenous peoples with a voice in their relationship with BAM was never examined again in a formal setting. The only subsequent treatment of this question portrayed the indigenous peoples in the BAM Zone as completely satisfied with the project's contribution to their lives.[106]

In 1975, the USSR Academy of Sciences sponsored the first formal gathering of scientists and other academics whose work dealt with the project—the conference on BAM construction and environmental protection—in Irkutsk. The mostly young participants addressed such pressing issues as the difficulties of rail-laying on permafrost and coping with seismic activity and extreme low temperatures when building bridges and tunnels. The participants empathized with the BAMers' dilemma of creating the necessary infrastructure (that is, the construction of electrical, telephone, and water lines) to complete the railway on the one hand while remaining cognizant of their duty to protect the environment on the other.[107] Along with a similar conference held that same month in Khabarovsk, this gathering of concerned scientists produced a small but dedicated core of academics and others who continued to sound the alarm on BAM's adverse impact on the local ecosystem until 1984 and beyond. Similar BAM seminars were also convened in Gorky in 1975 and in Ulianovsk in 1976.[108] After the Irkutsk and Khabarovsk conferences, many participants were involved in the promotion of such environmental causes as the protection of Lake Baikal from the Baikalsk paper plant.[109] During the Gorbachev years, these same individuals noted the dangers of underground nuclear testing on the Arctic island of Novaya Zemlya as well as the April 1986 accidental meltdown at the Chernobyl nuclear power station in Ukraine.[110]

In 1977, the BAM Zone Komsomol Central Committee and the project's VOOP Central Council sponsored another gathering, the "Scientific-Practical Conference on Environmental Protection and the Rational Use of Natural Resources in the BAM Zone," held in Khabarovsk. This meeting included representatives from fifteen different union- and RSFSR-level governmental ministries as well as delegates from the Komsomol. In a broadcast on local radio, E. G. Lysenko (of the twelve-thousand-member strong Russian Federation VOOP) noted that the conference participants concluded that the issue of BAM Zone environmental protection had not yet received sufficient attention and that their specific concerns centered on the impact of logging and of railway and housing construction on the BAM Zone ecosystem.[111] In a series of interviews published in local newspapers, Lysenko revealed that a number of BAM Zone Komsomol organizations insufficiently utilized "propaganda and organizational work" to promote the cause of environmental protection among the BAMer population.[112]

Although the Tenth Five-Year Plan (1976–1980) allocated eleven billion rubles for environmental education and protection measures throughout the Soviet Union, Lysenko remarked that Komsomol and Ministry of Transport Construction officials in Moscow dispensed only meager sums of this total to their subordinates throughout the BAM region. This number is quite small when compared with the 621 billion rubles allotted for agriculture.[113] Lysenko attributed the program's lack of success to an acute shortage of trained specialists—particularly geologists, agronomists, and foresters—who could provide environmental protection education to the railway's workforce. At the end of the conference, delegates affirmed that "the question of environmental protection is always . . . [at] the center of attention of the Communist Party and government of the Soviet Union" and that the Twenty-fifth CPSU Congress should adopt new measures for the further protection of water and air from industrial emissions and residential runoffs.[114] The conference participants also pronounced that more survey work must be conducted before railway construction continued anywhere in the BAM Zone; GlavBAMstroi completely ignored this suggestion, however, as construction was already behind schedule in 1977. The delegates concluded that commonly hunted mammal and fish species should be protected to bolster the appeal of the region to prospective tourists.[115]

Media Coverage of Environmental Protection in the BAM Zone

Local publications tended to stress the importance of ecological awareness and education among the BAMer population to a greater degree than national newspapers and journals. One illustrative example was journalist T. Andreeva's report on members of two construction-erection subdivisions who declared: "We will defend the forests, lakes, and rivers. We will not tolerate a barbaric attitude toward the forest, toward those who seek to murder our green 'friends' and to clog rivers and waterways."[116] An editorial in the newspaper *BAM* noted that "such a gigantic project as ours cannot fail to exert some influence on [the BAM Zone's] ecology."[117] The editors stressed that this influence must be minimized as to prevent "the death of nature" in the area. They remarked that the Komsomol and the USSR Ministry of Transport Construction directed insufficient attention to the plight of those BAMers who attempted to prevent the environmental degradation of their new homelands.[118] Unnamed "careerists" were also taken to task for "ignoring one's socialist duty" by being more interested in advancing their careers than defending the BAM ecosystem from pollution and careless exploitation.[119] The editorial concluded with the assertion that the duty of BAM residents was to "protect flora and fauna and struggle for clean rivers, lakes, and air"—not to abuse nature for personal gain.[120]

BAM reporter P. Cherepanova conducted an interview with Olga Eremenko of the BAM Zone Hydrochemical Laboratory in February 1983. Eremenko sounded the alarm regarding water pollution and noted with some sadness that two brigades, working at remote outposts in Larba and Khorogochi, had failed to reduce significantly their emissions of water pollutants in nine years of existence. Only after "fines and formal reprimands of brigade personnel," said Eremenko, did the violating detachments begin to meet even the most minimal requirements of the USSR Water Codex. Eremenko concluded her remarks on an even more somber note: the thirty- to one-hundred-ruble fines levied against the polluters, she said, served as only marginal deterrents and failed to prevent BAMers from fouling the water near their encampments in the rush to meet their construction quotas on time.[121]

V. Lavrinenko, secretary of the Tynda Komsomol Committee, espoused a similar sentiment. He noted that although "technology is the most notice- able element of BAM . . . those young people who employ this technology possess little life or professional experience to assist them in employing mech- anization effectively and responsibly."[122] This observation was borne out in a March 1983 *BAM* article by correspondent V. Vozin, who commented that human waste as well as petroleum products from the South Iakut territorial production complex threatened the delicate natural balance of the region.[123] Although Vozin cheerfully said that "a modern sewage system is being in- stalled in Neriungri," he also admitted that previous dearth of water treat- ment facilities in South Iakutiia and the BAM Zone generally had already dirtied the local limnetic environment as much as industrially produced contaminants.[124]

A pair of 1981 *BAM* editorials pointed to the need to not only train work- ers in the use of bulldozers and other equipment in building the railway, but also to instill in the BAMers an appreciation of nature's fragility and the need to use a gentle hand in the region's taiga.[125] In a very sanguine obser- vation, the newspaper's editors noted that although many BAMers strove to improve their careers by serving with the project, they ignored the fact that their activities would leave a lasting impression on the BAM ecosystem long after their departure. The editors claimed that the protection of nature was not only a concern to the residents of the BAM Zone, but in the interest of *all* people.

An Embryonic Ecological Movement?

The powerful proponents of "big science" within Soviet officialdom cast the Baikal-Amur Mainline Railway in a distinctly Promethean light as a great connector that would link the Soviet Union's eastern frontier with the rest of the USSR and expose the region's immense natural resources for immediate and complete exploitation. Although this "gigantomaniac" signal radiated from the center's most potent ideological dynamos of the Komsomol headquarters as well as the middle-aged men of the USSR Ministry of Transport Construction, it lost some of its strength the farther it traveled. By the time the Promethean theme reached those who actually worked and lived along the railway, the idea that nature could in effect be raped in the name of socialist progress struck some of those BAMers who possessed high levels of education and held positions of prominence within the BAM hierarchy as foolhardy and inimical to Leninist teachings.

These concerned citizens produced a counter rhetoric of environmentalist sentiment. Whether from such extra-Komsomol organizations as VOOP or from within the youth league itself, a number of academics and bureaucrats noted the environmental degradation surrounding them. While sounding the alarm, they purported to maintain their faith that Soviet-state socialism contained the panacea of officially generated environmental protection that would cure the project's woes. They involved local schoolchildren in the nationally spawned green and blue patrols, established green zones around BAM settlements, and produced reports of careless workers' habitat and permafrost destruction in the pages of the regional press. In these ways, the self-consciously ecologist BAMers belied their actual numbers through their enthusiasm and visibility rather than through their success.

The tragedy of the germinal BAM environmental movement—and that of the entire Soviet Union—lay in the simple truism that awareness and activism did not necessarily produce concrete and lasting results. While striving to preserve the BAM Zone's unique ecosystem from the encroaching railway, the small but highly motivated nucleus of ecologists were always cognizant that their activities had limits due to economic and political considerations. These conservationists realized that the Party's (and thus the nation's) priority was to finish BAM in ten years, regardless of the financial or ecological cost. The efforts to combat ignorance and apathy among the general BAMer population regarding environmental issues met with limited success. The bureaucratic apparatus in Moscow shunned conservationism and as a result doomed the BAM ecological movement to general ineffectiveness more than any other factor. Not until the BAM environmentalists finally withered away like so many of the BAM Zone's acid rain–soaked birches could the debate over whether to give priority to the ecosystem or the railway be fully joined.

3 / Crime and Corruption in BAM Society

The battle against drunkenness and hooliganism must be waged
with a spirit of Communist morality!

Resolution of the Komsomol Central Committee, 1976

A s the BAM project progressed, the attitudes of BAMer youth became increasingly restive as their attention turned away from the building of a Communist society to the more practical goal of improving their
own material status. As one report stated: "When asked the question 'Why did
you come here [to work on the BAM railway]?' several young men working
with SMP-391 in the settlement of Magistralnyi replied: 'To make connections and seek our fortunes.'"[1] BAMer Vladimir Poleshak responded similarly:
"I am already past Komsomol age, and I don't need your romantic notions
of camaraderie. I need money and only money, and that is why I came here."[2]
These attitudes were not unique to BAM, as young people throughout the
Soviet Union were orienting themselves more toward capitalist rather than
socialist goals. In an attempt to thwart this shift, the Komsomol used its
propaganda outlets to present BAM in heroic terms that would motivate
young people both within and outside of the endeavor. The project's makers

hoped that as a "symbol of worker valor and mass heroism," the railway would inspire self-confidence and enthusiasm for the state among BAMers, who would then transmit this positivism to the wider population.[3] Another reality was the development of criminal habits among some BAM workers. What was the nature and scope of these habits as engendered by the experiences of BAMers? The BAM administration had a specific conceptualization of these "deviant behaviors," both in the public and private spheres.

With the arrival in the spring of 1974 of the All-Union Pacesetting Komsomol BAM Construction Brigade, thousands of young Komsomolers, railway personnel, and their children descended upon the taiga of eastern Siberia and the Soviet Far East. These BAMers strove to lay the rails of the "path to the future" that would open the USSR's eastern reaches to economic development and greater prosperity. The Komsomol also expected them to create a new, more progressive society among the pines and firs of the territory. As construction on the railway and worker housing began, the BAMers encountered onerous living conditions that few had ever experienced before. Officials in the Komsomol and other state organizations faced the dual challenge of fostering a pioneering spirit and a strong esprit de corps among the project's young builders. The Komsomol leadership also struggled to provide a sufficient number of outlets for the BAMers' leisure time, the enjoyment of which was considered the "right" of every Soviet citizen, according to the state.

While building the "society of tomorrow" and a "twenty-first-century civilization," however, BAMers had to contend with the area's harsh climate and with the rigors of life in a far-flung collection of isolated communities separated by bogs, impassible mountain ranges, and accessible only by helicopter even in good weather. Towns in the BAM Zone lacked the basic infrastructural components of reliable electricity, sewage, and transportation. As a consequence of the BAMers' overwhelmingly youthful and demographically transient composition, the towns were also deficient in the societal networks of family and friends that typically hold together the social fabric. The Komsomol attempted to fill this void by manufacturing a protean "BAM civilization." Many everyday BAMers ultimately turned to crime, thus failing to become the harbingers of an elysian culture that would blaze a path to Communism, which the rest of the Soviet Union would follow.[4]

More than any other organization involved in the railway's construction, the Komsomol shouldered the burden of selecting sufficient numbers of qualified members to send to the project. Workers were provided occupations to ensure the railway's completion within a decade. The Komsomol was to police those individuals who failed to carry out their assigned duties or violated the law. As construction progressed, however, the Komsomol became increasingly less able to fulfill any of these functions because of the growing size of the project and a chronic staffing shortage. As the project's viability became more doubtful, the youth organization's leadership came to conceive of BAM not as a reward for exemplary Komsomolers, but as a repository for those cadres whose behavior it deemed to be too embarrassing or dangerous to be managed by their home Komsomol committees.

Of those Komsomolers who experienced difficulties with the law, a significant percentage (a cross section of Soviet and non-Soviet sources suggest some 40 percent of them) were children of prominent Party or government functionaries whose dismissal from the organization would serve to embarrass their parents and the group as a whole. The maximum age for Komsomol membership was thirty, and after reaching this age, many former lawbreakers simply disappeared into the local bureaucratic abyss after serving on the railway. By 1984, a surprising number of positions along the railway were staffed by a ragtag collection of wayward Komsomolers who, for a multitude of reasons, could not be expelled from the BAM Zone. The presence of such uninspiring cadres helped to transform many citizens' perceptions of the "project of the century" from an "All-Union Pacesetting Endeavor" to the butt of jokes. This one was told across the country: "What sound does Brezhnev's head make when you hit it with a rail? BAM!" Interviews of former BAMers and others connected to the project mentioned a bevy of BAM "anecdotes," many of which employ lewd railroad imagery to achieve comic effect. Former BAM chief Valentin Sushchevich, an archetypal BAM positivist, cracked several such jokes when interviewed.[5]

Fostering "Communist Morality" in an Amoral Climate

After World War II, Soviet criminology had coalesced into a staid and highly rigid discipline that, along with most other academic realms, walked lock step with official precepts, with little divergence among scholars. A representative Brezhnev-era perspective on hooliganism and criminal tendencies among Soviet youth is *Preduprezhdenie prestupnosti nesovershennoletnykh* (The prevention of youth crime), edited by V. N. Kudriavtsev of the USSR Academy of Sciences Institute of Government and Law.[6] The word "hooliganism" (*khuliganstvo*) was borrowed from the English term for a ruffian or hoodlum. In the Soviet context, the moniker "hooligan" (*khuligan*) described those who instigated public disturbances and fomented disorder. BAMer hooligans (to be differentiated from the hardened criminals who were also present in the BAM Zone) struggled to find their identity and expressed their unwillingness to be molded by officialdom through their so-called misbehavior.

Kudriavtsev's study, rooted in the fundamental Marxist-Leninist concept of the progressive nature of history, argued that man (or *chelovek*, which unlike its English equivalent, does not specify a particular gender) is perfectible and that only Soviet-style socialism could recast the offender in a superior form. The book differed from earlier studies in its avoidance of the vitriolic condemnation of criminal behavior in the Soviet Union as the product of nefarious bourgeois (read: capitalist) forces originating from outside the USSR; traditional views held that these forces must be purged by any means necessary, including the use of violence. But Kudriavtsev and his colleagues concluded that crime—regardless of its severity, frequency, or target—represents a "deviant" act that could be prevented by understanding the motive of the young perpetrator as the result of a lack of ideological education. This, in turn, could be remedied through rehabilitation rather than coercion. Since motive is a function of one's environment rather than the psyche, the contributors maintained, the "criminal-deviant personality," including its subtype the hooligan, could thus be reformed within the Soviet Union's ever-progressing socialist society with a resulting eradication of an individual's desire to engage in wrongdoing. This rehabilitationist philosophy defined Soviet criminology until the Gorbachev years.[7]

Although Kudriavtsev and his associates understood hooliganism as "deviant behavior," by the 1960s some Western scholars perceived the hooligans of nineteenth- and twentieth-century Eastern and Western Europe not as societal marginalia in need of rehabilitation, but often as unwitting cultural mouthpieces whose activities expressed the despair, conflict, and even aspirations of the "laboring classes" (those who held traditionally "blue-collar" jobs, to borrow an American term). Such social and cultural historians as Joan Neuberger, E. P. Thompson, and Eric Hobsbawm as well as the philosopher Michel Foucault instead argued that these individuals on the societal periphery deserve a legitimizing perspective that acknowledges both the deliberateness and the rationality of what the Soviet criminologists deemed "deviant behavior."[8] BAMers of both blue- and white-collar backgrounds who engaged in bribery, theft, drinking to excess, and even rape were not a small minority of troublemakers. In fact, they represented the majority of the railway's all-too-human population. In reality, those within the Komsomol and other BAM Zone organizations who attempted to dictate the norms of morality were often the deviants within the project's frontier world. Many who condemned the lasciviousness of their comrades were themselves guilty of rank hypocrisy.

Most reports of wayward BAMers were kept classified after the resolution of a criminal case. One illustrative example is the 1979 secret letter written by A. A. Karamyshev, head of the Iakutsk city *Lineinoe otdelenie vnutrennykh del* (LOVD, or Line Division of Internal Affairs), in which Karamyshev informed BAM chief Valentin Sushchevich that in the previous year, Komsomol members had committed ninety-three crimes (nearly 20 percent of all offenses that year) within his jurisdiction. Karamyshev angrily noted in the letter that a number of regional Komsomol organizations had permitted many convicted felons, all of whom were Komsomol members in good standing, to be sent to the BAM Zone and that these individuals continued to break the law as new BAMers. Although crime on the railway may have been underreported by the Komsomol, the amount of administrative attention given to discussing, adjudicating, and later cloaking each episode of worker malfeasance strongly suggests that the project's administration took BAMer "deviant behavior" seriously.[9]

From 1974 to 1984, the Komsomol and its allied BAM Zone organizations noted with growing alarm that the behavior of many BAMers, the majority of whom were under thirty, failed to adequately represent the BAMers' official image as hardworking and morally upright Soviet citizens who maintained constant vigilance against "antisocialist notions" and "deviant tendencies."[10] In an effort to curtail an array of "amoral behaviors," the Komsomol instituted a propaganda campaign that emphasized the experimental nature of life on the railway as a "laboratory of socialist development." They promoted an amorphous notion of "Communist morality," in which all BAMers, regardless of age or occupation, would grow together to form a cohesive and progressive society. Instead of teaching so-called Communist morality directly, the Komsomol leadership viewed the philosophy as a way of life that all the project's participants would follow instinctively upon their arrival in the "virgin taiga."[11] The onus for maintaining this self-imposed code would fall upon the Komsomolers themselves, who would blaze the path to Communism as the Soviet Union's foremost ideological pioneers.[12]

Among these moral and physical trailblazers, some were established troublemakers, while others who had never previously engaged in criminal activity began to run afoul of the law. Many reports from the local police, the BAM Zone Interior Ministry, the Communist Party, and the Komsomol attribute this to the stresses associated with the area's primitive living conditions.[13] This turn by formerly law-abiding citizens to crime, corruption, and in some cases social unrest was the direct result of a serious deficiency in the number and quality of leisure outlets available to the average BAMer. These outlets might have included sports enthusiast groups, clubs, and voluntary associations. The profound lack of diversion in the BAM Zone led to high rates of alcoholism, rape, petty crime, and other "violations of public order" whose genesis and scope the BAM apparatus failed to comprehend or manage. Of course, the BAM Zone was not the only area of the Soviet Union that faced increasing crime rates beginning in the mid-1970s.[14] Nationwide, trends in law enforcement of incompetence, corruption, and apathy combined with the railway's relatively small law enforcement organs stretched the state's ability to regulate the BAMer population to the breaking point.

The project's overtaxed law enforcement network included the *Ministerstvo vnutrennikh del* (the MVD, or the Ministry of Internal Affairs), to which the Komsomol turned to help reign in its chaotic members. The MVD suffered from organizational and personnel problems of its own, which undermined the project's prospects for success. Foremost among these was the serious corruption of MVD officials who were assigned to BAM as part of the LOVD, who investigated and prosecuted cases involving Ministry of Railways personnel or property. As with many Komsomolers and others with checkered pasts who were sent to lay the rails, the MVD headquarters in Moscow often transferred substandard officers to the BAM Zone, an area which few officers were familiar with and even fewer found desirable, in an attempt to rid itself of these individuals. Former BAMer Nikolai Nikitin stressed this fact when he stated that "all of us knew that they [the MVD] had sent the worst of the lot to us. It was like a trash can for policemen!"[15] Daily existence in the BAM Zone for workers and law enforcers alike produced boredom and hardship that spawned lawlessness in some and immorality in others. Ultimately, rather than serving as a "laboratory of socialist development," BAM served to atomize a Soviet society that Moscow touted as the most progressive in the world.[16]

In addition to possessing a lackluster policing force, the Komsomol had another problem: its inability to recruit quality cadres who were willing to serve as volunteers to build the railway. BAMers who served on the railway for the standard three-year tour received substantial financial inducements in the form of hardship wages that were equal to three times the standard monthly rate, according to one's specialization and experience. In addition, BAM "veterans" were to receive new car vouchers upon their departure from the project. But none of the vouchers were ever honored by the Soviet government, and by the mid-1980s, the BAM administration had stopped issuing them altogether. In an April 1975 report from Central BAM Segment Headquarters, twelve of the twenty-two Komsomol organizations within BAMstroiput, one of the largest BAM construction trusts, were said to have not brought any new workers to the project in 1974 and 1975.[17] BAMstroiput's answer to this dilemma was to screen a tedious three-hour-long film, entitled *Chelovek i zakon* (Man and the law), which contained interviews with law-abiding Soviet men and women, Party members all, who discussed the joy with which they shouldered the legal responsibilities of Soviet citizenship. The division's bosses believed that the film would instill a sense of "morality" in the worker population, but not surprisingly, the numbers of workers in attendance fell far short of official expectations.[18]

The lack of "moral control" among the BAMers greatly concerned other railway organizations, and many of them devoted significant resources to addressing the problem. For example, the BAM Zone CPSU apparatus reported in October 1975 that the city committee in the settlement of Ust-Kut had "failed to foster a good moral atmosphere" while allowing the pace of construction to slow to the point that projects slated to begin the following year had to be postponed. According to the committee secretary, the "moral climate" of Ust-Kut had degenerated to the point that "labor discipline [has] disappeared," and he noted with some trepidation that the "antipodes of Communist morality" were winning the "struggle to maintain civic order among the labor collectives."[19] Such sentiments were not uncommon among Party and governmental officials in the BAM Zone as all were concerned about their ever-loosening hold over their cadres. Despite their anxieties, however, the dilemma of how to reimpose "moral control" over the BAMers was never formally addressed either by the Komsomol BAM Construction Headquarters in Tynda or the Komsomol Central Committee in Moscow.

Attempts at Self-Regulation: The *Druzhiny*

The BAM administration's solution to crime—whether personal or state, petty or serious—was a near monolithic reliance on the standard criminological practices of "rehabilitation" and "prophylactic action." With an overburdened and understaffed police force, the Komsomol found itself left with the primary responsibility of policing its young members as well as others who had joined the BAM project. The methods the Komsomol employed were national-level policies that had been designed to encourage faith in the system among Soviet youth and to channel their energies away from hooliganism toward such activities as child "militias" and "deputy brigades" that the state deemed important in the maintenance of social order.

In a desperate bid to maintain control over what it considered to be a restive population, the BAM Komsomol headquarters developed the concept of "discipline days." These weekend festivals were cosponsored by local branches of the Ministry of Internal Affairs and the district police; specially chosen "deputy brigades" led public gatherings in an effort to bring peer pressure to bear against those who had violated public order or those who might be considering such activity. While the Komsomol used these festivals to rehabilitate chronic drinkers, other types of violators were also compelled to meet with their peers as part of the normalization process. In the BAMer settlement of Urgal, for instance, some eighteen mentors encouraged "rehabilitated violators," mostly convicted petty thieves, to work with them to curb the incidence of further disturbances in the area.[20]

Another form of self-regulation undertaken by the Komsomol included the use of young adults and even children as surrogate law enforcement officers. In an eventually frustrated effort to combat a growing crime rate and proselytize among the youngest BAMers, the youth organization implemented a special BAM version of a child- and teenager-run policing organization known as the *druzhiny* (the singular is *druzhin*), or young persons' militia. The *druzhiny* was organized by the Ministry of Internal Affairs in 1958 to assist in maintaining public order, combating hooliganism, and preventing all forms of crime. The corps numbered more than a thousand young people at its height. In the BAM Zone, the Komsomol headquarters exercised operational control over the *druzhiny*. The *druzhiny's* duties appeared in a 1975 handbook entitled "Instructions for the Organization of Operational Komsomol Young People's Militia Detachments along the BAM." It stipulated that all prospective members must be over eighteen, come well-recommended by their peers, and maintain themselves in a "businesslike and upright manner." Also, they must meet "the proper political, moral, and physical standards to fulfill the functions of defending public order." The BAM *druzhiny* swore to defend and protect "civic order"; they also made a pledge to engage in sporting events regularly.[21]

As conceived by BAM chief Sushchevich and Colonel D. G. Postnikov, Sushchevich's equivalent within the MVD apparatus, the *druzhiny* were to conduct themselves as examples of socialist morality and righteousness who would be emulated among the BAMer population young and old.[22] These "citizen-police" were to serve as a "force for the preservation of social order . . . among the youth" of the BAM Zone by "combating drunkenness in all its forms, conducting raids to fight hooligan tendencies among youth, and to educate the entire BAMer population about the dangers of drink, idleness, and irresponsible conduct around railway and other transport facilities."[23] Sushchevich himself, however, admitted that many *druzhiny* did not take their responsibilities seriously. Furthermore, while the Komsomol lavished praise upon the young and mostly Slavic militiamen who received the "For Active Work in the Preservation of Social Order Award," most young people fell far short of the Komsomol's lofty expectations.[24] They seemed to have a greater interest in "socializing with members of the opposite sex" than in patrolling among their peers.[25]

Along with the *druzhiny*, the Komsomol sought to include younger children in its amateur self-policing force. The Young Dzerzhinskiite Youth Movement consisted of fourteen- to eighteen-year-olds, along with a junior division of twelve- to fourteen-year-olds known as the "young friends of the police," who served as liaisons between the police and children in the "struggle to maintain public order." Named after Feliks E. Dzerzhinskii (1877–1926), the first head of the Soviet secret police, the group was known originally as the Cheka and later as the GPU and the OGPU. Dzerzhinskii was also head of the People's Commissariat of Internal Affairs (or NKVD), which was subsequently renamed the KGB. This organization was reorganized after the dissolution of the Soviet Union in 1991 and is currently known as the *Federalnaia sluzhba bezopastnosti* (the Federal Security Service). The Komsomol emphasized the physical prowess of potential members, who had to demonstrate skills in marksmanship, swimming, and the Russian martial art of sambo as well as a knowledge of first aid.[26] Before joining, each prospective member swore the following oath to an assembly of his or her peers: "I, a member of the All-Union Leninist Communist Youth League, upon entering the Feliks Edmundovich Dzerzhinskii Brigade, do solemnly swear to always carry the Dzerzhinskii banner high, to faithfully execute all requests and orders of my commander, to be honest, disciplined, and principled at all times, to never hesitate before hardship, to laugh at danger, to be trustworthy of my comrades, to struggle for the maintenance of civic order in my school and neighborhood. If I should violate this oath, then let my comrades scorn and punish me!"[27]

As the project wore on, the BAM administration became more concerned with increasing the numbers of *druzhiny* and Young Dzerzhinskiites without placing as much emphasis on the quality of the new members. As a part of the "I Am the Master of the Project" campaign, nearly seven hundred so-called Young Pioneers (a junior division of the Komsomol), who were divided nearly equally by gender, served as *druzhiny* within forty-four Dzerzhinskii brigades in Tynda between 1977 and 1979.[28] With the help of nearly four hundred Komsomol and LOVD "sponsors," the young militia investigated thirteen crimes in the Tynda area, which led to the arrest and conviction of some nineteen indivduals. The Dzerzhinskiites engaged in "prophylactic work" among their cohort and within the BAM laborer population to strengthen the ties between young people and the law enforcement organizations in the BAM Zone. These youth also published their own newspaper for children that employed humor to emphasize the respect all BAMers should show for their police force.[29] In 1977, BAM chief Sushchevich applauded the efforts of nearly five hundred *druzhiny* in several BAMer settlements for opening "civil order stations." From these stations, young militiamen and -women spoke against theft and alcoholism and for the need to preserve socialist morality.[30]

Sushchevich later turned critical in his evaluation of the *druzhiny*, however. In conjunction with the one-hundredth anniversary of the birth of Feliks Dzerzhinskii and the sixtieth anniversary of the formation of the Soviet police force, the young militia personnel were expected to reduce the frequency and severity of crime in their districts, but in fact rates of theft of state and private property as well as hooliganism increased.[31] Sushchevich cited MVD figures that theft of government and private property within the BAM Zone had multiplied by a factor of three in 1976, hooliganism and murder had quadrupled, and incidence of rapes had doubled.[32] Under the rubric of petty theft, Sushchevich revealed a sharp rise in the number of offenses committed in 1977 by Komsomol members and others under thirty, including "petty hooliganism," "public drunkeness," "violation of internal passport laws," "illegal possession of firearms," "disregard for railway and automobile safety directives," and "violation of fire-prevention codes."[33] Despite his apparent candor, Sushchevich neglected the fact that the BAM administration's sole punishment for these offenses was either to fine the young perpetrators or to arrange a meeting between Komsomol officials and the offender's parents.

Ultimately, Sushchevich and Postnikov's ideal *druzhin* failed to materialize. In the Severobaikalsk and BAM settlements, attempts by the voluntary militia to include younger citizens in their activities also failed. In several towns, *druzhiny* visited middle schoolers in a bid to recruit them for the Young Dzerzhinskiites, who would in turn "prevent violations of the law," but these ideologically-based trips fell into chaos after dozens of male schoolchildren publicly refused to join the organization.[34] Female students, while probably also disenfranchised, were apparently less vociferous about their dissatisfaction. In Tynda, libraries and other public buildings supposedly under the protection of the *druzhiny* became "dangerous places" after the young peacekeepers started selling black market goods while on guard.[35] For the adults in the BAM administration, their attempts to co-opt the *druzhiny* had failed as the supposedly best youth of the railway became an added headache for those who faced the already thorny problem of youth disorder.

Because of the chaotic nature of life for the *druzhiny* and others along the railway, the regime needed to find heroes and heroines that it could present through the local media to an occasionally disgruntled and often apathetic public. In August 1975, Aleksandr Kolesnikov, an MVD policeman, encountered a "drunken hooligan" who had been reported to the police by an observant citizen in Amur Oblast. After the officer attempted unsuccessfully to negotiate with the man about coming to the station peacefully, the drunkard fired a shot at Kolesnikov, who claimed to be "stunned" by his adversary's aggressiveness. The officer decided not to return fire since he was standing close to an occupied apartment building. Suddenly a woman exited the building, and in trying to save her from certain death, Kolesnikov was shot in his left side by the assailant. Ignoring the pain, Kolesnikov and his fellow officers were able to apprehend the criminal, who had been arrested several times in the past.[36] The BAM press presented Kolesnikov as an archetypal BAM hero whose bravery and compassion was to be emulated.

In 1980, G. Khakhanov, head of the Khabarovsk Krai LOVD and a *BAM* correspondent, penned an obituary of Vladimir Timofeev, a MVD sergeant killed in the line of duty. While relaxing off duty at home one evening, Timofeev received a phone call about a domestic disturbance at a nearby BAMer dormitory. Upon arriving at the dorm, he was confronted by a drunken father who had beat his wife and twelve-year-old daughter with a set of keys. Timofeev ordered the man to surrender the keys, but instead the man struck Timofeev on the head and proceeded to beat the policeman to death in a drunken rage. Khakhanov presented Timofeev's death as an example of the heroism a typical BAMer, who had come to the railway in search of a new life, could find not only in life but in death as well.[37] If one considers official crime statistics to be somewhat credible, the number of BAMer police heroes should have been higher, but such heroic representations constitute only a small portion of newspaper and other media coverage of life in the BAM Zone. This paucity can be explained by a number of factors, the most compelling of which is that the official media apparatus was wary about discussing violent criminal episodes in print, even if a positive spin was put on the outcomes of these events. By confirming that crime was as much a part of everyday life in the BAM Zone as in the rest of the country, the local press would point to the lack of a progressive and futuristic (that is, crime-free) society along the railway. Rather than confirm the obvious, the state was thus determined to stick to its own version of history, where only a few BAMers died at the hands of "deviants."

Alcoholism along the Railway

In the years preceding the alcohol sales restrictions of the Gorbachev era, the state enjoyed only a nominal control over the sale of spirits in the BAM Zone despite its official monopoly over this trade. In 1985, the Soviet government initiated a program to curb alcohol abuse that included a temporary prohibition and the reduction of the USSR's alcohol-producing capacity. By 1987, however, these measures had largely failed because of bureaucratic intransigence and a turn to distilling homebrew (*samogon*) by many of the Soviet Union's chronic alcoholics. According to some observers, chronic alcoholics composed more than half of the country's adult male population.[38] Boredom and a lack of alternative forms of entertainment combined with halfheartedly enforced strictures on the distribution of drink and the production of moonshine ensured that a sizable number BAMers imbibed to excess in bars, in clubs, and in their homes. A bulletin issued by Vladimir Kosei of the LOVD indicated that of all criminal cases reported in BAMer dormitories during 1977, nearly half were "related to drunkenness."[39] The term "dormitory" includes both general-use accommodations for BAM workers that were built by the Ministry of Railway Construction and special Komsomol-sponsored and constructed "youth housing projects," known as *molodezhnie zhilie kompleksy* (MZhKs), in which only Komsomolers (usually single) could reside.

Another representative report delivered to the RSFSR Council of Ministers by GlavBAMstroi in 1975 revealed that of two thousand inhabitants of the BAM Zone town of Zvezdnyi, nearly five hundred were sent to "medical sobering-up stations" (*medvytrezviteli*), where they spent the night and then were released. Of these, fifty-nine were arrested for hooliganism and seven for "criminal activity."[40] In a 1974 communiqué to Komsomol headquarters in Moscow, Komsomol official Iurii Galmakov discussed the death of GOREM-21 member Nikolai Gerasimov.[41] While raising electrical lines with a co-worker, Gerasimov electrocuted himself by grabbing a live wire in an attempt to steady himself. The investigating commission concluded that Gerasimov's death was "alcohol-related," although the boss of GOREM-21 received only a "strong rebuke" for allowing Gerasimov to work while intoxicated.[42] Interestingly, administrators from GlavBAMstroi blamed Gerasimov's death on unspecified "technical deficiencies" rather than on incompetence or intoxication. Ultimately, the responsibility for investigating many on-the-job mishaps like this were relegated to the specialized design-technical bureau (*spetsializirovannoe konstruktorsko-tekhnicheskoe biuro,* or SKTB), which had no authority to prosecute or punish offenders. Espousing a Leninist labor philosophy known as the "scientific organization of labor" (*nauchnaia organizatsiia truda,* or NOT), the SKTB strove to accelerate the pace of construction while improving quality.[43]

Such incidents were common in the BAM Zone, especially during the colder months. In another example, A. N. Kashirskii, a sleeper rigger, was last seen drinking at the *Iunost* (Youth) social club in Tynda; he disappeared later that night during a heavy snowfall.[44] None of Kashirskii's acquaintances realized he was missing until several hours later, and only following an intensive search did they discover his body frozen a few feet outside the club. The investigating Komsomol official identified the deceased only as Kashirskii (meaning a "known instigator") and remarked that he often drank to excess.[45]

In another incident, loader Aleksandr Safonov was killed by a passing train in 1974 as he tried to run from the Tynda rail yard to the conductor's hut, where a drinking bout was already in progress.[46] Edmund Miachislavovich, a previously exemplary member of the Eighteenth Komsomol Congress Pacesetting Brigade, became so intoxicated while serving as a foreman in the BAMer settlement of Kichera in 1978 that he died from alcohol poisoning. Although Miachislavovich had received several reprimands for his public drunkness, the Kichera Komsomol organization never forbade or restricted him from purchasing alcohol. He had been decorated only months before as "Hero of Socialist Labor," one of the highest civilian decorations in the Soviet Union. This award was presented to a citizen who exceeded his or her work quota by a significant, often exponential, percentage.[47]

Other representative BAMers whose alcohol abuse resulted in social disorder included twenty-three-year old Georgii Korneliuk, who before arriving in the BAM Zone had been convicted of aggravated assault. Although Korneliuk had spent a year and a half in prison for his offense, Komsomol officials dispatched him to the BAM Zone either erroneously (by failing to check his records) or intentionally (to rid themselves of a troublemaker). Korneliuk paired with Petr Gridtsev, an old schoolmate from Kobrin, to "foment disorder" and distribute illegally obtained spirits among their colleagues in SMP-578 (*stroitelno-montazhnoe podrazdelenie*, or specialized construction-assembly subdivision).[48] Another former criminal, Aleksei Terekhin, arrived in Iakutsk after spending three years in a Voronezh Oblast prison for attempted rape. As a member of SMP-591, Terekhin resumed his previous pattern of behavior until his arrest and deportation from the BAM Zone in early 1979.[49]

The BAM Zone Komsomol and MVD organs devised a series of "discipline days" to raise the level of BAMer consciousness regarding the amount of alcohol-related crime in the region. Those found guilty of committing petty crimes were expected to meet with their peers to discuss their transgressions and formulate ways in which they could improve their behavior.[50] Within the SSMP (*spetsializirovannoe stroitelno-montazhnoe podrazdelenie*, or specialized building and erection subdivision) detachment Ukrstroi, a BAM construction division based within the Ukrainian Soviet Socialist Republic, twenty-five upstanding cadres formed an Anti-Drunkenness and Alcoholism Commission. These members interrogated those accused of alcohol-related offenses, toured bars and social clubs where many BAMers socialized, and visited stores and kiosks where spirits were sold to verify vendors' compliance with state alcohol sales rules.[51] A similar organization, the Commission to Combat Drunkenness and Alcoholism, worked within Ukrstroi to determine both the rate and the type of alcohol-related misdemeanors and felonies committed among the group's members. Its mission was to identify those charged with public intoxication, to determine what merchants had violated Soviet laws concerning the sale of alcohol, and to organize the subdivision's antialcoholism campaign.[52]

Despite these efforts at mobilizing BAMers against alcohol abuse, the near total lack of enforcement of statutes restricting the sale of liquor contributed to an outbreak of "mass disorder" fueled by drink. A 1975 report related the exploits of three members of the prestigious N. Kedyshko First Belorussian BAM Construction Brigade, a wholly Belorussian formation analogous to the All-Union Komsomol BAM Construction Brigade. The three Komsomolers organized a "night of collective drunkenness," in which they spent their monthly wages to purchase vodka for themselves and their associates. After exhausting their supply of liquor, the trio beat a coworker whose only crime was having a relationship with a young woman in whom the perpetrators had taken an interest. BAM Zone officials recommended that the three be dismissed from the project, but the national Komsomol organization refused to provide them with housing outside of the region, thus ensuring that the men would remain on the railway.[53]

Deputy project chief Iurii Galmakov reported that three members of the Riazan Komsomoler brigade were to be expelled immediately from the BAM Zone for "constant drunkenness." They had ignored the orders of their commissar and the train's conductor to behave themselves while on a labor reassignment voyage and committed "drunken debauchery" by threatening the conductor and "insult[ing] and interfer[ing] with the relaxation of the passengers." In a separate incident, the individuals in question jumped off a train traveling between Moscow and Khabarovsk and headed to the settlement of Shimanovsk on their own accord without first receiving permission to go there. After securing falsified documents by bribing an official from the Department of Visas and Registration (all Soviet citizens required an internal passport to travel within the USSR) and obtaining living space in a Shimanovsk dormitory, they got drunk repeatedly and "disturbed public order." The men entered neighboring rooms occupied by women, cursed at them, "leaned up against them, grabbed their skirts, and threatened them with physical violence and rape." After the trio's detainment by a surprisingly brave band of *druzhiny*, the other members of their detachment voted to dismiss the three from the brigade and return them to their previous place of work.[54] Such incidences of alcohol-induced sexual harassment were quite common in BAMer dormitories.

A similar event involved young Tamara Davydchik, an upstanding graduate of the Minsk Higher Komsomol School. She had been sent by the Belorussian Komsomol committee to work with SMP-578, a mixed-gender detachment that specialized in railway engineering. Although most BAMer brigades were single-sex formations, a select number of elite detachments contained both men and women. Upon her arrival in the BAM Zone, Davydchik was reported to have demonstrated a "careless relationship" to her work and a low level of discipline. In 1975, she used her wages to buy vodka in a store and afterward organized a "massive sale of vodka and spirits," which precipitated a "collective drunkenness" in which Davydchik was assaulted by her comrades once her money ran out. Unlike the aforementioned male violators, however, Davydchik was expelled from SMP-578 for "engaging in amoral conduct."[55]

In an effort to mold civic behavior through the use of negative psychology, the BAM press provided examples of behavior not to be emulated. A 1983 article in the newspaper *BAM* related the story of a particular BAMer who had fallen asleep with a cigarette after a drinking bout. The smoldering ash ignited a conflagration that killed him and his drinking companion and destroyed the brigade's wooden dormitory. The article's author strove to put a positive spin on this tragedy by praising the surviving members of SMP-573, none of whom had training as carpenters or electricians, who had managed to rebuild their dormitory from the ground up. In another misfortune, the improper use of firewood to heat a living compartment sparked a blaze that resulted in the deaths of two intoxicated laborers working with the chronically understaffed North Muisk Tunnel project. In the following month, two railway engineers were incinerated when the contents of a broken oil lamp started an electrical fire on their train.[56]

MVD detective V. Barichko in 1983 reported a fuel tank fire that caused the destruction of imported machinery. The blaze, which began inside the Ministry of Transportation's *Mosgidrotrans* headquarters (this was a specialized detachment within Mostransstroi that performed hydrology assessments of rivers before they were bridged by the railway), was caused by the drunkenness of several staff members. While inebriated, they had allowed sparks from a heating stove to fall onto the wooden walls of the headquarters building, which in turn erupted in flame and spread to the fuel storage depot nearby. The resulting conflagration destroyed the structure, a fueling station, and several pieces of heavy earth-moving equipment that were parked nearby. The station manager's sole punishment was to spend his weekends lecturing local schoolchildren on fire safety.[57]

In 1974, the Komsomol attempted to silence the story of a drunken locomotive engineer attached to Angarstroi who had accidentally caused the explosion of a coal-fired locomotive after falling asleep at the controls. In the process of passing out after a drinking episode, the railwayman slumped over the engine's steam valve, allowing pressure to build inside the furnace. This led to a blast that killed both the conductor and a nearby signalman. The official efforts to deflect attention from this incident failed for the most prosaic of reasons, however. The deafening sound of the explosion itself awakened the ten thousand residents in the nearby city of Ust-Kut.[58] While trumpeted by the state as examples of BAMer resiliency in the face of rare incompetence, such mishaps were all too familiar to those BAMers, and citizens throughout the Soviet Union, who had lost their homes and personal property in similar incidents.[59]

Sexual Crime, Theft, and Refusal to Work

The extent, severity, and frequency of sexual crime throughout the BAM railway project remains difficult to determine based on the limited treatment given to such incidents in the archival literature. Such crimes as rape and molestation are completely absent from official secondary sources; many rapes went unreported. Thus interviews and newly declassified documents play an important role in determining the minimum frequency and extent of this especially personal form of malfeasance. A secret Komsomol report on sexual crimes committed by its workers in 1978 revealed that several groups of young men and even boys engaged in rape that year. The three profiled offenders, all of whom were under thirty, participated in a gang rape. In an attempt to understand the motivation behind this incident, the Komsomol examined each youngster's family history and his activities after arriving in the BAM Zone. A common factor in each of the men's lives included alcohol abuse as well as the lack of a strong father figure. The youth organization chose not to imprison any of them; rather, the men were to be "rehabili-tate[d]," with the assumption that their "deviant nature" could be reformed. In a project where the recruitment of workers was difficult, the Komsomol strove to maintain all of the labor it could.[60]

Another sexual criminal with a representative story was the carpenter Evgenii Gromov, whose poor work record began with a "strict reprimand" for being absent from his job for five consecutive days in 1975 because of drunkenness. One night, Gromov entered a women's dormitory at the Shi-manovsk Industrial Complex and attempted to rape several females who were sharing a room. After several women stepped forward to bring charges, a plenum of Gromov's comrades voted unanimously to dismiss him from the brigade and petitioned the Komsomol to return Gromov to his previous place of work.[61] Aside from his loss of occupation and residence, Gromov managed to avoid any further punishment. The system was used by the Komsomol to vote for representatives or to condemn a comrade. This pro-cedure, in which ballots were cast openly and the candidates (or the accused, in this instance) were allowed to talk with each member before and after his or her vote had been tallied, underwent a fundamental revision in the late 1980s, when Komsomol membership declined dramatically.[62]

More information about the importance of the Shimanovsk Industrial Complex is in order. This facility, located in southern Amur Oblast, was the first and foremost territorial-production complex (*Territorialnyi Proizvod-stvennyi Kompleks,* or TPK) to be built in the BAM Zone. Although its pur-pose was to provide the railway with a convenient source of construction materials and processed fuels, the Shimanovsk production nexus never lived up to its potential. The main reason was the unwillingness and inability of several state ministries—most notably the Ministries of Transportation, Transport Construction, and Fuels—to divert enough personnel and re-sources from the industries of the European USSR to allow the Shimanovsk complex to function independently.[63]

Despite the efforts of the BAM apparatus to silence gossip, news of even more outrageous episodes of worker promiscuity circulated among under-standably curious and occasionally shocked BAMers. One individual in a detachment from Volgograd was responsible for a 1979 outbreak of venereal disease that resulted in the unknowing infection of several females, who then spread the disease to others before learning of their condition. Another infected individual was determined to be "mentally deficient" after several women reported having "forced encounters" in which they were offered money in exchange for sexual favors. Many accused BAMers fled before they were to face "comrades' tribunals" to answer for their misdeeds and were never heard from again. While the Komsomol blamed these incidents on the prevalence of alcohol, young male BAMers in particular were singled out for their debauchery and "reckless behavior." Such sexual skulduggery, which was widely discussed among the BAMer population, stymied Komsomol efforts to recruit new young people and to convince those who were already in the BAM Zone to remain for another tour of duty in exchange for increased wages and special job and housing considerations upon their return home. For many law-abiding railway personnel, especially women, the stories of mass drunkenness, physical assaults, and rapes made BAM's automobile vouchers and triple hardship pay much less appealing.

For many BAMers, the project offered an almost irresistible opportunity to steal, "borrow" scarce materials, or engage in bribery as a means to ameliorate one's financial or material situation. As the signature construction endeavor of the Brezhnev years that possessed the general secretary's personal seal of approval, the railway received large quantities of high-quality machinery and electronics. The fact that a substantial percentage of these goods were imported and bore Japanese, European, and American "name brands" that were recognizable even to members of the supposedly "closed" Soviet society added a further inducement for even the most scrupulous but generally underpaid BAMer to at least dabble in thievery. At the project's midpoint in 1980, BAM Zone procurator E. Kazakov noted a high level of theft of goods in BAM railway cars and warehouses. He remarked that the value of stolen construction materials from SMP-567's building site totaled more than 100,000 rubles.[64] Kazakov observed that although nearly every brigade had experienced some theft, an average of 146,300 rubles of materials was removed annually from each of the nearly four hundred individually named BAM construction detachments.[65] Ironically, the esteemed sociologist Liudmila Medvedeva praised SMP-567 and its leader V. Vepritskii specifically for their achievement of "N. Ostrovskii Brigade" status and recognition of its "for labor prowess" (*za trudovuiu doblestiu*) award.[66]

It is difficult to estimate the relative value of the Soviet ruble during any given year, but a ratio of ten 1980 rubles to one 1980 U.S. dollar would result in an annual loss of $14,630 worth of goods per brigade, or a total of $5,852,000 in 1980 dollars. For most of the USSR's history, the official Soviet exchange rate has hovered between $1.50 and $1.60 to the ruble, while the rate on the street ranged between three and ten rubles to the dollar until the collapse of the ruble in the Gorbachev years. When multiplied by the ten years in which these detachments were active, theft alone cost the BAM project more than $58 million, if one uses Kazakov's conservative statistics. In addition, some kleptomaniac quartermasters appropriated dry goods and foodstuffs intended for workers' settlements along with construction materials, selling them for personal profit instead. In most cases, the only punishment for such "petty theft" was a small fine.

Stories of theft abound in the archival literature of the BAM railway project.[67] A representative report from the Komsomol archive describes the "antics" of thirteen members of SMP-585 who were involved in a 1975 disappearance of tools, special winter clothing, and construction materials. After being questioned by Komsomol BAM headquarters about the missing items, the accused were unable to say what had happened to the goods. Although twelve members of SMP-585 were expelled from the Komsomol, the brigade's leader received only a reprimand.[68] In a 1977 letter to the Komsomol Central Committee in Moscow, Iurii Galmakov, then the associate head of BAM headquarters, reported that dozens of vehicles, especially cars, were missing from many locations. Galmakov bemoaned the fact that the theft of these expensive and relatively rare conveyances belonged to brigades that worked in the remotest sectors of the BAM Zone, with some laboring hundreds of miles from any town or settlement. One project along the railway suffered from automobile theft most acutely. In dozens of separate instances, workers who were laboring on the North Muisk Tunnel "borrowed" automobiles and other motorized conveyances, never to return. To guard their vehicles, some drivers were forced to sleep inside their trucks in winter, leading to a colossal waste of fuel and several cases of driver hypothermia. Galmakov echoed the sentiment of many other BAM administrators by observing that each manager is concerned only with meeting his project's quotas, and as a consequence some unscrupulous bosses "borrowed" vehicles to accelerate the pace of construction. Galmakov and his subordinates had to divert precious human and material resources in searching for missing vehicles; the deplorable condition of those "borrowed" vehicles that were returned made the chronic shortage of spare parts even more acute. After Galmakov repeatedly requested help from his direct superiors, he admitted that "the routine 'borrowing' of equipment [has] made meaningful construction work impossible."[69]

Although Galmakov failed to name any thieving individuals by name, a 1979 secret report implicated an official who maintained close ties with the Komsomol BAM construction headquarters in Tynda. The accused, one

E. A. Efimov, obtained shipping manifests that were bound for BAM, including a curious collection of "motorcycles and rugs," and "systematically diverted" goods to his "acquaintances and friends" in exchange for a percentage of the price when these items were sold on the black market. Efimov apparently had a weakness for Japanese stereo equipment, which he still possessed when officials from the Kemerovo Interior Ministry and Department for Combating Theft of Socialist Property raided his residence.[70]

In 1978, BAM Zone security organizations investigated fifty-two instances of theft from railcars and warehouses. In the majority of these cases, the stolen materials were imported and of a "sophisticated nature," which was BAM jargon for precision measuring equipment and electronics. No suspects were ever detained or arrested in any of these investigations, and a handful of Ministry of Transportation personnel deemed to have been irresponsible in their implementation of security measures, as with so many other corrupt bureaucrats, had to pay only small fines for their carelessness.[71] The culture of bribe-taking, skimming, and "fencing" stolen merchandise on the infamous *chernyi rynok* (black market) was well ingrained among BAM conductors and freight loaders. Former BAMer Nikolai Shtikov related his personal experiences with the black market, commenting that that "fencing" served as a major source of revenue for many BAM participants. He recalled: "I knew many people that did it [fencing]. Those were the ones [one] had to look out for."[72] Only after the collapse of the Soviet Union, however, was the true extent of theft by railway employees discussed openly.

A 1979 investigation by the BAM Procurator's Office discovered that a manager at the Komsomol BAM headquarters had acquired undisclosed "scare goods" in exchange for various luxury products, including caviar and imported electronics. In another case, this individual gave motorcycles to his cronies rather than the survey teams and winners of "socialist competitions" in the region who had been promised the vehicles by the local Komsomol authorities.[73] When informed that the manager and his accomplices had stolen the motorcycles and they could not be recovered, several BAMers demanded automobile vouchers as compensation for their lost reward. Although the local CPSU organ grudgingly approved this request, former BAMer Nikolai Nikitin recalled that "the socialist competition winners never received their vehicles. It was a joke."[74] This was true for most BAMers who were rewarded with such vouchers for their railway service.

Also in 1979, the Komsomol committee in the settlement of Severobaikalsk reported on a series of "raids" it had undertaken on the city's stores in search of stolen goods that unscrupulous shopkeepers were trying to sell. In all, nine individuals working in seven stores were discovered to have stolen state property. When confronted by the local MVD, several of the guilty merchants offered bribes in exchange for leniency, another shopkeeper physically blocked the police from inspecting his store, while three others attempted to flee when the raiders approached. Also implicated as "engaging in the deception of the buying public and speculation" were an inspector from the state automotive inspectorate (*Gosudarstvennaia avtomobilnaia inspektsiia,* or GAI), a high-ranking member of the Operational Komsomol People's Militia Detachment (*Operativnye komsomolskie otriady druzhinnikov,* or OKOD), as well as five inspectors from the Department for Combating Theft of Socialist Property, which was supposed to be preventing this type of crime.[75] The kingpin of the Severobaikalsk operation was one Viktor Kolontai, a driver with the Nizhneangarsktransstroi automobile depot. (Nizhneangarsktransstroi was a division of the USSR Ministry of Transportation, based in the BAM Zone town of Nizhneangarsk.)

Apparently, these "fencers" approached potential sellers of their stolen goods at discos and even Komsomol-sponsored "propaganda-agitational bonfires," where they could negotiate without drawing attention to themselves. Once a deal was agreed to, the parties met in the dormitory room of a third party who had been paid to stay out of his or her room and watch for the authorities while the exchange took place.[76] The sale and distribution of stolen goods within BAMer dormitories leads to the conclusion that the railway's administrators, although surely not all involved in theft themselves, were aware of its existence. Either they were too afraid of retribution to report these activities or, more likely, they received bribes to ignore the goings-on in the "houses of workers' solidarity."[77]

In a 1979 communiqué, a frustrated Iurii Galmakov reported several instances of BAMers who, having disembarked in the BAM Zone, refused to honor their pledge to work on the railway during the previous year. Galmakov noted that a "significant percentage" of Komsomol laborers and professionals invited to the project by their local Komsomol organizations never arrived, while their sponsors either refused or were unable to provide any information as to their whereabouts. These apathetic BAMers included many Komsomolers from the Russian Republic who arrived in the BAM Zone, took one look around, and jumped on the first outbound train before they could be stopped. One Ivan Malyshev from Estonia was reported to have abandoned his post and stumbled off in a drunken stupor after engaging in "amoral behavior" with five women from his Komsomol detachment, which was building desperately needed housing in the recently founded town of Nizhneangarsk. Two eighteen-year-old female radio technicians from the Latvian Soviet Socialist Republic refused to operate equipment at the Nizhneangarsktransstroi headquarters and offered to have sex with the conductor in return for allowing them to stow away on the next train home.[78]

A 1975 letter of condemnation issued by the BAM Komsomol headquarters revealed much about the general sentiment shared by many of the project's participants. Thirty-three-year-old Vladimir Poleshak deliberately avoided participation in the "party and social life of [his] collective." Poleshak was reported to have stopped working during the hardest period for his brigade and demonstrated himself to be a person "concerned only with the material side of life."[79] The Komsomol recommended that he be dismissed from the BAM construction and his prized car voucher seized. Such disenfranchised Soviet citizens as Poleshak represented the marginalia of Soviet society. This characterization is in direct contrast to the image of the BAMer as the highest evolution of Homo Soveticus. This image had been put forward by those in the Soviet Union as well as by some individuals abroad who defended the railway from criticism. American socialist author Mike Davidow, for example, has lionized the school-age "BAM buddies" of the Kichera BAM settlement. For Davidow, himself a child of Bolshevik émigrés, these individuals exude none of Poleshak's crudely materialist sentiments or cynicism.[80]

The Verbitskii and Shcherbinin Affairs

Corruption and graft were daily facts of life in the BAM Zone, as in the USSR generally. Perhaps the most prominent and far-reaching of such scandals involved Iurii Verbitskii (BAM headquarters deputy head) and Iurii Shcherbinin (head of the Nizhneangarsktransstroi housing construction division). In 1981, Verbitskii faced widespread public criticism for his lavish lifestyle and frequent junkets to Moscow and elsewhere far from the BAM Zone. The controversy began when a group of BAM Zone women accused Verbitskii of ignoring the "apartment question." Specifically, they charged Verbitskii with ignoring the acute housing shortage in the area and assigning scarce apartment space to his extended family. They claimed that he had forced many families with children to wait out the winter months in temporary housing, which often took the form of converted boxcars and prefabricated cargo storage containers.[81] One irate mother of four lamented Verbitskii's "inadequate, disdainful, and boorish attitude" toward those such as herself who had a critical need for more adequate housing. Others accused the BAM bureaucrat of appointing favorites, whom Verbitskii's critics described as "uneducated and illiterate non-Party members," to fill vacant positions while more qualified candidates worked in jobs outside their specialty and skill level. That summer, Verbitskii drew even more ire when he was spotted leaving for Kiev in his personal car during a time when the BAM Zone population was facing a dire shortage of such public services as water and electricity. A team of local Komsomol officials dispatched to glean peoples' impressions of Verbitskii reported that he "allows things to break but cares not a bit to repair them."[82]

Amid the public's call for an official condemnation or even dismissal of Verbitskii, Komsomol head Dmitrii Filippov came to the defense of his embattled subordinate. In 1981, Filippov denied all of the accusations against Verbitskii and explained that his associate's absences—including a trip to North Korea, Vietnam, and the Philippines—were all work-related and thus unavoidable. Filippov promised to transfer Verbitskii to a Komsomol post in Moscow in an effort to appease the angry BAMers, but the Komsomol head later chose not to honor this pledge. Apparently, Filippov was concerned that rescuing Verbitskii would damage his own stature within the organization that he had run since Brezhnev's ascension to power in the late 1960s.

Verbitskii could not manage to avoid further scandal after the events of 1981. In a 1982 report to the Komsomol Central Committee, an anonymous Internal Affairs official claimed that Verbitskii paid MVD officers throughout the BAM Zone to ignore crimes in which Verbitskii's "associates" stole various items for sale on the "black" or "gray" markets. The most damaging accusation made by the unknown whistleblower concerned Verbitskii's purchase of a set of "two Japanese stereo systems" valued at 2,500 rubles (approximately $250 in 1980 currency), when his monthly salary totaled only 300 rubles.[83] Another suggestion of financial impropriety on Verbitskii's part pegged the deputy BAM chief for his expenditure of 850 rubles on various gifts for a delegation of visiting West German Communists. Another accuser claimed that Verbitskii spent more than a thousand rubles to fund "payments and advances" for his coterie to conduct "business" (a term that carried a pejorative connotation during the Brezhnev era).[84] The end result of the Verbitskii affair was not an expulsion of Verbitskii from the Komsomol or the Communist Party, but rather a simple reprimand from his superiors.

The Komsomol's leadership in Moscow chastised Verbitskii for "numerous deficiencies" in the conduct of his job as BAM's associate head.[85] It is conceivable that Verbitskii's actions caused considerable embarrassment to the railway project, and that public knowledge of his wrongdoing might have damaged the already poor reputation of BAM in the eyes of both Soviet citizens and foreigners alike beyond any hope of repair.

Ordinary BAMers' knowledge and disdain for the corruption they witnessed among their leaders, whom the Moscow bosses continued to herald as "moral compasses," were not confined to secret reports. Soon these attitudes spilled into the local press. The 1978 publication of an open letter to the BAM administration, published under the headline "The Labor Front Is Absent" in the newspaper *Severnyi Baikal* (North Baikal), signaled that public sentiment was beginning to turn against some members of the BAM bureaucracy. The letter's author, a leader of a brigade attached to Nizhneangarsk-transstroi, condemned his direct supervisor, Iurii Shcherbinin, for "fostering a climate of recklessness and danger" by skimping on construction materials while building workers' dormitories. The writer accused Shcherbinin of blatantly ignoring the welfare of his own charges by erecting dormitories that lacked even the most basic amenities, including adequate heating and running water, necessary to support the population of Nizhneangarsk. In commenting on the disappearance of scores of expensive cold-weather tools and earthmovers, Shcherbinin's accuser described the sanitary conditions in the living areas along the north shore of Lake Baikal as "abysmal." In a not-so-veiled innuendo, he remarked that while Shcherbinin was enjoying the comforts of "his female personal secretary," many average laborers had no choice but to turn to drink and other forms of "unproductive socialization" (that is, gambling and sex) because of the lack of recreational facilities in the area.[86]

Although the casual observer could interpret the controversies that swirled around Verbitskii and Shcherbinin as aberrations, criticism of lax building regimens and worker apathy, both public and private, resounded throughout the railway's territory. One of the earliest castings of such aspersions came from those laboring in the Western BAM Segment, which was the first of BAM's five administrative divisions to see a substantial influx of new laborers in 1974. A group of some three hundred Komsomolers arrived to find that they would have to build their own housing before beginning work on the actual railway. To their chagrin, the Irkutsk battalions possessed neither the knowledge nor the proper materials to construct shelters that could withstand the area's raging winters.[87] Writing to the editors of *Sovetskaia molodezh* (Soviet youth), the newspaper of the Irkutsk Oblast Komsomol Committee, the disenfranchised "trailblazers" expressed their dissatisfaction but also their desire not to publicize this embarrassing shortcoming in the railway's planning. The editors' reply, which along with the Irkutsk youth's original correspondence was never published, was more concerned with damage control and with preventing an increase of laborer disenfranchisement than addressing the problems at hand.[88]

Understanding Deviancy

A profound consequence of the BAM project's high level of corruption was the damage done to the railway's official representation as a panacea for a system increasingly dependent on exports of raw materials for revenue.[89] Although some lucrative foreign trade did roll along BAM's tracks by the late 1970s, much of the revenue from the sale of these expensive goods ended up in the pockets of grafters instead of in the hands of the aging and obsolete industries of the European USSR.[90] Many who were aware of its shortcomings continued to view the railway as the "great connector" between the Soviet Union and the quickly growing markets of the Pacific Rim after its announced completion in 1984. Nonetheless, skimming (the sale of stolen property for personal gain) and a public perception of general shadiness continued to haunt the endeavor. These factors helped relegate BAM to obscurity by the early 1990s.[91]

The presence of criminals, profiteers, and generally materialistic builders along the railway revealed that BAM society was not as progressive or futuristic as the state purported it to be. Instead, the dynamics of crime and control that intersected in the taiga revealed that the peculiarities of Soviet human nature, not "Communist morality," were ultimately the superior forces in defining the inhabitants of the BAM Zone. Although such "immoral behaviors" as theft, rape, and graft were certainly not unique to the undertaking or to the Soviet Union, their frequency and the frankness with which the Komsomol apparatus reported them, if only within its inner circle, reveals that the state's control over the populace may have been at its weakest in the BAM Zone, which not coincidentally was the farthest outpost from the center both geographically and culturally. Ironically, while struggling to create a society that would exalt the best traits of socialism, including self-sacrifice and a rejection of materialism, the Komsomol and its attendant organizations actually helped to produce a retrograde, not dynamic, civilization. Within this social milieu, "socialist fire" was replaced by the most atavistic characteristics of humanity in general and contemporary Soviet society specifically.

The state's trust that the BAMers would intuitively chart a course toward a perfectible society was betrayed by a collection of young people who were not the "constructors of Communism," but in most cases were bored and lonely, looking for a way to improve their lives or for a good time. These individuals were not deviants, but members of a generation who, only seven years after BAM faded from the public eye, took an active role in establishing new rules of social and cultural discourse in a post-Soviet environment. These once spurned "amoral" qualities were now considered indispensable for survival. The persistence and even growth of criminal behaviors among the railway's population spoke volumes to the social and psychological condition of the Soviet Union as a whole, which by the mid-1980s had begun to experience personal crime at a rate that would eventually match that of the West.[92]

ДОРОГА
В ГРЯДУЩИЕ
СТОЛЕТИЯ

"The Path to the Coming Century." Note the gender role juxtaposition of the man with sledgehammer and the woman with the camera and flowers, as well as the dove of peace and the diamonds—symbols of the harmony and wealth the railway was supposed to provide.

BAMers crossing the icebound Taiura River.

The Baikal Tunnel under construction.

A Lithuanian BAMer camp.

"First Steps in the
BAM Zone."
BAMers traveling
to a construction
site by helicopter.

An Armenian BAMer camp.

СТРОКИ, ПРОДИКТОВАННЫЕ БОЛЬЮ И НАДЕЖДОЙ

"Projects Dictated by Pain and Hope." This is referring to earlier construction projects in Siberia and the Far East, including the Trans-Siberian Railroad.

АВТОГРАФ ЭПОХИ, АВТОГРАФ ПОКОЛЕНИЯ

"Autograph of an Era, Autograph of a Generation." Note BAM's rails lead to a shining future of construction, jewels, and aviation.

Buriats, a Siberian indigenous group, in national costumes.

BAMer Iurii Podaliak and two Evenk (indigenous Siberian) girls.

4 Working Alone

Women on the Railway

THROUGH ITS OFFICIAL PROPAGANDA CHANNELS, the Soviet government emphasized the equal ability and dedication of male and female BAMers in all aspects of the railway's construction. The Soviet Union was still concerned with solving the long-debated "women's question" (*zhenskii vopros*) —namely, the dilemma of achieving economic and social parity between the sexes. But official recognition of women's accomplishments within a project that severely lacked tangible results was rarely forthcoming. The so-called women's question was debated openly in the pages and airwaves of various media outlets in the BAM Zone, reflecting a growing national trend of discussion on the issue. By the early 1970s, the overall population of the Soviet Union was more than 50 percent female due to the demographic "echo" precipitated by loss of males during World War II. The female population, which represented more than half of the national workforce, was targeted as the key to the establishment of a permanent population in the desolate BAM Zone. Women were also targeted as a constituency of railwaywomen and service industry personnel.[1] Media outlets encouraged Soviet women, especially those under thirty, to volunteer for the BAM project by eliciting a sense of heroism, adventure, romance, and individual pride. The project's overwhelmingly male leadership constructed a notion of the female BAMer, and the recruitment campaign emphasized courage in a thinly disguised attempt to bring women to staff decidedly nonheroic occupations.

Another purpose of the women's recruitment campaign, although it was somewhat understated, was to provide a source of potential wives for young male BAMers, who represented more than 60 percent of the railway project's workforce.[2] Many railway proponents felt that women might remain with the project longer if they felt a sense of familial connection and personal responsibility with BAM. They hoped that women who came to the "project of the century" seeking to further themselves professionally could also be convinced to serve as the mothers of future generations of BAMers and thus help to ensure the endeavor's viability as a social and economic institution.

The 1970s and 1980s witnessed an increasing self-awareness among Soviet women of their inherent self-worth as wives, mothers, and individuals.[3] The mostly young female BAMers strove to make their own contributions and define their societal and cultural roles for themselves within the patently patriarchal railway society.[4] The lack of attention within Soviet officialdom regarding women's "double burden" of wage-earning and household duties and the growing sense of independence among some young women were certainly not exclusive to the BAM Zone. Examining how BAMers, both male and female, ignored or conceptualized these issues reveals much about the gender dynamic of the Brezhnev years in general. The state hammered home the notion that the railway's women (and men) were part of an "experimental" society and participants in a "forum for the discussion of social questions."[5] Although women in the BAM Zone made undeniable contributions during the railway's decade of prominence, they fared no better than those living elsewhere in realizing the difficult goal of a creating a truly gender-equal society.

An Overview of the "Women's Question"

For a decade after the 1917 revolution, *zhenskii vopros* (or "the women's question") occupied a prominent position in Soviet national discourse. The twin issues were (1) how would the state achieve gender equality, and (2) how would women fulfill their dual reproductive and labor roles in the push to establish a proletarian workers' state?[6] Many women played an integral part in the women's emancipation movement during these early years of Soviet authority. Bolshevik feminist Aleksandra Kollontai argued for greater female representation within the government, the liberalization of the marriage code, and the revision of legislation dealing with prostitution and abortion, which were ultimately incorporated into the Family Code of 1918.[7] Nadezhda Krupskaia, the wife of Soviet leader Vladimir Lenin, argued for the adoption of more comprehensive reproductive freedoms and pro-female labor statues into Soviet law; she also helped to establish women-specific institutions within the Soviet bureaucracy.[8] Revolutionary activist and radical feminist Inessa Armand had organized Bolshevik activities in Western Europe before the revolutions of 1917, and between 1917 and her death in 1920 was the first director of the Women's Bureau of the Communist Party of the Soviet Union. Known as the Zhenotdel, the Women's Bureau was dissolved in 1930 under pressure from Soviet leadership.[9]

After Stalin's rise to power in the late 1920s, however, the state effectively silenced such feminist voices as Kollontai's and Krupskaia's. Instead, it turned to patriarchal pro-natal policies, which included the abolition of abortion in June 1936 and the reversal of the Family Codes of 1918 and 1926. These documents had permitted women a substantial degree of sexual, economic, and reproductive rights.[10] Some scholars view these events as an imposition of a "cult of motherhood" upon Soviet women, in which the state sought to boost the population of the Soviet Union by promoting the institution of motherhood. This was considered a critical element in the construction of a rapidly industrializing and progressive Soviet society; and the state granted awards and financial incentives to those women who bore multiple children.[11]

The state appropriated the rhetoric of the women's emancipation movement for itself by announcing that it had leveled men's and women's salaries, created a comprehensive childcare system that allowed women to work outside the home, and reformed the educational system to permit women to pursue technical and professional careers that had been mostly closed to them before 1917. With the exclusion of any contrarian voices in the forum of women's rights after 1930, the government by mid-decade had proclaimed the women's question to be solved. The state boasted that women's emancipation had come to pass as inevitably as had the liberation of the laboring classes from the shackles of capitalist oppression.[12] This assertion of gender equality in the Soviet Union, despite women's double burden of wage-earning and household duties, persisted until after Stalin's demise in 1953.

The apex of Soviet patriarchal policies occurred during World War II, when the nation's women were called upon to produce even more children and to provide vast quantities of armaments for the war effort. Many women also served in the country's armed forces and partisan detachments alongside their male comrades.[13] Official expectations of women, already heavy with the demands of the Stalinist crash industrialization and agricultural collectivization drives, became even more onerous during the war years as the general population of men declined dramatically due to war losses. During and continuing after the conflict, women filled many positions in government and industry that had been vacated by fallen men as they continued to shoulder the lion's share of domestic responsibilities, including raising children.

The post-Stalin official sentiment on the women's question was perhaps best expressed by Soviet political scientist Vera Bilshai, who stated in her 1959 treatise *Reshenie zhenskogo voprosa v SSSR* (The solution of the women's question in the USSR) that "the practical experience of nations within the socialist camp clearly confirms that the complete liberation of women both as individuals and laborers has been attained as a result of the victory of socialism over capitalism."[14] Although the Khrushchev regime was eager to initiate change in such areas as the treatment of the Stalinist past, agriculture, and foreign policy during the "thaw," the still present dilemma of women's status in Soviet society remained of little interest to the dominant patriarchy, with the notable exception that it lifted the prohibition on abortion in 1955.[15] Despite the assertions of Bilshai and other scholars that the liberation of women from the domestic and reproductive constraints of the past had been achieved, the debate over gender parity continued to spark interest among the larger female population (at least privately, if not publicly).[16]

Although the official relaxation of social and cultural controls that accompanied the so-called thaw ended abruptly with Khrushchev's removal from power in 1964, the atmosphere of debate and questioning it engendered remained and helped to contribute to a reexamination of the women's question and the veracity of its purported resolution. The primary causal factor in the return of this question to the public sphere centered around the state's need to add workers (females in particular) to a diminishing national pool of labor, which had been stricken by an increase in abortions and a trend toward smaller families. Thus the addition of more workers would heighten the Soviet Union's industrial capacity.[17] The "new public atmosphere" of relaxation and critical thinking that defined the thaw years allowed women to gain a new confidence to express their desires, discontents, and hopes for the future.[18] This emerging women's consciousness would endure beyond 1964.

Table 4.1

BAM brigade composition by gender and age, 1981, all divisions (percentages)

Sex	Age			
	20 and under	21–24	25–28	29 and over
Male	48.6	65.6	70.9	69.4
Female	51.4	34.4	29.1	30.6

Source: Argudiaeva, Trud i byt molodezhi BAMa, 24.

Later, "developed socialism" during the Brezhnev years allowed some further room for ideological maneuvering on the issue of women's equality. It permitted a partial recasting of the discussion of women's positions in Soviet society that attempted to transcend the traditional roles of wife and mother. In asserting that the achievement of socialism was an ongoing process in the USSR, the state admitted that the attainment of gender parity, while still a possibility, was as yet incomplete. The return of the women's question to official vogue precipitated a wave of scholarly and popular attention on women's roles as mothers and care providers for children. The government adopted legislative measures designed to curb the rapidly rising divorce rates and promoted the monetary and social benefits of having larger families.[19] The revisiting of the women's question pointed to an official awareness, if not a tacit admission, of the persistence of patriarchal control in the supposedly gender-equal Soviet Union. As such, this matter contained an element of danger for those who sought to hold together the unraveling threads of the USSR's social quilt.

By the beginning of the Brezhnev years, the majority of Soviet women worked outside the home in addition to undertaking such responsibilities as childbearing and rearing, which the state declared to be the backbone of domestic society. These duties, however, were not considered part of the masculine social function.[20] This double burden of family and work gained currency among Soviet women and contravened the official orthodoxy that women were eager and willing to fulfill their duties as wives, mothers, and economic contributors without complaint.[21] Women who contemplated joining BAM had to contend not only with the project's primitive working and living conditions, but also with the realities of their double burden.

The majority of *bamovki* (female BAM workers) in the BAM detachments were in their twenties. Older males (those older than twenty-five), who often held supervisory positions over female BAMers, represented a sizable demographic presence in the railway workforce.[22] Table 4.1 details brigade composition for all divisions by gender and age in 1981. It includes information for approximately three hundred thousand laborers with Komsomol BAM organizations (such as GlavBAMstroi) and administrative units (such as the BAM Division of the Union of Professional Railway Workers, which fell under the control of the USSR Ministry of Transportation). As for the other two hundred thousand BAMers who participated in the project between 1974 and 1981, statistical data for determining the gender ratio of this population is not available. One possible supposition in explaining this lack of data is that the number of males versus females on the railway became a more important priority for the BAM administration after 1980. That noteworthy year was the first time the railway reached a sufficient level of completion to support a permanent population, at least in the minds of Soviet planners.[23] The amount and quality of statistical data on BAMer men and women improves noticeably after 1980.

The *Bamovka* as Heroine

The mostly male cohort of BAM administrators and media directors sought to entice women to the railway by launching a campaign that emphasized the strong characteristics and heroic deeds of those who were already there. This promotional effort, which described the *bamovki* as hard-working citizens, was intended to convince those women of Komsomol age that they could also achieve heroism through labor and childrearing. Many women were interested in BAM for its exotic appeal or financial incentives (most BAMers received triple hardship pay). The project's boosters entertained the idea that a substantial portion of the female BAMer population was amenable to joining the railway due to their sense of adventure or escape rather than civic duty. The male hierarchy failed to consider that a substantial cohort of Soviet women would not want to remain *bamovki* indefinitely, regardless of the incentives or appeals used to recruit them. Reluctant to acknowledge the complexities of the "women's question," BAM leaders and publicists in effect weakened their efforts to recruit and retain a large female presence on the railway. This revealed their ignorance of the fact that Soviet women's self-image and expectations of true equality had grown by the early 1970s.[24]

How then did the BAM administration undertake the daunting task of drawing females to the railway? Recruitment lay in the state's frequent assertion and genuine belief that BAM was not a temporary undertaking, but the opening salvo in a long-term battle to increase the number of inhabitants in and the industrial capacity of the BAM Zone as well as the entire eastern third of the Soviet Union. With the realization soon after the project's inception that such a goal could never be realized without a significant proportion of women, BAM propagandists dedicated a decade's work to bringing them to the project in large numbers. One of their core strategies was to deemphasize women's reproductive potential and instead to foster the notion of the railway as a place far from home where the young BAMers' dreams of independence and freedom could be realized while building a new and progressive "BAM society."[25]

The idea that self-realization was a concomitant result of BAM service was reinforced by such institutional rituals as the swearing of oaths to the Komsomol and the Communist Party. At the beginning of their service, the nearly 80 percent of BAMer women who served in all-female formations were expected to affirm the following statement publicly before beginning their tour on the railway: "I am a Komsomol woman. This gives me the right to choose my own career path. The Komsomol membership card is a mandate, one that opens the door to true happiness, real happiness both at work and leisure. I believe in the Komsomol and I want it to believe in me."[26] Although this affirmation was designed to instill a sense of belonging among female BAMers, it also included the expectation that loyalty to the Komsomol was one's most important responsibility as a BAMer. The most ubiquitous and refined trope employed by BAM propagandists in their recruitment of was that of the BAMer heroine as a worthy representative of the liberated and progressive socialist woman in the Soviet Union. The image of such individuals embodied a number of positive qualities, including industriousness, humility, and selflessness—the purported hallmarks of all BAMers but women especially.[27]

In an effort to recruit enough women to create a permanent population base, BAM journalists produced glowing accounts of women who worked hard but also managed to preserve their femininity. Reporter B. Musalitin of *Gudok* described the archetypal *bamovka* heroine in his profile of Construction Brigade Number 544, an all-female group under the leadership of one Vladilena (a name derived from Vladimir Lenin) Danilova. The writer characterized Danilova as a "shining example of female initiative, wisdom, and compassion."[28] Her charges were said to have overfulfilled their track-laying norms and, in some instances, surpassed the output of male teams. Musalitin singled out Danilova's group because it was led by a female and participated in actual railway construction instead of auxiliary duties.

Gudok contributors A. Pobozhii and Iurii Fokin, in articles entitled "Trailblazers" and "A Tale of the Line" respectively, used warriorlike language to laud *bamovki* who "assaulted" the taiga by helicopter during the project's first spring to survey the railway's future route.[29] Pobozhii noted that the "heroic women" combated mosquitoes and ticks in a Promethean triumph over nature, but they also "maintain[ed] their delicate female features."[30] Fokin related the story of how Russian women of the past, especially Cossacks, had helped to expand the nation's frontiers during the imperial era. Now, instead of bringing "primitive capitalism" to the borderlands as the Cossacks had, today's BAM women served as the "shock troops of Communism" as they struggled to integrate Siberia and the Russian Far East more closely into the national economy and society.[31]

Polish journalist Marek Sechkovskii, who visited the BAM Zone in 1975 to learn more about women's roles on the railway, espoused a similar perspective as his Soviet colleagues. In "The Girls of the Line," Sechkovskii profiled several female members of the Seventeenth Komsomol Congress Brigade who had "eagerly" ventured to the BAM Zone during the project's first days and found themselves serving not as railwaywomen but as waitresses at a cafeteria in the newly founded town of Zvezdnyi.[32] He expressed amazement at their capacity for hard labor and self-sacrifice and went to great lengths to point out that these BAMers were "pacesetters who blaze the path for women around the world," their prosaic occupations notwithstanding.[33] For Sechkovskii, these individuals represented sui generis Soviet women who, despite the fact that they served as service-industry personnel along with most other *bamovki*, were successfully forging new lives amid the region's primitive conditions. His choice of BAMer women who worked in a service capacity (rather than in the actual construction of the railway) exposed his not-so-subtle attempt to recruit women for the large numbers of menial jobs. As a state-sponsored propagandist, Sechkovskii understood that although they were essential to the project's success, these more service-oriented positions were difficult to fill due to their undesirable location and salaries.

A 1976 issue of *Avangard* (Advance guard) looked at Anna Zbrueva, who was a member of a brigade laboring on the border of Amur Oblast and the Iakut ASSR in the railway's northeastern sector. A professional railway builder, Zbrueva had come to the BAM Zone straight from her collective farm in southern Russia. Her "working heroism and courage" had helped her to build the "path to international women's unity" as a tractor driver turned sleeper layer, who was responsible for positioning the railroad ties (or sleepers) in their correct orders along the railway.[34] Also in 1976, a series of *bamovki* profiles entitled "Young BAM Pacesetters" appeared in *Baikalo-Amurskaia magistral* (the Baikal-Amur Mainline newspaper) and included the story of bricklayer Tania Vasina, whom the editors described as a "tall, shapely girl" from the Russian Soviet Federated Socialist Republic (RSFSR). Their photograph-enhanced account of Vasina, a deputy to the RSFSR Supreme Soviet and a recipient of the *Znak pocheta* (badge of honor), lacked any concrete information about her accomplishments on BAM. Instead, the journalists hinted that Vasina's good looks were not an impediment for her, noting that "her well-known beauty has opened a large and interesting path for this attractive girl."[35] The purpose of this article and others like it, which stressed the physical attributes of a particular *bamovka* over her professional qualifications, was to drive home the fact that female BAMers could preserve their beauty and hence their attractiveness to men while also serving the nation—an important consideration to those women who were looking for husbands among lonely BAMer men. By the mid-1970s, incidentally, the divorce rate in the Soviet Union had increased to well over 50 percent.

In another profile detailed in "Young BAM Pacesetters," the reader is introduced to Liubov Churaeva, a delegate to the Seventeenth Komsomol Congress who went to the BAM Zone after the conclusion of the congress. The same editors of *Baikalo-Amurskaia magistral* who had ogled Tania Vasina exclaimed that "Churaeva speaks with pride" about the dormitory in Tynda she and her "sisterly comrades" helped to construct. Also highlighted is Churaeva's participation in the USSR-sponsored 1975 World Congress of Young Women, in which BAMer women traveled to Havana, Cuba, to publicize their accomplishments as the women "on the frontlines of the first proletarian achievement to employ twenty-first century technology." Churaeva was a perfect representation of *bamovki* excellence that could be shown to the world, particularly those nations within the Soviet sphere of influence that Moscow wanted to impress. The newspaper's editors pointed out that Churaeva's freedom to leave the Soviet Union (a highly desirable liberty that most BAMers could not enjoy) was available to all BAMers; they hinted that other *bamovki* could follow "friendly and self-effacing" Churaeva overseas if only they excelled in their tasks.[36] Proportionally speaking, however, few BAMers ever left the USSR during their tours of duty.

The militarized language that dominated other forms of BAM propaganda also permeated the women's recruitment genre. In 1977, Nina Raspopova, World War II veteran and Hero of the Soviet Union, traveled around the BAM Zone aboard the agitational train *Komsomolskaia pravda*. Having served as a pilot in the Red Air Force, she now delivered a series of lectures on the role of Soviet women during the conflict. The talks were held in conjunction with the sixtieth anniversary of the Bolshevik revolution. The administration presented Raspopova as a heroic older *bamovka* worthy of emulation whose valor was attainable by the younger generations through their participation in the quasi-military BAM undertaking.[37] In a military-worded broadside that was posted in common areas in many BAMer settlements, the Komsomol compared Raspopova's bravery in the skies over Leningrad and Stalingrad to the triumphs of BAMer women on the railway's "front" and "rear," referring to both construction and support services.

Nina Nesterova of Cheliabinsk was another *bamovki* heroine. The Komsomol honored her in a nationally circulated poster as the "best young electrician" within a Buriat ASSR tunneling brigade, known colloquially as TOs (*tonnelnye otriady*).[38] Nesterova's success within the male-dominated profession of tunneling revealed that female workers could further their education and refine their freely chosen specializations while living on the rails. The poster contained language that ordinarily was reserved for males within the project: "fearless" (*besstrashnaia*), "powerful" (*moshchnaia*), and "strong" (*krepkaia*). This message was intended to appeal to young women who were thinking about joining BAM as well as those already on the railway who might be persuaded to remain if they could be convinced that a long-term commitment to BAM would serve as a catalyst for their professional careers.

Larisa Komarova and Tatiana Gruzdova, both cashiers at a BAM Zone grocery store, were profiled as "glorious providers of sustenance" in the struggle to defeat the harsh winter conditions in the region.[39] By "gladly offer[ing] nourishing food," Komarova and Gruzdova served as an encouragement to the USSR's older women, whom the project's boosters believed might be moved to volunteer with the railway's support staff.[40] In 1982, O. Vasilev of *BAM* submitted a report on brigade leader Liudmila Sergeevna in recognition of International Women's Day. Sergeevna's "Work Without Retreat" campaign emphasized brisk but attentive construction work within her all-female detachment. Since 1976, stated Vasilev, Sergeevna and her young charges had proven that a highly motivated and skilled battalion could work successfully without any male supervision "in conditions that women outside the socialist world would find overwhelming."[41] As "pacesetters of Communist labor," Sergeevna and her team were dedicated socialists who in previous years had devoted much of their spare time to building a school and a children's clothing store. As a prime representative of a self-effacing *bamovka,* Sergeevna declined to take any credit for her detachment's successes. Instead, she proudly reported to Vasilev that one of her subordinates had recently been elected as a deputy to the regional Communist Party council of Amur Oblast, where she "serves not as a woman, but as a freely chosen ambassador of the people."[42] The message that the potential for social advancement and even Party membership could result from one's BAM service appeared frequently in this permutation of the women's recruitment genre. It was echoed in non-BAM literature that sought to bring more women into political life and thus strengthen the CPSU's societal role.

Another *BAM* article in 1976 detailed *bamovki* accomplishments in honor of International Women's Day. Valentina Monina and Nina Lavrova, two assistant principals at the Tynda high school, were "not only the able educators of the next generation, but also outstanding workers—the builders of our Communist future."[43] Monina and Lavrova set examples of diligence and attentiveness within the service industry corps that other BAM women, including female children, were encouraged to emulate. (According to archival findings, Tynda had a population of approximately twenty thousand children out of its total of one hundred thousand). Entitled "Happy Holiday!" the article emphasized that these traits could best be learned during one's service on an undertaking such as BAM. The transmission of the railway's positive image to children was crucial to the center's goal of perpetuating both BAMer and non-BAMer enthusiasm for the project after the invariable dissipation of initial interest. The message was expressed by Monina herself: "My greatest joy has been telling our young BAMers about their role in this great moment in history."[44]

A 1975 article from the Sverdlovsk (now known as Ekaterinburg) Komsomol newspaper contained excerpts from the "journal" of Liudmila Makeeva, a twenty-year-old worker with the Urals BAM Construction Division.[45] In

"All Is Peaceful and Radiant in the Spirit," Makeeva displayed her intense pride in being a *bamovka* and spent several paragraphs describing the natural beauty of her Amur Oblast worksite. The journal entry devoted little attention to the actual work being undertaken at her location and instead commented on the alacrity of the changing seasons and the exotic animals such as the Siberian lynx that inhabited her area. This form of recruitment article, in which the region's rich ecology was emphasized rather than the project itself, was popular with local journalists. They hoped that this type of article, replete with lavish descriptions of the natural splendor that surrounded the railway and with hints of conservationism, would resonate with those prospective and current BAMer women who felt an affinity with nature. Makeeva also stated that she felt "cleansed" after a few months of life in the BAM Zone, suggesting that one could engage in self-purification by joining the endeavor. BAM recruiters sought to foster a sense of inclusion among those women who might otherwise be unmoved by the tedious descriptions of the railway's technical specifications and colossal scale that dominated much of the popular literature.

Women from the Soviet Union's numerous ethnic minorities, particularly those residing in Siberia and the Far Eastern sectors of the RSFSR, were also the targets of a specific and individualized form of railway propaganda. Reporter A. Ignatenko profiled one such woman, a forestry expert and *komsomolka* from Kazakhstan named Roza Li.[46] The child of a Russian botanist and a Chinese technician who had forsaken his homeland to live among the "peace-loving and friendly people of the USSR" after the Sino-Soviet split of the late 1960s, Li was bilingual and had written Chinese leader Mao Zedong several times about the successes of BAM and its potential to "strengthen proletarian ties" between the Soviet Union and the People's Republic of China. The article stressed BAM's possibility as a unifying, rather than an atomizing, force in the relationship between the Chinese and Soviet peoples. When not studying economics during spare moments in her Tynda dormitory, Li traveled throughout the country to popularize the project and "build Communism among our young women as we are building BAM" in the process.[47] Li was promoted as an educated and well-traveled professional who, like Liubov Churaeva, possessed the freedom to leave the project periodically. The message strove to encourage minority women, only a few thousand of whom ever served on the railway, to volunteer for BAM service, demonstrating the project's "multinational" character.[48]

A 1975 article in *Pobeda* (Victory), a newspaper published by the Shimanovsk Industrial Complex, a CPSU organization, examined several female *udarniki* (pacesetters). Close friends Ekaternina Shkuro, Klavdiia Sevriuk, and Olga Pavlenko worked as machinists and had volunteered for double shifts to produce more building materials for the railway's dormitories and railway stations. As with Liudmila Sergeevna's brigade of philanthropists, the self-sacrifice of these three young women for the greater good of BAM provided clear examples of innovation and industriousness that other bamovki were to follow.[49] The BAM Zone was thus described not only as a forum for professional achievement, but also as a territory where true self-confidence, forthrightness, and contentment could be realized.[50]

A 1981 *BAM* article entitled "One's Place in Life" introduced the reader to Anna Gribkova, who chose to be a railwaywoman after grade school due to her "romantic notions of travel" as well as her affinity with the symbolism of Soviet railways as "beacons of socialist accomplishment."[51] As a locomotive operator at Volkhov station along the October Railway that runs between Moscow and Leningrad (now St. Petersburg), Gribkova grew to love the sounds, smells, and "intense rhythm" of the rails. As her time as a railwaywoman increased, she yearned to see the farthest reaches of the Soviet Union; this "romantic enthusiasm" drew her to join the BAM project. Serving as a Komsomol secretary at the BAM station of Zolotinka, Gribkova exclaimed that she was "happy to be a part of an endeavor that is both great and necessary for the nation."[52] By sacrificing her chance to raise a family and dwell in the relative comfort of the European USSR in favor of advancing her career with BAM, journalists had found in Gribkova an ideal *bamovka* who would appeal to many women. As a resolute and determined woman, Gribkova served as an example to those contemplating a move to the BAM Zone of a young woman who had succeeded without male intervention and the constraints of a family.

In a 1982 contribution entitled "Happiness Serves People," *BAM* reporter O. Chudnovskii explored the "BAMer character" (*bamovskii kharakter*) in a visit with Liubov Murashova, a railway veteran of thirteen years who served as the chief custodian at the remote station of Skovorodino. Murashova became well-known for the lavish International Women's Day celebration she prepared at the station each March 8 for travelers and her fellow workers. Chudnovskii's real interest, however, lay in Murashova's background. After arriving in Tynda without her husband and her children, all three of whom had remained behind to continue their education, Murashova found a maintenance job with the Trans-Baikal Railway (a line that circumscribes Lake Baikal under the administrative jurisdiction of the Trans-Siberian Railway) in 1970, some four years before BAM construction began. She decided to become a BAMer, which she described as "the best decision of my life," and was elected as her department's delegate to the regional party congress.[53] With the encouragement of her family, Murashova forged her own path as a "compassionate woman" by serving as a surrogate mother for the younger *bamovki* who had been assigned to the Skovorodino station. The image of Murashova as a caring and nurturing figure was intended to be a direct appeal to the maternal instincts of older women whose potential willingness to work in such an occupation was in short supply.

Valentina Basova, a warehouse official in the BAM Zone settlement of Berkakit, also served as a surrogate parent. Female journalist M. Dymova of *BAM* noted that Basova's desire to find "challenging and interesting work" led her to the railway, where she proclaimed herself to be "the happiest I've been in my entire life."[54] Rather than include an extended interview with Basova herself, Dymova chose to write about her discussion with Basova's supervisor, M. N. Babiichuk. Babiichuk delievered a long-winded description of Basova in the article, including a commentary on Basova's "caring personality" and her ability to "put everyone around her at ease."[55] Dymova's contribution closely resembled Chudnovskii's look at Liubov Murashova in its effort to evoke in the reader a sense of family and closeness in this often anonymous endeavor of a half-million people.

Another older *bamovka* profiled in the local press was Liudmila Golovnina, the general manager of the food kiosk at Bam Station. Not to be confused with the BAM railway itself, the station of Bam is located along the Trans-Siberian Railway at the southern terminus of the "Little BAM." A. Kozenko of *BAM* described Golovnina in his September 1982 contribution "Dreams Personified" as an "interesting and serious person."[56] Kozenko concentrated on Golovnina's knowledge of the region's flora and fauna, which she had gleaned during trips with her husband, Valerii, whom Kozenko wrote had taught her how to drive an automobile. Here, the reader learns that other activities besides those connected directly to the functioning of the railway are available to all *bamovki*, regardless of age. BAM propagandists viewed the attainability of a daily existence along the remote and exotic railway that was as normal as any other throughout the Soviet Union as a powerful inducement.

E. Kokhan of the BAMer newspaper *Zolotoe zveno* (The golden spike) profiled *bamovki* Valentina Sidorova and Lidiia Vorobeva, who had left their homes in the RSFSR to help in the final push to finish the railway. Kokhan noted that Sidorova and Vorobeva had become adults during their service and had both gained confidence and even a feeling of "personal independence" that they would carry for the rest of their lives.[57] The fact that these two women had voluntarily left the safety and comfort of their homes to live a new and exciting life on the railway was considered a propaganda bonanza by those who wanted to channel the spirit of such young women into building a BAM society out of nothingness. In propagandizing the image of the *bamovka* as a pioneering heroine and benevolent mother figure, the BAM media sought to promote social mores among a female population that certainly contained a percentage of heroines and mothers but was also defined by the attitudes of more prosaic individuals.

The Contented BAM Woman

The creation of a passive and satisfied *bamovka* in the local and national press constituted another attempt to guide women's beliefs about themselves and the BAM project. But not all images of the project's female population were designed to encourage resoluteness among the railway's women. An interview by the famous BAM correspondent Leonid Shinkarev with four female BAMers stated in not-so-subtle fashion that the women's boss was their "honored father," an older man who had helped the four young women to "maintain their diligence and Communist morality" since their arrival on the railway.[58] Without his guidance, one of the women declared, "we would have been lost. We are so thankful for such a caring man!"[59] In a *Gudok* article Komsomolers Natasha Shishkina and Vaspura Sarkisiana characterized themselves as "occasionally absent-minded sisters" who were in the capable hands of their "benevolent and fatherlike [male] supervisor."[60] Some *bamovki*, particularly those young women under the direct supervision of an older male, were undoubtedly willing to sublimate themselves to their superior's will or endure the frequent berating that characterized many of the railway's professional and personal relationships. It is equally conceivable, however, that some women resented male interference and were simply saying what they had to in order to keep their jobs. Former Komsomol member Galina Mironova expressed this sentiment in an interview. Now an employee of the

Molodaia gvardiia (Young guard) publishing house, she had met her husband while serving on the railway. According to Mironova: "We said what we had to say [about the project]. That was all there was to it. Any words against the project meant problems with the local Komsomol committee."[61]

Perspectives in the media of women who held jobs that had not been traditionally held by females stressed these individuals' ease with their unique position in BAMer society. For example, BAM media coverage contained positive representations of female tunnelers and tended to emphasize the tunnelers' emotional state rather than their tangible contributions to such a critical area of railway construction. In *Baikal-Amur Railway—A Panorama of a Multinational Endeavor*, a number of women building the North Muisk Tunnel declared their "happiness at labor among the North Muisk hills" while ironically working under the slogan "Real Men Build BAM's Tunnels."[62] Women who staffed positions in the service industry sector were portrayed subordinately in the BAM Zone media. A 1977 account in *Baikalo-Amurskaia magistral* looked at "The Faces of BAM," including saleswoman Galina Panchenko. Panchenko and her "doting" husband had decided to come to BAM, where she "brightened the lives of those with whom she has served and worked" while serving as a cashier in a Tynda clothing store."[63] The article's female author praised Panchenko's "satisfaction with her job" and categorized her as a woman who "exuded the spirit of the railway" through her selflessness and infectious optimism.[64]

Genuine Enthusiasm Ignored

In an interview, Mironova explained that BAMer women lived, worked, and socialized within a segregated and marginalized gender cohort: "We lived apart in what they said was a 'community of comrades.' That wasn't so bad, being away from the men and all. But the problem was that we wanted equality and some thought that we might find it there. We didn't."[65] Dominated by concerns of equal pay and plans for the future, the latter of which included the key decision of whether one should stay on BAM or not, women faced economic and social considerations that differed starkly from that of BAMer males. With the launching of the mammoth BAM publicity campaign in the spring of 1974, images of the railway as the "key to the twenty-first century" and "the path of courage" flooded local and national media outlets. For a variety of reasons—from adventure to familial pressures to careerism—

thousands of women contacted the Komsomol's Moscow headquarters and expressed their strong interest in becoming a part of the project.

While the vast majority of these women were unaware of the living conditions and work realities that would be expected of them in the BAM Zone, some four hundred declared themselves willing and able to contribute to the "path to tomorrow" by writing to the Komsomol's leadership in Moscow. A rare example of such requests in print can be found in the 1975 edition of *Baikal-Amur Railway—A Panorama of a Multinational Endeavor*, a yearbook published by the CPSU committee of Khabarovsk Krai. These communications were not part of the BAM recruitment campaign, as such letters were rarely published and were normally forwarded to the Komsomol archives. It is unclear why the BAM administration chose not to exploit these sincere letters, although it is conceivable that many of the letter writers were too young or lacked the proper credentials to be assigned to the railway.[66]

One letter written by four young women to Komsomol Secretary E. M. Tiazhelnikov reads: "Please send us to BAM! We will be very, very thankful!"[67] In a letter sent from western Siberia, a young woman who identified herself only as "Young Miss Evdokimova," revealed a deep concern that she would remain "undisciplined" if the Komsomol denied her request to come to BAM as a radio technician. In another example of what appears to be legitimate enthusiasm for the project, young Komsomoler Alla Gladkova wrote that although she was only in the tenth grade and possessed no professional skills, she was willing to go BAM and serve in any capacity as long as she could "experience the power of Soviet technological and industrial prowess" for herself while completing her studies as a geologist.[68] Nina Zueva sent Tiazhelnikov this impassioned plea: "Please understand that I simply must be together with you [the Komsomol] to find real happiness." In an expression of her personal faith that the youth organization had her best interests at heart, Zueva declared: "I believe in the Komsomol and I want it to believe in me."[69]

A letter from a prospective *bamovka* who identified herself only as "Comrade Afanaseva" requested that "My Esteemed Secretary and Comrade Tiazhelnikov" send her to BAM despite the fact that she possessed none of the skills designated as desirable:

> Excuse me for interrupting you when you have other important business, but please understand that I have no other alternative but to contact you directly. I have no idea what to do with myself. You are my last hope. I must go to

BAM. Please understand that this is absolutely necessary. I must be there and only there. It is the one and only place that I can work. Do you understand? It is my duty to build BAM. I cannot accept any other life for myself. Please understand that this is not an idle request. I live with one wish, one dream. And if you tell me "no," then I am not sure what will happen next. I am certain only that something must be done. I am being completely serious—this is not a joke. I know that I will continue to be unhappy unless some action is taken. I will go to BAM myself if I must. I have left myself no other option.[70]

Without acknowledging Afanaseva's threat of what she might do if denied a BAM appointment, Tiazhelnikov responded with a promise that BAM would continue "for the next eight or nine years," and consequently Afanaseva could join the project in the future after learning a skill needed by BAM construction headquarters.[71] Afanaseva's emotional appeal must have been a serious one because her correspondence with Tiazhelnikov was never published. It was sent from the Komsomol BAM headquarters to its organizational archive in Moscow, most likely because of its strong emotionalism and the fact that Afanaseva's youth and possible mental instability made her of little propaganda value to those who sought to bring more women to the railway. Such emotional appeals, while rare, reveals that women did respond to the official call for them to join the BAM project.

Marginalization and Retention Problems for Women

Lowbrow humor was one of several marginalizing phenomena BAMer women faced. The carefully crafted representations of BAMer women in the propaganda as heroines and blissful nurturers could not hide the stark realities that each *bamovka* encountered on the railway. Not only did they face difficult living and working conditions, they also struggled against a male-dominated social structure. In direct contradiction to official proclamations on the existence of an equal and harmonious relationship between the sexes, the endeavor's male hierarchy opposed an effort to promote female independence. Manifestations of overt and subtle forms of patriarchy and misogyny were rampant throughout the Soviet Union, the realities of which were exacerbated by the railway's difficult living and working conditions. A form of "humor" played a key role in perpetuating sexism along the BAM Zone. Supposedly amusing anecdotes, which were more offensive than entertaining to most women who were frequently targets, revealed the polarized character of BAM gender relations. Although such jokes certainly were not used by all male BAMers, former BAMer Mironova made frequent mention of the off-color humor that she and her female friends heard both within and outside the project: "These jokes were sometimes funny and we would tell them too, just like the men. Some of the other anecdotes weren't so funny, though."[72] The following *chastushka*, a short poem with an ostensibly witty or vulgar theme, enjoyed considerable popularity among the railway's male population:

> I went to BAM
> And dug a trench,
> And if it doesn't look just exactly like my pussy,
> Then I must be going out of my mind.
>
> I wrote a letter to my Vania:
> "I don't want you to screw me on the sofa—
> But instead come to me on the BAM,
> And I'll give myself to you on the rails."
> Come to me on the BAM
> With your fleshy suitcase [that is, penis],
> And then leave me
> With your prick frozen off.[73]

Such denigrating examples were employed frequently by the male BAMer cohort, either consciously or unconsciously, as a means of social and cultural commentary. The woman in this poem was worthy of male ridicule for two primary reasons: (1) she has a strong libido, which gives her the confidence to ask her lover for sex, and (2) she demonstrates her competency in the task of ditch-digging, a chore that all BAMers, but especially railroader men, found distasteful.[74] Both the vociferousness of this tale's "heroine" about her carnal desires and her pride in a rather mundane accomplishment point to the fact that some BAMer men, who took great pride in laying track and blasting tunnels, used this offhand brand of humor to demean those females who expressed their individualism by volunteering for any assignment, regardless of its prestige or lack thereof, for the good of the project.

Often working under male supervision, women were assigned to tasks that were seen as sufficiently easy or enjoyable in an effort to reduce the risk that large numbers of BAMer women would resign their commissions.[75] This was

Table 4.2

BAMer monthly salaries by gender, 1984 (percentage)

	Under 100 rubles	More than 300 rubles
Male	14.3	80.3
Female	85.7	19.7

Source: Argudiaeva, *Trud i byt molodezhi BAMa*, 48.

coupled with ultimately hollow promises of advancement within the BAM bureaucracy in a bid to sweeten the railway's appeal even further. What BAM administrators neglected to mention, however, was that these new recruits would also be expected to adhere to the traditional expectations of family and marriage. The great amount of BAM media attention given to women's responsibility as nurturers of the family revealed a return to traditional pronatal policies. This emphasis on women as childbearers and rearers characterized the Brezhnev years as a whole.[76]

Contrary to official proclamations of "equal pay for equal work," both skilled and unskilled BAMer women faced monetary discrimination. Table 4.2 reveals BAMer monthly salaries by gender in 1984. *Bamovki* received far less pay on average than their male counterparts, a fact of which both sexes were well aware. Although some women performed service industry tasks such as cafeteria and sanitation duties that brought a lower wage regardless of one's gender, many others labored in all-female track-laying or building construction detachments that the two main BAM umbrella organizations (the Komsomol and the USSR Ministry of Transport Construction) chose to classify as "nonessential" or "nonprofessional."[77] By categorizing the tasks of these elite women in a subordinate labor classification, the BAM bureaucracy could pay them a smaller salary and thus economize within an undertaking that faced constant budgetary shortfalls despite the generous funding lavished on it by the Komsomol.[78]

Although women's contributions to the railway's progress were as important as those of men, financial discrimination against women defined BAM throughout its operational lifetime. Despite the attention received by the BAMer "heroines" in the media, the accomplishments of BAMer men were more prevalent within the BAM public discourse than their numbers warranted, especially when one considers that *bamovki* constituted 40 percent of the project's labor force.[79] Of the approximately five thousand BAM-related newspaper and journal articles that appeared in the national and local press between 1974 and 1984, fewer than 10 percent concerned the activities of female BAMers.[80] The railway's media also failed to note the gender imbalance of elite formations in the BAM Zone. Within the elite Eighteenth Komsomol Congress Pacesetting Brigade that arrived in 1978, for example, only one of fifteen Order of Lenin recipients was female.[81] Among the fifteen representatives from Orel, only two were women.[82] Furthermore, only one of thirty-nine brigade members from Leningrad Oblast was female, while three of forty Lithuanian Brigaders were women. There were no women among the forty Moldavians who composed their republic's contribution to the elite Komsomol formation.[83]

This underrepresentation of women was acknowledged in a report made to Komsomol headquarters. In his attempt to explain why he had authorized the sending of only one woman among the fifteen young people who represented Estonia within the Eighteenth Komsomol Congress Brigade, a Komsomol representative identified only by the last name of Doronin remarked that "an insufficient number of adequately qualified females [had] chosen to apply for admission" to the brigade during the previous year.[84] According to former Komsomol BAM chief Valentin Sushchevich, what Doronin did not admit was that female requests and applications for BAM service had exceeded those of men nationwide. The fact that women requested BAM duty more than men, Sushchevich recalled, "really surprised us. To be honest, we didn't know what to do with these female applicants. There wasn't enough work [on BAM] that was suited for them."[85]

As did the nation at large, the BAM project suffered from an organizational shortage of women in supervisory positions and an overrepresentation in those assignments that often involved menial chores. While necessary, these jobs were viewed with contempt by those who engaged in the more glamorous professions of rail-laying and building construction. Former BAMers Nikolai Nikitin and Nikolai Shtikov confirmed this. Nikitin stated that "women in charge were practically absent from the project," and Shtikov remarked that "the only [women] I saw worked in the cafeterias, the canteens, and the health clinics."[86] In late 1974, only one of the eleven Komsomol committees that were operational within the BAM Zone at that time possessed a female first secretary.[87] Within the Buriat ASSR, approximately 10 percent of laborers within the over eighteen-thousand-strong railway builders were women, but they constituted more than 90 percent of the service industry–related labor pool.[88]

Nearly 30 percent of all new arrivals in any given year between 1974 and 1984 were women with children. Thus the Komsomol declared itself "institutionally unable" to cope with the influx of female BAMers and their families due to a severe shortage of nurseries, daycare facilities, and schools.[89] This dearth of childcare left many *bamovki*, whose traditional parenting networks of grandmothers and other female relatives were often located far from the BAM Zone, to look for scarce and low-paying part-time jobs that would allow them to work and also look after their children. The result of the railway's shortfall in family services was a widespread unemployment and underemployment of young BAMer women (more than eight hundred *bamovki* in the Buriat ASSR were unemployed out of a total female population of ten thousand, for example).[90] They became increasingly frustrated with their continued inability to find meaningful and sufficiently paying work that would also allow them to spend some time with their children. After learning of these childcare deficiencies, many young mothers joined the large numbers of single women who left the railway after fewer than two years of service. Table 4.3 details the length of women's duration in the BAM Zone, based on marital status. The decision to leave entailed the breaking of one's three-year service contract, resulting in a pay reduction. All nonmilitary BAMers, whether male or female, received triple "hardship pay" for their BAM service.

Recognition of BAM service with the granting of medals and certificates was a nationwide phenomenon, and official recognition of one's excellence as a BAMer was of particular importance because honorees received special housing assignments and the right to partake in all-expenses-paid trips outside the BAM Zone. The proportion of *bamovki* who received awards and commendations was much lower than that of their male counterparts. According to a 1984 special issue compiled by correspondents from the newspapers *Avangard*, *BAM*, and *Mosty magistrali* (Bridges of the railway), fifteen of sixteen "heroes of socialist labor" who received the Order of Lenin and/or the Hammer and Sickle Gold Medal that year for their BAM service were male.[91] The distribution of awards among women who received commendations revealed that the BAM administration confirmed its subordination and marginalization of the *bamovki* by choosing to recognize those who per-

Table 4.3

Length of women's duration in the BAM Zone,
based on marital status (percentages)

Duration	1980		1984	
	Married	Single	Married	Single
1 year	62	58	61	56
2 to 3 years	27	30	31	31
4 to 5 years	8	11	7	11
More than 5 years	3	1	1	2

Source: Argudiaeva, *Trud i byt molodezhi BAMa*, 53.

formed auxiliary occupations rather than those who worked in those professions that it considered to be honorable careers *for men only*. For example, the women honored in 1984 with the "for participation in BAM construction" award included a journalist who wrote for a magazine that covered "club and dancehall management," a "morally upright and modest senior clerk" with BAMstroiput, and a "pacesetter of the Tenth Five-Year Plan" who received the title of "best in profession" while working as a cook with SMP-581.[92]

In addition to the perilous working conditions, women also faced physical dangers because of the pervasive climate of sexual harassment that permeated BAM culture. A 1975 report from the Komsomol Spotlight organization details one such incident. After receiving several complaints of assaults on women within the dormitories and cafeterias of the Shimanovsk Industrial Complex, the Komsomol Spotlight initiated a "raid." Residents Liudmila Rostovshchikova and Roza Serebriakova had filed reports after refusing to sleep with their male brigade members in exchange for money, cigarettes, and food chits. The Spotlighters learned that Rostovshchikova and Serebriakova had received numerous threats of rape and violence from some of their comrades after their report became known publicly.[93] Although they demanded to be exempted from their service agreements so that they could return home, the tribunal that investigated their case determined that Rostovshchikova and Serebriakova had "brought these problems upon themselves" by engaging in "idle flirtation rather than ideological collaboration" with their male coworkers.[94] Many women chose not to remain with the BAM project because of the gender-specific hardships they faced, including intense sexism as well as their isolation from the traditional network of family and friends that provided camaraderie and childcare.

The Denisova Affair

Tatiana Denisova, musical director of the Komsomol BAM headquarters, was a well-known guitarist and singer in the BAM Zone. The tragic fate of Denisova, who once enjoyed a promising career as one of a handful BAMer women who held one of the railway's few high-level positions, points directly to the envy and misogyny of some male and female BAMers. Many BAMer women who held positions of authority and attempted to make a name for themselves faced such challenges. The first mention of Denisova in the archival record, dated 1983, notes that the twenty-two-year old *komsomolka* had received a recommendation from Valentin Sushchevich (who had by this time been promoted from his position as the chief of the Komsomol BAM headquarters to the leadership of GlavBAMstroi) to travel as a member of a Druzhba [Friendship] group to Cuba, East Germany, and Hungary as a member of the elite Moskovskii komsomolets brigade. Describing Denisova as a "loyal and dedicated" cadre, Sushchevich proclaimed that she "could be trusted to preserve state secrets" while representing the railway abroad.[95]

Unfortunately for Denisova, Sushchevich's description of her as a "pace-setting" BAMer and a highly trusted cadre who could successfully motivate others did not endure. After their return to the Soviet Union, other Druzhba participants reported that Denisova had spoken negatively about BAM and its workers while abroad by supposedly remarking that "we [that is, Soviet young people] should not be traipsing about the world when our country needs all the help it can get."[96] More damning for Denisova, however, were the rumors that began to circulate about her. Although she was married, the rumor was that she was a homosexual who had used her dynamic personality and relative renown to seduce young Soviet and foreign women during her travels. After Denisova's return to the BAM Zone, Sushchevich's subordinate, Iurii Verbitskii, the current head of the Komsomol construction headquarters, gave voice to the whispers that had surrounded Denisova since her return. He alleged publicly that she was an adulteress who had engaged in several homosexual relationships both within and outside the Soviet Union. Verbitskii demanded that Denisova make a public confession of her lesbian lifestyle and resign immediately or be removed from her position, expelled from the Komsomol, and denied any hope of attaining Communist Party membership. When Denisova refused to admit any wrongdoing, Sushchevich approved her dismissal as musical director but stopped short from expelling her from the project entirely. "I didn't believe she should be sent home because of this," he recalled. "While we all disapproved of her [Denisova's] behavior, sending her back would have been bad for morale. After all, she still had a lot of friends around."[97]

The reasons for Sushchevich's rather cautious handling of what came to be known in BAMer circles as the "Denisova affair" lay in the fact that after Verbitskii's accusation of Denisova's homosexuality, dozens of outraged BAMers, many of them women, initiated a letter-writing campaign in which they protested Denisova's removal from her post and insisted that she was a BAMer worthy of emulation.[98] These individuals risked discrediting themselves and possibly even losing their Komsomol or Party membership by refuting the charges made against Denisova, but nevertheless they penned dozens of anonymous and public appeals to Sushchevich urging him to exonerate Denisova. In the national newspaper *Sovetskaia Rossiia* (Soviet Russia), respected transport engineer Tatiana Kultysheva defended Denisova and expressed outrage at the ferocity of the attack against her.[99] Simultaneously, several prominent individuals within the railway community, both male and female, spoke publicly about Denisova's innocence.[100] While the imploring of Denisova's colleagues failed to convince Sushchevich to retain Denisova as the project's musical director, the telegrams and letters did influence his decision not to banish her from the BAM Zone, an action that would have resulted in her loss of Komsomol and Party affiliation.[101]

The Denisova saga had yet more twists. The nation at large was introduced to Denisova in an April 1984 profile in the Moscow-based journal *Sobesednik* (Interlocutor) by correspondent Natalia Osokina, who had first met Denisova in August 1979 during the annual BAM Music Festival, where she learned of Denisova's previous troubles.[102] Some BAMers who lived in Tynda at the time have conjectured that Osokina had privately envied Denisova's accomplishments ever since their first encounter. Even before the publication of her apparently complimentary look at Denisova in April

1984, some Tynda residents believed that Osokina had hatched a plan to first popularize and then disgrace the woman whose celebrity she herself could not enjoy.[103]

Denisova's difficulties continued with the August 1984 publication of an interview with the regional newspaper *Avangard*, in which she criticized both the Komsomol BAM construction headquarters and the BAM Music Festival's *orgkomitet* (organizing committee) for their poor administrative decisions that had resulted in a significant decline in the quality and quantity of participants in the annual musical festivals. When asked in private by Sushchevich to confirm her remarks as they had appeared in the newspaper, Denisova reiterated her displeasure with the BAM administration's handling of that year's festival planning and informed her boss that she had simply expressed the sentiments of dozens of colleagues. Denisova told Sushchevich that her view of the festival was shared by many Tynda residents, some of whom had approached her in the street to express their regret that the event's significance had been "cheapened."[104] Former Komsomoler Galina Mironova recalled that she and her friends in Tynda "told Denisova that we appreciated her contribution to [the BAM Music] festival . . . despite the regrettable quality of this year's event."[105]

News of Denisova's complaint ushered forth a tidal wave of accusations and attacks against her character and professionalism from persons unknown within the upper levels of the BAM bureaucracy. A series of local Komsomol-produced posters condemning Denisova as a "negative influence on the development of the youth of the BAM Zone" began to be distributed throughout Tynda and other railway towns that summer. BAM headquarters was quick to label Denisova as the instigator behind the declining quality of the music festival. In addition, rumors that Denisova had engaged in sexual liaisons with both male and female festival participants began to surface among the BAMer population.[106] The possibility that Denisova could have been a sexual initiator was threatening to those who attempted to control a public discourse that demanded female subordination within an ostensibly "progressive" BAM society.

The role of Natalia Osokina in the distribution of this anti-Denisova literature was investigated during a September 1984 meeting between the journalist and Sushchevich, in which she was asked to corroborate the charges she had leveled at Denisova, who publicly stated that Osokina's accusations were "distorted" and "untruthfully reported."[107] Osokina responded that she had "reported only that which I had seen with my own eyes" and that she had written her April article in *Sobesednik* "without full knowledge of [Denisova's] real personality or antisocial tendencies."[108] When Sushchevich pressed Osokina to comment on whether she had participated in the smear campaign against Denisova and the distribution of the slanderous broadsides in particular, Osokina replied cryptically during her private interview with Sushchevich that "BAMers must know the truth."[109] Osokina's role in the "Denisova affair" was never pursued further by Sushchevich or anyone else in the BAM Komsomol organization after this.

A stream of telegrams from concerned individuals such as Galina Mironova arrived at the Komsomol offices in Moscow and Tynda. These messages implored the youth organization to permit Denisova to defend herself against Osokina's "groundless accusations."[110] Deputy project chief Vladimir Shcherbin also penned an impassioned letter that the allegations directed against Denisova by Osokina and others were groundless. Despite these attempts to exonerate the embattled music director, the Komsomol announced in October 1984 that Denisova would be expelled from the Komsomol for "violations of disciplinary order."[111] In explaining its decision, the organization noted that Denisova did not appear for a meeting scheduled in Moscow for that September (even though Denisova was never given permission to leave the BAM Zone during these troubles) and that her absence abrogated any right to defend herself.

To maintain the fiction that Denisova had avoided a full disclosure of her wrongdoing, the Komsomol attempted to arrange another hearing on the affair in the BAM Zone settlement of Kuanda during the "driving of the golden spike" that October. This much-publicized event marked the official completion of the railway and assumed nearly mythic proportions in the weeks leading up to the ceremony. But Denisova "again failed to appear," despite the fact that she was present in the small settlement at the time.[112] The Moscow headquarters issued a statement the following month that Denisova had been "dismissed from [her] duties as an instructor with the Komsomol BAM headquarters at her own request."[113] Denisova left Tynda for Moscow on November 4, 1984, and she never returned to the BAM Zone. Denisova's main offense was not that she had a strong sexual appetite, but that she, as a woman, held a position of authority within the highest echelons of the BAM bureaucracy and had attempted to speak her mind about the state of affairs along the railway. The vitriolic attacks leveled at

Denisova by those who resented her popularity and feared her vociferousness revealed the lack of progress made in gender equality in the ostensibly egalitarian Soviet Union.

Women's Voices Unheard

The experiences of Tatiana Denisova and other BAMer women directly contradicted the male hierarchy's assertion that all *bamovki* could become heroines while pursuing their own destinies. In reality, a woman's ability to achieve heroism was limited to traditional forms of female endeavor, including the nurturing of children or colleagues, food preparation, and the all-important role of maintaining a stable domestic front for BAMer men, who were expected to make the greatest contribution to the railway. Faced with these myriad and often unanticipated expectations, many *bamovki* chose not to remain in the BAM Zone for long. They left because of the insufficient remuneration, the difficulties of an extended separation from home (where the labor and emotional support networks were), and an overwhelmingly male supervisory apparatus that struggled and ultimately failed in motivating its female charges to work hard on a project of questionable utility toward the amorphous goal of blazing the "path to the future."

Although the state expended a significant effort in tailoring the BAM message to females, the project's leadership ignored the fact that those inducements that might appeal to some potential *bamovki*—say, those who desired families and would possibly stay in the region as a consequence or those who wished to seek their fortune in an exotic region—would not resonate with all women. Those who did take to heart the message of the BAM project as a road to greater personal freedom and self-realization, however, quickly learned that such promises were utterly hollow after experiencing marginalization and denigration. Most damaging for those women whose goal it was to bring and maintain the railway within the national consciousness, was that many *bamovki* encountered the same prejudices and societal constraints in an even more stressful environment than the one they had left behind.

Ultimately, those who conceived of BAM were incapable of providing the social environment of equal labor and equal representation that had been promised to female laborers during the Brezhnev years. The project's arduous working and living conditions, combined with the presence of traditional strictures and expectations that weakened the endeavor's appeal, made a long-term existence unthinkable to many of the railway's female recruits. Indeed, the vaunted "progressive" BAM society demonstrated not an enlightened attitude toward gender relations but a decidedly atavistic dynamic of patriarchy and misogyny that revealed the retrograde, not the futuristic and utopian, qualities of the railway.

5 // National Differentiation and Marginalization on the Railway

Unfortunately, many of the good traditions of the past, in which all areas of our country cooperated on such an All-Union endeavor as BAM, have been forgotten. Participants from the cities of Tallinn and Vilnius have lost all interest in fostering any relations with their non-Baltic comrades on the railway, while those from Moldavia and Azerbaijan choose not to interact with any of the Party and state committees within the BAM Zone that do not include comrades from their own republics.

Report by the Komsomol BAM construction headquarters, 1983

Among the BAMer representatives of the USSR's multiple nationalities along the railway project, there were many tensions as well as constructive relationships. Soviet officialdom was keenly aware of the potentially disastrous consequences of ethnic tension within the railway's population and, by extension, throughout the USSR. Through its propaganda network the state consistently proclaimed the BAM project to be a forum where the center's claims to multinationalism and ethnic equality were visible. Despite these claims, however, Slavic labor formations dominated and non-Slavs were relegated to tasks of little importance. The Komsomol BAM construction headquarters put quite a propaganda spin on these phenomena, but in private they were often discussed differently. The complex and often divisive factor of nationality contributed to BAM's ultimate failure to realize one of its main goals: namely, the improvement of relations between on the one hand ethnic Russians and other Slavs who labored on the "path to the future" (that is, the "majority") and the Soviet Union's non-Slavic nationalities (that is, the "minority" or "ethnic minorities") on the other hand.

For the project's administrators, the arrival of brigades from all corners of the USSR posed a challenge of ethnic integration that it had neither planned for nor wanted. But in promoting the "project of the century" to the larger populace as an enterprise worthy of attention and support, Moscow viewed the railway as a showcase for all of the Soviet Union's attributes, including its vaunted ethnic cohesion. Faced with the dilemma of how to overcome the linguistic and cultural barriers that nonetheless separated the BAM workforce, the undertaking's authorities dealt with the thorny problems associated with the amalgamation of BAMer units by consciously segregating Slavic and non-Slavic laborers at nearly every location. The Komsomol BAM construction headquarters, which itself "was staffed almost entirely by Slavs" according to former Komsomol BAM headquarters chief Valentin Sushchevich, viewed the BAMer ethnic minorities with a combination of mistrust and derision.[1] These twin attitudes, the products of Russian nationalism and railway policies that masked Slavic supremacy within the USSR while ostensibly celebrating the project's ethnic diversity, combined to mold BAM into a socially and culturally divided undertaking. These understandings exacerbated ethnic tensions within the Soviet Union, which depicted itself as a happy family of nations.[2] Amid officialdom's professions of BAMer ethnic harmony and solidarity—called the "unification theme"—lay the atomization of Soviet society along national lines that, while always a latent characteristic, was increasingly visible and worrisome to the center.[3] The rift and occasional hostility between Slavic and non-Slavic laborers represents one of the fundamental tensions that defined the entire BAM effort.

Nation and Nationality

In beginning any discussion of nationality and its expression within the political milieu of the nation, the meaning of these two commonly used but often oversimplified terms must be defined. The concept of "nationality" remains a contested issue. One school of thought, which remains popular among a number of post-Soviet and Western academics, views nationality as an organic construct that emphasizes the value of birth affiliations and geography above all other factors, most notably industrialization, education, and the impact of increasingly efficient methods of communication.[4] This perspective, called the "genetic" school, attempts to rehabilitate the study of nationalism and elevate national identity to an equal level with other criteria of analysis, including class and gender. Regardless of their theoretical persuasion, most scholars of the former Soviet Union and traditionally marginalized areas such as sub-Saharan Africa and Asia admit that the study of nationalism has languished somewhat behind other methodologies.[5] By studying nationalism for its own sake, the "geneticists" seek to explain the atomization and frequently atavistic ethnically spawned conflict that has plagued many areas of the post-1945 world.

A contrasting method is the "deconstructionist" approach to nationality. Its exponents do not deny the importance of nationality; rather, they understand the nation as an imagined construct that falls squarely within the realm of myth and popular culture.[6] Advocates of the deconstructionist school (Benedict Anderson, Eric Hobsbawm, Karl Deutsch, and Anthony D. Smith) stress that nationality is not a timeless concept that has defined our species since its beginning as the "geneticists" maintain, but a fairly recent phenomenon that has been shaped by such factors as political integration, the advent of the printing culture, and the development of extensive transportation networks throughout Europe as well as non-European industrialized and industrializing societies.[7] Most deconstructionists agree (although it is not a unanimous sentiment) that nationalism is a nondeterministic (that is, socially and/or culturally rather than historically determined) phenomenon that is molded by ethnic identity. It also contains social and cultural characteristics that did not appear in many areas of the world until after the beginning of the nineteenth century or even later.[8] The deconstructionists postulate that while ethnicity has existed for centuries, the assumption of some geneticists that the creation of a nation out of one or more ethnic groups represents an inevitable outcome of national struggle is a completely modern belief that lacks any historical antecedent.[9]

Answering the Nationality Question

Before tracing the relationships among the different nationalities that labored throughout the BAM Zone, it is instructive to look at the official Soviet understanding of the "nationalities question" and how this evolved from the 1917 revolution to the early 1980s. One of the original planks of the Bolshevik program was the liberation of what Vladimir Lenin called the "prison of peoples"—namely, the tsarist empire in which all non-Russian nationalities were trapped in a society where their cultural language and heritage could not be celebrated publicly.[10] During the debates in the early 1920s in which the Bolshevik leadership discussed the structure of a federalized Soviet Union and what role such preexisting nations as Russia and the Caucasian states would play within it, Lenin characterized the imperial conundrum of suppressing all but one nationality within a polyethnic state as the "nationalities question." Lenin and other early Bolsheviks insisted the young Soviet Union would have to contend with this pivotal issue to ensure its own viability. To free the "imprisoned" peoples of the Russian empire, the Bolshevik regime adopted a policy of nativization (*korenizatsiia*) during the early 1920s. Within a predetermined socialist framework, the empire promoted native language education and a limited degree of national identity expression by the USSR's constituent republics.[11]

By attempting to control and thereby appropriate the expression of nationalism through nativization, the Bolsheviks sought to eliminate the specter of national liberation and direct these energies toward the creation of the world's first proletarian state. This would be a nation in which one's self-identification as a Russian, Georgian, or Buriat, for example, would be forgotten and replaced with a new, supranational consciousness—that of the *sovetskii narod,* or Soviet people.[12] Indeed, as late as the early 1920s, modern national consciousness had only begun to gain currency among many of the newly incorporated Soviet peoples, especially those located in Central Asia. Such innovations as the relatively recent adoption of a written language and mass-media outlets contributed to the gradual growth of nationalism in these territories, which were previously within the Ottoman or Persian spheres of influence. The primary impetus behind the Bolsheviks' decision to transcend existing national affiliations by regulating their articulation derived from Lenin's interpretation of Marxism. Its core tenet was the primacy of class struggle over nationalism, which Lenin viewed as a vestige of the tsarist past, and all other considerations in the young USSR's transition from primitive capitalism to socialism.[13] While the state was moderately successful in capturing the national discourse for itself through *korenizatsiia*, the nativization campaign had the unintended effect of awakening and in some cases catalyzing the growth of national consciousness, particularly among the non-Slavic peoples of Caucasus and Central Asia and later the Baltic populations of Estonia, Latvia, and Lithuania.[14]

After achieving a dominant position within the Communist Party by the late 1920s, Joseph Stalin, Lenin's successor, adhered to the nativization policy early in his tenure, but by the mid-1930s he realized the paradoxical nature of promoting separate and distinct national cultures on the one hand while advancing the concept of Soviet nationality on the other.[15] Stalin's campaign of rapid industrialization, the collectivization of agriculture, and the strengthening of the USSR's military forces witnessed the end of official support for nativization, as the government and the Party now proclaimed that national unification (*sliianie*) would be realized as the Soviet Union marched inexorably toward Communism.[16] After witnessing the Soviet Union's severe beating at the hands of Nazi Germany at the start of World War II, however, Stalin forsook the remaining vestiges of his Georgian heritage and demanded that his representatives in the republics abandon the supranational message. Instead, he made an impassioned appeal to Russian national sentiment as an inspiration to drive the foreign invaders from the *rodina*, or Mother Russia.[17]

At the same time, a center fearful of disgruntled nationalities that might assist the enemy deported hundreds of thousands from the European USSR to remote eastern sectors of the country. This group included a large number of Crimean Tatars and Volga Germans, who along with other deportees would later be known as the "punished peoples." Some members of ethnic minorities did assist the Nazis during their occupation of the Soviet Union, but the vast majority of the "punished peoples" were innocent civilians. Some of these relocated individuals served as forced labor in the removal and transport of rails from the 1930s BAM project to the European front, while others worked on the second BAM undertaking that was abandoned in 1953 after Stalin's death.[18]

Stalin's demise ushered in a new era in the treatment of the "nationalities question." After a near rebellion that year in Poland, which included anti-Soviet sentiments, and a strident anti-Soviet outburst after the USSR's intervention in Hungary in 1956, the Soviet leadership reconsidered its ethnicity policies both at home and abroad. In his address to the Twenty-second CPSU Congress in 1961, General Secretary Nikita S. Khrushchev outlined the course that Soviet nationalities policy would follow in the era known as the political and cultural "thaw."[19] As part of his Third Party program, Khrushchev acknowledged that while the final fusion of all the USSR's peoples would come to pass soon enough, for the moment the various ethnic groups of the Soviet Union would "flourish" as they grew ever closer to one another (*sblizhenie*).[20] Khrushchev also implemented a plan in which more authority was given to regional councils (*sovnarkhozy*), which in turn allowed Party functionaries at the republic and district levels to enjoy a degree of independence from the center that had been unknown during the Stalin years.[21]

The leeway given to elites at the republic and Autonomous Soviet Socialist Republic (ASSR) level increased markedly after Brezhnev's consolidation of power in 1968.[22] In conjunction with the declaration of the official policy of "developed socialism," this period witnessed a trend in government policy commonly known as "trust in cadres"—a Party program introduced in 1965 that permitted entrenched Party functionaries, both Russian and non-Russian, to enjoy a relatively wide latitude to administer their districts as they saw fit.[23] While the domestic *nomenklatura* (those high-level officials appointed to their posts directly by the CPSU Central Committee in Moscow) maintained influence over their individual fiefdoms, the official position on dissent within the Soviet bloc hardened, as the 1968 invasion of Czechoslovakia and the government's reaction to internal criticism of this action revealed that the intellectual and cultural freedoms of the Khrushchev years were a thing of the past.

The limits of the "trust in cadres" policy became clear as the state compelled Party bureaucrats to follow an aggressive policy of Russification, which included an emphasis on Russian and the fourteen other union-level languages and cultures to the exclusion of other traditions, in the realms of education and the media.[24] The increasing birthrate among the Soviet Union's non-Slavic peoples, especially among the Muslim populations of Central Asia, and a concomitant reduction in population among Russians and other Slavs played a major role in the center's decision to stress pro-Russian linguistic and cultural programs.[25] Officialdom feared that if current demographic trends continued, Slavic hegemony within the USSR might eventually end and, even more troubling, a rising awareness of and interest in Islam could precipitate an outbreak of fundamentalism in the country's southern areas that could threaten the viability of the Soviet Union itself. After the 1979 Islamic revolution in Iran and a near revolution in Afghanistan that same year, the possibility of a similar religious upheaval occurring within the Soviet Union became an obsessive concern to those in Moscow.[26] The Institute for the Study of Nationalities, a governmental institution that carefully noted the increase in the relative and numerical population of non-Slavs within the Soviet Union, reported findings to a concerned Party elite that scrambled to maintain the primacy of Slavs who were in danger of becoming a minority in the USSR at some point in the future.[27]

Another feature of the Brezhnev-era Russification policy was a shift in cadre policy. The position of republic- and ASSR-level Party second secretary, an office that had influence over linguistic and cultural policies, had increasingly been staffed by Russians.[28] By Brezhnev's death in 1982, most of the major administrative regions outside of the Russian Soviet Federated Socialist Republic (RSFSR) were governed by an aging first secretary who was a member of the indigenous nationality and a Russian or Ukrainian deputy who held sway over the appointment of Party and government functionaries in his (such officials were almost always male) respective region.[29] For the BAM project, this process was mirrored within the railway's bureaucracy as Belorussians, Russians, and Ukrainians composed nearly 90 percent of the railway's leadership within the Komsomol and the Ministry of Transport Construction.[30]

By the mid-1970s, the state's Russification program, coupled with a proportional underrepresentation of non-Slavs within the Soviet media and education bureaucracies and burgeoning national consciousness in the Baltics and Caucasus, contributed to rising disenfranchisement among those non-Slavic populations who possessed an enduring cultural narrative and had enjoyed independence at some point in their respective pasts.[31] The growth of national dissent during the Brezhnev era belied the existence of a larger dissident movement in which Ukrainians and Roman Catholic Lithuanians, among other groups, began to challenge the state's message of ethnic cohesion throughout the country. In 1972 the Moscow leadership ousted Petr Shelest, head of the Ukrainian Communist Party, for encouraging Ukrainian nationalism and began a crackdown against "bourgeois elements" within the republic, which included the arrest and trial by the KGB of dissident intellectual V. Moroz in 1974. Moroz was convicted of distributing "anti-

Soviet literature" in the form of Ukrainian nationalist writings (the so-called Moroz Papers) and colluding with foreigners to distribute his work for publication abroad (known as *tamizdat*). Moroz was deprived of his citizenship and expelled from the USSR in 1979.[32]

One of the most visible examples of tension between Moscow and other regions occurred in April 1978, when a group of demonstrators marched in the streets of Tbilisi, the capital of the Georgian Soviet Socialist Republic, to protest the removal of a clause that proclaimed Georgian as the republic's official language from a Moscow-sponsored revision of the republic's constitution that was to mirror the updating of the Soviet constitution (popularly known as the "Brezhnev Constitution") in 1977. According to various accounts, the demonstrators numbered between five thousand and thirty thousand.[33] After several nights of public disturbances threatened to escalate into an ominous anti-Russian riot, authorities in the Kremlin decided to revise the document to read that Georgian was the sole "language of the republic."[34]

The Tbilisi demonstrations were not the only episodes of national resistance to Soviet authority in the non-Slavic republics during this period. Perhaps even more unsettled than the Caucasus were the Baltic republics of Estonia, Latvia, and Lithuania, where numerous religious and cultural protests took place in the late 1970s and early 1980s.[35] The most notable of these incidents was an August 1979 call by a group of intellectuals for the publication of the so-called secret clauses of the 1939 Molotov-Ribbentrop Pact, in which Germany acquiesced to the placement of the Baltic republics within the Soviet sphere of influence in exchange for Stalin's promise that he would not interfere in the 1940 Nazi invasion of Poland. Young people also took to the streets in Estonia and Latvia between 1976 and 1980 to note their disapproval over the banning of a number of rock concerts that were to feature native-language-singing groups whose lyrics, the Kremlin leadership worried, might stoke the fires of national pride.[36]

The Ethnic Composition of BAMer Brigades

BAMer detachments consisted of two primary types: those that were formed from a particular republic, district, or city, or all-Union elite formations that, according to the state, contained only the most outstanding Komsomolers. The composition of one such elite group, the Seventeenth Komsomol Congress Brigade, revealed an underrepresentation of non-Slavs that was in distinct disproportion to these groups' relative population within the Soviet Union. Those members of special detachments such as the Seventeenth Komsomol who happened to belong to ethnic minorities lacked the training and education of their peers from the Slavic republics.[37]

The exclusion of ethnic minorities from elite formations began at the project's start in the spring of 1974, when the Komsomol headquarters in Moscow approved the transfer of fifteen Armenian "volunteers." As part of the "trailblazing" Seventeenth Komsomol Congress Brigade, none of them were railway specialists; rather, they were chauffeurs in the practically roadless BAM Zone, a decidedly unglamorous profession among the railway's workforce. These Armenians possessed only a primary or secondary education, in some cases as low as a seventh-grade-level education. The rationale behind the Armenians' reassignment stemmed from the fact that no qualified young Armenians had asked to join the Seventeenth Komsomol and thus the republic's Komsomol organization was forced to select a substandard group that was willing to go to BAM despite its utter lack of railway construction experience.[38]

The representation of Slavs in elite formations was an equally complicated affair. Valentin Sushchevich, former director of the Komsomol BAM headquarters, expressed his surprise after learning that approximately half of the project's Slavs came not from the RSFSR, Ukraine, or Belorussia, but from Kazakhstan (a titular non-Slavic republic that possessed a slight Slavic majority by the 1970s) and the three Baltic republics, each of which was home to a sizable Slavic minority.[39] Within the delegations sent from Estonia, Latvia, and Central Asia to the Seventeenth Komsomol Congress Brigade, Slavs outnumbered the majority nationality (that is, Estonian, Latvian, or Central Asian) by a margin of three to one.[40] Those Slavs who held the majority of key positions within the Komsomol organizations of the various republics were able to manipulate the manifests of elite units to include many of their conationals, thus showing to an uninformed public that Slavs happened to be the superior type of BAMer. In addition, the youth organizations of many non-Slavic republics, including the Armenian Komsomol described earlier, could not find adequately qualified and ideologically reliable cadres in sufficient numbers. In many cases, it is entirely plausible that young people from outside the USSR's Slavic core were simply unwilling to leave their homes and join the railway.

Table 5.1
Regional origin of incoming BAM Zone residents (percentages)

	1975–76	1981	1984	Percentage of titular nationality within republic population
RSFSR	74	54	66	84
Ukraine and				73 (Ukraine)
Belorussia	15	26	16	80 (Belorussia)
Central Asia	7	9	14	57 (average for five Central Asian republics)
Moldavia and				64 (Moldavia)
Baltics	3	6	3	65 (average for three Baltic republics)
Caucasus	1	5	1	79 (average for three Caucasian republics)

Source: Argudiaeva, *Trud i byt molodezhi BAMa*, 9.

Officials outside of the BAM Zone were also aware of the poor quality and unrepresentative composition of the Seventeenth Komsomol Congress Brigade. In a secret letter commenting on the dearth of Latvian participation in that formation, the Latvian Komsomol committee requested that the youth organization's headquarters correct the ratio of Slavs to Latvians, but this notion was tabled by the committee's secretary, E. M. Tiazhelnikov, in Moscow. Although he admitted that the composition of the Latvian contribution to the brigade was overwhelmingly Russian, Tiazhelnikov maintained that they were Latvia's best-qualified young people and therefore should be sent to BAM without any further delay.[41] Tiazhelnikov's former assistant, Galina Tokareva, stated that Tiazhelnikov "had made the decision to send ethnic Russians and other Slavs [to BAM]" from such majority non-Slavic Soviet republics as Estonia and Latvia.[42]

The domination of Russians within elite units continued into the early 1980s.[43] Within the more than three-hundred-strong Nineteenth Komsomol Congress Brigade that began work in 1982, slightly over 30 percent of its members were ethnically Russian, while Belorussians and Ukrainians combined composed another 20 percent. Of the remaining 50 percent, Georgians, Armenians, and Lithuanians composed the largest percentage of non-Slavs, while representatives from the numerically significant populations of Central Asia were absent.[44] Those from this latter category had always struggled against both real and imagined aspersions cast upon them by some Slavs and Balts. Despite the official rhetoric to the contrary, the Caucasians and Central Asians were often looked upon with disdain as "second-tier" Soviet citizens due to a combination of traditions that differentiated these southern peoples: linguistic (a common demarcating factor among all the ethnicities of the Caucasus and Central Asia), cultural, racial, and religious (regarding the majority Islamic republics of Azerbaijan and those in Central Asia).

As with such high-profile formations as the Seventeenth and Nineteenth Komsomol Brigades, not all units from the Soviet Union's fifteen constituent republics accurately reflected their respective demographic profiles. Table 5.1 details regional origins of incoming BAM Zone residents in 1974–75, 1981, and 1984. Of the individual republic brigades that arrived in the BAM Zone in 1982, nearly 90 percent of Armenian brigade members were ethnically Armenian (the same percentage as in the republic as a whole), 75 percent of participants within the Belorussian detachment were Belorussian (compared with 80 percent of Belorussians in Belorussia), ethnic Lithuanians composed nearly 70 percent of their brigade's strength (80 percent within Lithuania), while 80 percent of the Georgian SSR brigade encompassed self-identified Georgians (69 percent within Georgia). However, only 9 percent of the Estonian brigade's membership identified itself as ethnically Estonian, while Estonians composed 65 percent of the population in the Estonian Soviet Socialist Republic by the late 1970s. In addition, native (that is, non-Slavic) populations constituted less than 15 percent of the total strength within Central Asian formations.[45] When one compares this figure to the data outlined in table 5.1, the underrepresentation of Central Asians on the railway becomes apparent. As table 5.1 reveals, the percentage of Slavic (that is, Belorussian, Russian, and Ukrainian) BAMers ranged from approximately three-fourths to two-thirds during the nine-year range of demographer Iulia V. Argudiaeva's study. These statistics are instructive if one makes the assumption that a significant majority of arrivals from any given republic were members of that area's dominant nationality, but my findings indicate that a substantial portion of project participants from Central Asia and the Caucasus were in fact Slavs and not members of those regions' primary ethnicity. Also, the general accuracy of Argudiaeva's data, which was gleaned from surveys that railway workers completed as part of their civil service requirement, must be questioned as accounts of BAMer ethnic origin varied widely within the contemporary BAM demographic literature.[46] Nevertheless, the unavoidable conclusion remains that Slavs, regardless of their specific numerical representation, dominated the project out of all proportion to their population within the Soviet Union. While this phenomenon was evident to the railway's administration, it persisted in hammering home the image of BAM as a forum for ethnic cohesion in a bid to entice those non-Slavs who had not yet come to the BAM project and were probably unaware of its national composition.

"The Whole Nation Is Building BAM!"

As the Komsomol struggled to find members of national minorities to include in its BAMer formations, it developed a static message of unity that it hoped would dominate the project's public discourse. The replication of the message was due in no small part to directives that emanated from the entrenched upper-level leadership in Moscow. Such catchphrases as "The Whole Nation Is Building BAM!" echoed throughout official representations of BAM during the 1974–84 period as a part of Moscow's desire to stress the ethnic cohesion and harmonization of the nation's various nationalities in the "building of Communism."[47] During BAM's decade of prominence, national and local media outlets stressed with little variation the theme that the Soviet Union's nationalities enjoyed a full and equal partnership.

The upper levels of the BAM administration repeatedly informed the public that all nationalities labored on projects of equivalent prestige and importance. L. N. Serdiuk, leader of a logging division within the construction trust Angarstroi, told a national television audience in the project's first weeks that "the vast majority of us are far from home, some from Moscow, others from Leningrad, Saratov, and Voronezh. Others came from Ukraine, Georgia, and Tajikistan. Now we all are here and must begin living as one family—and we will!"[48] A highly-profiled national minority included an Azeri, Nikolai Nasrullaev of Baku, who told his superiors that he had "read about [BAM] in newspapers and books" and "really wanted to see Siberia and the Far East."[49] As soon as he completed his education, Nasrullaev applied for and was accepted as a member of the Seventeenth Komsomol Congress Brigade. Despite the initial hardships of working on BAM, he "quickly learned a new specialization and became a highly qualified worker."[50] Another wide-eyed Muslim was Khamat Kaskapov, who came from the Tatar Autonomous Oblast. After learning of the BAM project, Kaskapov knew that he could fulfill his dream of working alongside other Soviet youth while discovering more about the USSR in general, which he termed "the union of workers and peasants, this greatest of nations."[51] While Kaskapov may well have been enamored with the railway, the boilerplate language attributed to him almost certainly came from a prepared statement that other minorities would repeat innumerable times.

As related in a documentary produced by the BAM Zone radio station *Maiak* (Lighthouse), two rail layers from Azerbaijan "set an excellent example" with their work on finishing a segment of track on the "Little BAM" railway connector. In temperatures sinking to minus fifteen degree Celsius, these rail layers loaded boxcars with desperately needed foodstuffs that were destined for the residents of Tynda.[52] In 1976, the BAM administration publicly congratulated a Chechen and three Azeris for their "pacesetting work" with MK-141.[53] Full of flowery praise, the announcement, which was broadcast on national radio, lacked any detail about why the men deserved accolades and failed to mention their respective professions or educational specialization. Furthermore, the broadcast did not include any information on the men's lives apart from the project. Such a disclosure might have revealed cultural peculiarities that would differentiate those whom the Komsomol deemed worthy of emulation by all national minorities.

Journalists who represented national newspapers and publishers echoed the unification theme as strongly as their colleagues in radio and television. Emphasizing that the railway's labor force reflected the USSR's national diversity, *Izvestiia* correspondent Leonid Shinkarev pushed the idea of the railway as an undertaking where the various ethnic groups of the USSR worked in harmony. Shinkarev made first mention of BAM's pan-Soviet composition in an article highlighting the beginning of construction in the spring of 1974. He reported that workers from the Armenian Soviet Socialist Republic who had arrived in the BAM Zone with the first wave of builders were the "best and brightest representatives of their respective regions."[54] This language reveals Shinkarev's disregard of the Armenians' minimal education and their semiskilled qualifications.

Another example of the unification theme that lauded BAMer "strength in ethnic distinction" was L. Fadeev's widely published book *BAM: Zolotoe zveno* (BAM: The golden spike), which appeared in 1984 with a print run of more than one hundred thousand copies. Fadeev's profile of a group of "new friends" from the Caucasus, Baltics, and Central Asia contained rich descriptions of how the workers used Russian as their common language and included passages extolling the scenic and gastronomic virtues of the fresh-faced BAMers' home regions. Emphasizing the "multinational atmosphere" that pervaded the area, Fadeev evoked the words of the well-known poet and *Bratsk Station* author Evgenii Evtushenko, who wrote after visiting the BAM Zone that upon catching sight of the Georgian-built settlement of Niia, he "nearly cried with nostalgia for I had just seen the ancient culture of Georgia in all of its radiant Caucasian splendor here on the BAM."[55]

Two 1974 *Gudok* articles devoted further attention to Central Asian and Caucasian BAMers by profiling a group of Komsomolers from Armenia, Georgia, and Uzbekistan who were sent by "[each] republic [as] the best of their youth in the first detachment of BAM builders."[56] In an article written from the "trailblazer" settlement of Zvezdnyi, another journalist lauded the accomplishments of Yerevan, Armenia's Pavel Sarkisian, who "abandoned viniculture" to work on the railway after attending the Seventeenth Komsomol Congress in the spring of 1974.[57] Young Pavel was so enamored with the promise of BAM's future achievements that he had convinced other members of his family to form a "dynasty" of Sarkisians who would venture from the vineyards of the Caucasus, push the railway forward, and then remain in the BAM Zone as emissaries of Armenian culture in Siberia. In all likelihood, however, the Sarkisians returned home to Armenia after completing their tour of duty. Findings in the Komsomol archive reveal that only a small percentage of non-Slavic BAMers, especially Caucasians and Central Asians, remained in the area after the expiration of their service contract. This was due in large part to the wide climatic differences between the BAM Zone and the USSR's southern reaches as well as the fact that most of these peoples were unwilling or unable to speak Russian on a daily basis.

Subsequent media coverage followed the trend of profiling non-Slavs by focusing on Caucasian and Central Asian "volunteers" who had arrived to work on unfinished sections of the railway in any area where the BAM administration needed them.[58] While discussing construction in Irkutsk Oblast, E. Bostrukhov of *Izvestiia* praised architects and builders from the Caucasus who had erected dormitories in their native architectural styles, but Bostrukhov failed to mention that these individuals' efforts created housing only for those BAMers who came from those three republics in a perpetuation of official segregationist policies.[59] Local journalists also promoted BAM as a "multinational endeavor" by making a determined effort to find and publicize "heroes" who were not Slavs. One such individual was Ivars Leimanis of Riga, Latvia, who had been killed while working as part of the *Kvant* (Quantum) Komsomol brigade, in which Leimanis was a rare ethnic Latvian. An active sportsman and participant in the life of his Komsomol collective, Leimanis was electrocuted while trying to prevent a live wire from falling onto a group of his coworkers laboring below. Portrayed by the CPSU secretary of *Kvant* in martyr-like terms as a "selfless hero who gave his life to protect his comrades," Leimanis was also described as "a self-effacing lad" whose self-sacrifice and determination to lead by example promoted the officially sanctioned theme that Slavs did not possess a monopoly on heroism along the rails.[60]

Another non-Slavic hero was Vladimir Titomir from the Moldavian Soviet Socialist Republic. Titomir was a highway bridge builder who, according to the editors of *Baikalo-Amurskaia magistral*, "never looked for a warmer place to work where he could have an easy job." Rather than seeking a cushy assignment, Titomir worked diligently in any temperature, even when his tools broke from the extreme cold. Titomir happily honored any request asked of him despite the fact that, as a native of "sunny Moldavia," he was unaccustomed to the harsh winter climate of the BAM Zone.[61] In an article entitled "A Fellow from Khashuri," a member of the *Stroitel BAM* staff profiled Otari Dzhaliashvili, a Georgian driver. Journalist A. Emelianov stressed that all BAMers, regardless of their national identification, shared as their foremost priority the completion of BAM and the establishment of the "close relations between the many peoples of the Soviet Union."[62] In "ArmBAMstroi Strengthens Its Position," another *Stroitel BAM* correspondent examined a handful of the two hundred Armenians building housing for the ten thousand future residents of Taiura.[63] Only in passing, however, did the reporter mention that ArmBAMstroi built housing solely for other Armenians who arrived later and worked in Taiura independently until the announced end of the project in 1984. As the segregated living arrangements for Slavs and non-Slavs ran counter to the theme of national unity, it was rarely mentioned by BAM Zone journalists and almost never by national writers.

In 1974, an Iakut ASSR party official wrote in *Molodezh Iakutii* (Youth of Iakutiia) of happy Iakuts working side by side with Slavs who had never seen an Asian before, although V. Zhuravlev did not mention any specific brigades and declined to indicate where these Iakuts and Slavs "coexisted."[64] In a subsequent article, "A Permanent Iakut Residence on the BAM," the same functionary made a bold recruitment pitch by inviting young Iakuts who "were interested in meeting their Soviet brothers" to contact their local Komsomol organization, sign a work contract, and bring as many friends as possible to the railway.[65] In a 1979 article in the newspaper *BAM*, journalist S. Fedina profiled a group of Armenian cafeteria workers in Tynda who all hailed from the same "quaint village" back in Armenia. Despite the fact that the villagers' singular contribution to blazing the "path to the future" consisted of serving meals to cafeteria patrons, Fedina proclaimed that "these Caucasian pacesetters are leading the way to a new era of Soviet progress."[66] The overarching message in such accounts was that non-Slavs were content and willing to risk their lives to help their comrades. The intended purpose of such articles was to show minorities that they should be appreciative, if not deprecating, toward those with whom they worked, particularly their Slavic supervisors.

After the 1979 Islamic revolution in Iran and the subsequent Soviet invasion of Afghanistan, the national and BAM Zone press went to even greater lengths to underscore the project's heterogeneous composition, with the intention of imparting a greater sense of belonging to BAM (and by association to the USSR as a whole) among the nation's non-Slavic minorities. This emphasis on the inclusion of non-Slavic peoples along the rails continued unabated until the 1984 completion ceremony, when both *Pravda* and *Izvestiia* detailed the accomplishments of Kazakh and Uzbek *bamovtsy*. That year, the Komsomol Central Committee presented several members of minority groups with a "For Participation in BAM Construction" award. These included an "initiating and work-loving comrade" Tatar, an Azeri MVD policeman who had defended the populace with a "strong sense of Caucasian pride," and a Jewish lumberjack whose timbering had helped to build housing in the Jewish Autonomous Oblast capital of Birobidzhan. Created by Stalin and located in the extreme southeastern corner of the Soviet Union, the Jewish Autonomous Oblast was promoted by Moscow as a territory where Soviet Jewry could enjoy a modicum of religious and cultural freedom. However, the true reason for the area's creation stemmed from an official desire to move Jews to a sufficiently remote location where they would remain isolated from the country's urban centers, the loci of Soviet power that some anti-Semitic elements within officialdom believed had been contaminated by Zionist or "cosmopolitan" influences. After the creation of the Autonomous Oblast, however, almost no Jews moved there; today, it remains an underpopulated and generally ignored borderland whose single importance is its proximity to the Chinese frontier.[67] Finally, one Buriat who desired to see the railroad improve the "quality of life in [the] land of his ancestors" also received a "For Participation in BAM Construction" award.[68]

Segregation and Criticism of Non-Slavic Formations

Such positive representations in the press aside, national minorities within BAMer brigades often labored in a negatively charged and unequal working environment that was the creation of the Slavic-controlled railway leadership. Aside from those elite formations that possessed a token number of national minorities, BAMers from the USSR's various republics and regions worked and socialized separately from one another in every sector of the BAM Zone. This segregation was intentional, as the Komsomol BAM administration consistently relegated admittedly semiskilled or unskilled non-Slavic detachments to difficult, manually intensive tasks, including sanitation and forest-clearing duties. Although non-Slavic republics did send some skilled personnel to BAM areas, such individuals generally found themselves placed with their conationalists. BAM authorities criticized these groups' predictable lack of accomplishment in the naïve belief that such commentary would not tarnish the image of the endeavor as a whole.

In 1976, the Komsomol committees of the USSR's Baltic, Caucasian, and Central Asian republics failed to send the promised numbers of workers to the project. Although the reasons for this shortcoming are not addressed directly in the archival literature, it is clear from the relatively low level of minority BAMer participation that non-Slavic republics struggled to recruit members of their titular republic nationalities. In short, non-Slavs were particularly unwilling to make the trek to BAM. Table 5.2 reveals future plans of BAM Zone residents by geographic origin for 1981. Nearly all non-Slavic republics and regions failed to fulfill their recruitment quotas as dictated by Moscow. Within the construction trust Angarstroi, only twenty-eight out of a promised one hundred thirty volunteers arrived from Azerbaijan, thirteen out of one hundred twenty from Armenia, nineteen out of a hundred from Georgia, and two out of fifty from the autonomous district of North Ossetia.

Table 5.2

Future plans of BAM Zone residents by geographic origin, 1981 (percentages)

	RSFSR	Ukraine	Baltics	Caucasus	Central Asia
Remain in BAM Zone	36.4	16.1	14.3	16.7	18.6
Return home	63.6	83.9	85.7	83.3	81.4

Source: Voronov and Smirnov, "Zakreplenie molodezhi v zone BAMa," 21.

Dagestan (a predominately Muslim region within the RSFSR) and Uzbekistan sent none of the fifty volunteers each had promised. Within the bridge-building division Mostostroi-9, Estonia, Latvia, and Lithuania failed to produce any of the one hundred workers promised by each republic respectively, while Tajikistan could not muster any of the fifty laborers expected of it. Despite the fact that the rail-laying detachment Nizhneangarsktransstroi operated wholly within its territory, the Buriat ASSR Komsomol organization sent only twenty of fifty participants. Kazakhstan, an important source of labor for the powerful tunneling division BAMtonnelstroi, sent none of the one hundred workers expected of it in 1976.[69] Noting what he termed a "lackadaisical attitude," Komsomol chief Dmitrii Filippov berated the Turkmenistan and Dagestan Komsomol organizations, which in 1975 and 1976 had promised to send one hundred volunteers in both years to BAM, but by 1977 had combined to send only three.[70] Filippov noted that among the BAM "volunteers" sent by the two regions, only 70 percent had completed the eighth grade or higher, and more than half of these were "insufficiently educated" cadres (the Komsomol required that potential BAMers possess the equivalent of an American high school diploma) who had managed to secure Komsomol membership cards despite their lack of schooling.[71]

An important factor in the unwillingness of many workers, particularly those who were accustomed to a climate far warmer and less severe than that of Siberia, to leave their homes and spend three years in a desolate sector of the country was the primitive nature of housing throughout the BAM Zone. The press was reticent on this subject, but stories of squalid living conditions and bitter cold were spread by word of mouth by railway "veterans" upon their return to their home regions. The low-prestige assignments to which the Komsomol invariably assigned non-Slavs were usually located in the most wild and inaccessible areas of the project, where accommodations were the most spartan. The paltry housing conditions faced by many were described in an October 1975 bulletin from the Buriat ASSR Komsomol apparatus, which remarked that members of Komsomol "shock brigades" who came to the region from the Baltics, Caucasus, and Central Asia lived in temporary housing constructed from prefabricated metal sheets. Although BAM construction headquarters expected these units to assemble more permanent facilities while simultaneously laying track, most of these "pacesetters" lacked the building expertise and construction materials with which to house themselves.[72]

In 1977, the Tynda Komsomol organization conducted a yearlong evaluation of BAMer formations that originated from the Caucasus. After a lengthy examination of these groups' common inability to meet the construction quotas assigned to them, the city's Party leaders labeled the underachieving detachments as "deficient" and sent nearly half of the five hundred BAMers in question back to their home districts without any financial compensation whatsoever.[73] In a related incident, the Komsomol bureaucracy decried the performance of BAMer detachments from the Caucasus and Eastern Siberia, in which more than 50 percent of members lacked any construction knowledge, railway or otherwise, despite the fact that many of these areas had historically possessed only small numbers of highly trained transport, especially railway, personnel.[74]

Party and government representatives in non-Slavic republics also were taken to task by the Komsomol for their lax personnel and planning standards. In 1977, the Turkmenistan Komsomol committee invited a former Komsomol member who had just been released from jail after serving a sentence for theft, to work on BAM under their sponsorship. In an example of the slowness with which the Komsomol bureaucracy functioned, the organization discovered its error five days after the ex-convict's departure.[75] Such postings of known criminals by republic-level Komsomol committees appears to have occurred more frequently in non-Slavic republics due to the acute shortage of qualified and motivated volunteers. In 1979, a governmental commission on BAM construction found that brigades under North Caucasian control undertook housing construction "unsatisfactorily." These brigades' inadequacies in building their own accommodations resulted in a postponement of track laying, which in turn produced a construction slowdown throughout the entire project.[76]

Construction mishaps and deficiencies were, in the eyes of project leaders, a constant problem that plagued minority brigades more frequently than

Slavic-run formations. In a 1977 report, deputy project head Iurii Verbitskii lamented "the generally poor quality of temporary housing construction" by singling out Armenia's construction trust ArmBAMstroi for its "low level of labor and social discipline," "poor labor organization," and mistakes by the Armenian Komsomol in the transfer of cadres who had amassed criminal records before coming to BAM. Verbitskii charged that ArmBAMstroi failed to fulfill any of its assigned plan and allowed expensive construction materials to disappear while dozens of brigade members left their worksites without permission.[77] Verbitskii later condemned the Komsomol organizations of Armenia as well as the Buriat and Iakut ASSRs for their failure to send the expected number of workers to the project while the Komsomol organizations of Moldavia and Turkmenistan "committed grievous errors by sending poor-quality cadres to BAM . . . [and] allow[ed] many substandard individuals to come to the railway without Komsomol membership cards or the necessary construction knowledge."[78] Within the Central BAM Segment, Iakuts composed less than 4 percent of the workforce within so-called multinational brigades laboring in the Iakut ASSR towns of Pervomaiskii, Ust-Niukzha, and Zolotinka during 1975 and 1976.[79] For comparison, Russians represented more than 60 percent of the membership of the same detachments.[80]

The amount a certain republic- or district-level formation spent of its allotted annual budget often factored into the center's evaluation of its overall productivity, regardless of the extent of that unit's tangible achievements. A set of statistical data for 1978 reveals that the thousand-member Gruzstroi-BAM was the most "productive" minority-sponsored division since it spent 62 percent of its allotted budget (some 623,000 rubles), while the eight-hundred-strong ArmstroiBAM could only manage to dispose of 53 percent of its allocated budget (424,000 rubles). The worst-performing detachment was the 250-member AzerbaidzhanstroiBAM, which used only 19 percent of its budget that year (47,000 rubles).[81] This waste of funds was directly related to the fact that AzerbaidzhanstroiBAM began work at Ulkan without an adequate number of technical specialists, logistical support, or sufficient administrative backing from its sponsor organizations in Azerbaijan. When an Azeri Party newspaper learned of these shortcomings, its editors contacted the Azerbaijan Komsomol to determine the reasons for the deficiencies. To the editors' dismay, Komsomol officials in Baku admitted their charges "relaxed" instead of working, with the predictable result that its members made no progress in housing construction. With the area's notoriously severe winter approaching, AzerbaidzhanstroiBAM had no choice but to purchase expensive prefabricated housing in the form of abandoned railway cars from the USSR Ministry of Transportation. While wintering in its meager temporary shelters, the brigade was unable to undertake work on permanent lodgings until a year after its arrival.[82]

In a 1980 annual report, Deputy Director Verbitskii noted that the performance of Georgia's GruzBAMstroi, at what the poet Evgenii Evtushenko described as the "paradise" of the Niia settlement, was severely lacking. Foremost, the brigade's engineers were "unprepared" to complete the tasks assigned to them upon their arrival due to a "complete lack" of training, which Verbitskii conveniently declined to mention was the responsibility of the Komsomol's partner agency, the USSR Ministry of Transport Construction, in permafrost building methods. In 1979, the formation received a few pieces of dated machinery from MK-131, but it failed to fulfill its earth-moving quota even with the help of the additional equipment. After a "disastrous" year in which several workers left their base camp without prior authorization, dozens of members of GruzBAMstroi abruptly decided to withdraw themselves from their assigned tasks and seek work elsewhere. Verbitskii also noted with disappointment that Chechen and Ingush BAMers had arrived at their worksites more than six months behind schedule. More disturbingly, many of the detachment's members developed certain "dependent tendencies" (a euphemism Verbitskii employed to describe alcoholism and a penchant for petty thievery), which threatened to destroy labor discipline and the group's already shaky morale. In the same report, Verbitskii praised a Slavic brigade for its "outstanding quality" of work, while he remarked on the Chechens' and Ingushs' "embarrassing antics."[83]

A 1983 communiqué from the Komsomol BAM construction headquarters roundly criticized a group of North Ossetians and Dagestanis for failing to meet their construction quotas for the previous year.[84] A 1982 report issued by Komsomol BAM headquarters revealed "gross errors" in the recruitment and mustering of brigades from the Caucasus. Among other mistakes, many of the newly arrived BAMers had been dismissed from their previous occupations for various offences, and several of them were former Komsomolers who had managed to rejoin the organization due to bureaucratic incompetence. Project head Sushchevich contended that the Komsomol committees of these three republics knowingly permitted young people who were of less than "ideal quality" to serve as members not only of their own brigades, but of the elite Nineteenth Komsomol Congress BAM Construction Brigade as well.[85]

While many non-Slavic workers faced the ire of their superiors for their disorganization and incompetence, a substantial portion of the minority BAMer component never began its assigned tasks along the tracks. Others fled the scene as soon as the opportunity arose. The Komsomol reported that a Latvian-sponsored group due to arrive at the still incomplete settlement of Taksimo, commissioned to begin its housing construction assignment, actually appeared some three months after its promised date. A similar group from Uzbekistan failed to arrive at all. Young peoples' brigades that arrived at Taksimo that year from Armenia and Turkmenistan were under strength by more than 50 percent and contained persons who "sowed the seeds of immorality and laziness" among their comrades.[86] The retention of non-Slavs proved as difficult as recruiting and motivating them. In a February 1982 bulletin, the Komsomol headquarters of the Western BAM segment reported "serious deficiencies" in the recruitment and quality of volunteers from Georgia, the Kabardino-Balkar and Chechen-Ingush ASSRs. Participants from Azerbaijan, North Ossetia, and Latvia had conducted themselves "poorly" due to their "complete antipathy toward work" and resistance to their superiors' orders. Of the 2,172 total volunteers arriving in the Western BAM segment in 1981, more than 30 percent had left the project by year's end.[87]

A 1975 dispatch regarding the Seventeenth Komsomol Congress Brigade revealed that more than 50 percent of brigade members who came from Armenia, Georgia, and Tajikistan were unwilling to work because of a "combination of apathy and, in some cases, an outright refusal to work." The report noted that a "general malaise" had gripped the brigade, which was supposed to be an elite formation among the BAM organizations, and also criticized the brigade's leadership for not taking an active role in combating idleness, ineptitude, and "passivity" among its members, who blatantly disregarded their assigned construction norms.[88] Within the Twenty-Sixth CPSU Congress brigade that arrived in the BAM Zone in 1981, 142 of the 290 Georgians who began with the brigade remained with it two years later, despite the presence of state incentives, including automobile vouchers and triple pay, which were designed to retain them for the entire duration of their three-year tour of duty. Paradoxically, while the Komsomol encouraged non-Slavs to come to BAM, it provided them with little opportunity to distinguish themselves or incentive to remain with the project. The semblance of national unity, not motivation and retention, was the aim of this facet of the BAM "myth."

Although the railway's authorities noted the difficulties of recruiting non-Slavic youth to join the BAM project, they did not put forth any serious attempt to address the societal or cultural problems behind the lack of minority interest. Many Komsomol officials privately believed a genuine BAM mobilization campaign to be too ambitious and even foolhardy to undertake. Could the railway experience have ever successfully fostered a sense of inclusion among the USSR's minorities? Yes, said some former BAMers and Komsomol cadres (all of whom are ethnic Slavs) who had occupied prominent positions in BAM hierarchy. Valentin Sushchevich, the former head of the Komsomol BAM headquarters, stated that "BAM really was about all of us as Soviet citizens. I can truly say that this was an all-Union undertaking."[89] Galina Tokareva, at the time the head of the reading room at the Komsomol archive, urged this author "not to forget about the 'little people' [non-Slavs generally and non-Russian specifically]" while at the Komsomol archive.[90] But the non-Party members interviewed, some of whom were not Slavs, were unanimous in their belief that such a goal had always been impossible.[91] For those who dominated the railway's hierarchy, however, the accomplishments of Slavic railroaders took precedence over any considerations of the project's ultimate viability.

The Primacy of Slavic Detachments

The vast majority of highly profiled and decorated BAMers came from select formations, such as the Seventeenth Komsomol Congress Brigade, and were nearly all Slavs.[92] A confidential list produced by the Komsomol Central Committee of those Order of Lenin recipients who had volunteered to join BAM revealed the preponderance of Slavs: among the fifteen honorees who arrived in the BAM Zone during the project's initial year of 1974, twelve were Russian and the remaining three Ukrainian and Belorussian.[93] Unlike their Caucasian and Central Asian counterparts, the Komsomol organizations of Belorussia, the RSFSR, and Ukraine distinguished themselves in the center's eyes with both the quality and quantity of "volunteers" they sent to BAM. In addition, the youth organization praised these groups' performance in meeting annual construction norms that were often formulated arbitrarily by the Komsomol leadership in the capital.[94] The Komsomol organizations of the Soviet Union's three "core" republics met (and in many cases exceeded) their recruitment quotas—in 1976, for example, the city of Leningrad sent more than the required number of workers, while Belorussia provided "several dozen" more laborers for assignment over its quota. Many RSFSR Komsomol committees surpassed the expectations of the BAM construction headquarters that year by providing "volunteers" who signed contracts before leaving home that bound them to remain with the project for the next three years.[95] The signing of such contracts before one's arrival in the BAM Zone assured that those who had second thoughts about participating could not easily renege on their commitment.

A critical factor in the success of Slav-dominated formations was the financial and technical backing they received from government and Party organizations in the home republics. Brigades from the Slavic republics received lucrative "donations" of money and equipment from their home CPSU committees to build BAM towns in the architectural styles of their home regions. For instance, brigades from the RSFSR cities of Kransnodar and Stavropol received 44 million rubles in locally generated "sponsorship" funds to establish the town of Ust-Kut, Leningrad nearly 140 million for Severobaikalsk, Belorussia more than 100 million rubles for Muiakan, Moscow nearly 250 million rubles for Tynda, and Ukraine over 200 million rubles for Urgal.[96] Ukrstroi received an additional grant of nearly 19 million rubles, while its equivalent in Moscow and Leningrad secured sums of 17 million and 7 million rubles, respectively.[97] The positive impact of these additional funds on the efficiency of Slavic formations was made clear when Komsomol General Secretary Filippov himself praised several of his RSFSR organizations for exceeding his expectations by completing construction of their sponsored towns ahead of schedule.[98]

Accolades for Slavic brigades did not stop with Filippov. In a 1976 letter, other members of the Komsomol Central Committee extolled the "Communist righteousness" of participants, all of whom came from the Slavic regions of the Soviet Union.[99] In addition, the brigade of Ukrainian Valentin Prikhodko set a new record by laying nearly two thousand meters of track in a single night in 1975, in honor of the thirtieth anniversary of the Soviet victory in World War II. The brigade, which contained railroaders from Prikhodko's homeland as well as Belorussia, was composed entirely of Slavs. In a sign that the official interpretation of Soviet history was one in which Slavs occupied a position of superiority that tended to exclude the contributions of all others, this so-called "Thirty Years of Victory Detachment" received a lion's share of publicity during the BAM Zone media's coverage of anniversary festivities along the rails.[100]

Near the end of the project, the entire country was exposed to the Slavic dominance of BAM through L. P. Kaminskaia's *BAM—doroga druzhby* (BAM—The path of friendship), a book published in East Siberia but distributed nationwide.[101] Full of color photographs and song lyrics designed to attract a potential reader's attention, the work's purpose was to evaluate and celebrate the national unity created by the common experience of building BAM. In her attempt to proudly display the "multinational unity" brought forth by the railway's completion, Kaminskaia revealed that the majority of technical and logistical support had come from Belorussia, Russia, and Ukraine, while the non-Slavic areas of the Soviet Union, especially Caucasian and Central Asian republics, had provided only laborers with little or no railroading experience. While Kaminskaia proclaimed that "one hundred nationalities" participated in the project, she devoted the majority of her attention to extolling the physical achievements of Slavs laboring at high-profile bridge and tunnel construction sites.[102]

Hostility between the Majority and National Minorities

Along with soldiers and lower-class city dwellers, members of the BAM workforce expressed their displeasure with the circumstances of their lives.[103] Stories of violent behavior within supposedly harmonious elite formations abounded during BAM's decade of prominence. During a drinking bout in 1981, a group of Georgians began fighting with local police after the authorities attempted to dismiss a gathering that was being conducted entirely in Georgian, a language that none of the Slavic militiamen could understand. According to witnesses, the rowdy group's leaders attempted to throw the outnumbered militiamen off an unfinished dam that stood several hundred feet over the rolling Neriungri River. A public hearing ensued and the offending BAMers, all of whom had been specially selected to come to the BAM Zone by the Georgian Komsomol Central Committee in Tbilisi, were expelled from the region without receiving their prized automobile vouchers or hardship wages. In another incident the following year, two Georgian housing construction bosses apparently transplanted their black market ring from their home republic to the BAM Zone. After failing in an attempt to bribe local officials, the pair colluded to murder the chief detective of the Neriungri police department but were ultimately foiled.[104] Although the Georgians' fate is not discussed in the Komsomol archive, it is plausible that these individuals lost their Komsomol memberships and served only a short jail sentence. Long-term imprisonment was not a common punishment in such cases.

In 1976, BAM deputy chief Verbitskii filed a brief about the behavior of a non-Party member from Dagestan who suddenly abandoned his post, throwing his group into "chaos" and resulting in its complete dissolution. Remarking that "the majority of the suspect's former brigade members are only interested in higher pay," Verbitskii noted that of the thirty-seven original members of the detachment, only six remained in the BAM Zone after their leader's defection.[105] Of these, two headed to the small town of Bodaibo in northern Irkutsk Oblast to "look for gold," while the whereabouts of the thirty-one unaccounted for Dagestanis remained unknown.[106] Verbitskii also provided details another national minority resistance, in which a woodcutting brigade under the direction of two Azeris was to be transferred to an assignment that involved loading and unloading barges at the Ust-Kut River Port. After learning of their new assignment, the duo decided that they did not wish to move their families away from the Azeri community in which they lived; therefore they instructed their conationals not to obey the order. After the ringleaders' arrest, the Komsomol committee that adjudicated the matter decided to reconstitute the brigade under new leadership and to revoke the Party memberships of the two in question. The highly skilled Caucasians had no alternative but to return home after surrendering their Komsomol and Party membership cards.[107]

Other incidents involving minority BAMers mirrored the ethnic tensions at play throughout the country. In 1975, the chief Komsomol officer of the Shimanovsk Industrial Complex reported that three detained Armenians held revoked Komsomol membership cards and in fact had not enjoyed Komsomol membership for several years. In approving the trio's dismissal from service, the official chastised the Armenian Komsomol for permitting such "unsuitable residents" to come to BAM on an all-too-frequent basis.[108] Later that year, BAM Zone headquarters lambasted two Azeris for "disrupting social order" at the Andizhan Cotton Industry Institute, an "international experimental cooperative of people's friendship" located within the Shimanovsk Industrial Complex. After drinking on the job, the pair in question encouraged their fellow countrymen to instigate a fight with their Slavic supervisors. All of those who participated in the fracas were dismissed from Shimanovsk, and the two fomenters were forced to return to Azerbaijan to face charges of "antisocial conduct resulting in an ethnically motivated disturbance."[109]

Considering that many Caucasian BAMers viewed life along the rails with distaste and even contempt (a sentiment certainly shared by others), such a penalty may not have been unwelcome by the two men. In another incident of unrest involving ethnic minorities, two Azeri masons stated publicly after an afternoon of drinking that they would "leave the BAM Zone tomorrow" if they could find work elsewhere. This defiant announcement incited a "series of unfortunate events" that included a disturbance between the Caucasian pair and several Russian workers that resulted in several serious injuries.[110] The close interaction between Slavs and ethnic minorities working along the BAM railway provided fertile ground for long-brewing feelings of racial animosity, bigotry, and resentment to find expression, among Slavs and non-Slavs alike who lived far from Moscow's strict ideological controls.

Competing Expressions of Unity and Dissolution

After a decade's worth of confident assertions about the "eternal brotherhood" enjoyed by the disparate BAMer nationalities, the Soviet government announced that its twin goals—the completion of the railway on schedule and the strengthening of ties among workers of different cultural and linguistic backgrounds—had been achieved in a testament to the strength of ideology and labor organization. Behind this insistence, however, lay the far-from-ideal reality that the coexistence between majority and minority workers was tenuous at best and potentially explosive at worst. In addition, another equally damaging truth lay in the fact that while trains rolled along BAM, they did so sporadically and not across the entire railway.

Such realities were of little importance, however, to the project's proponents in Moscow and throughout the BAM Zone. For them, the main challenge had been to promote the unification theme of national harmony in the press, an ultimately futile bid to elicit minority support for the endeavor. The media pushed the public "heroization" of national minorities, despite the ethnic tensions evident to those inside and outside the BAM Zone. By promoting the fiction that non-Slavs played a prominent role in BAM construction, the state could point to the fact that the project represented a microcosm of the happy and peacefully coexisting patchwork of peoples that was the USSR. For those in Moscow and the BAM Zone whose job it was to impart legitimacy to the endeavor, much of BAM's utility centered around its potential to serve as an example of cohesiveness that others at home and abroad could admire and emulate. In making explicit overtures to its minority groups through the promotion of BAM, the state revealed the truism that the sheer numbers of non-Slavs who lived in the Soviet Union by the mid-1970s dictated that their opinions simply could not be ignored.

BAM was a microcosm of the existing dynamic of the country's many nationalities during the Brezhnev years, but this characteristic was revealed in its internal not external correspondence. While trumpeting ethnic fraternity in public, the BAM bureaucracy privately eschewed national harmonization as it provided the railway's non-Slavic workers with substandard equipment and training, sent them to the remotest sectors of the BAM Zone, and then criticized their performance behind the not-too-tightly closed doors of Komsomol headquarters from Tynda to Moscow when these groups failed to live up to the regime's inflated expectations. In short, representatives of the USSR's geographic periphery lived and worked on the margins of BAM. The critical disconnect between the image produced by the BAM mythmakers and the realities of life on the railway lay in Slavic officialdom's implicit mistrust of its non-Slavic cadres (and vice versa), whom it viewed with a mixture of disdain and mistrust due to growing concerns about demographic shifts, renewed expressions of national consciousness, and religious reawakenings that threatened the Soviet Union. As a result of this deliberate policy of segregation and marginalization of non-Slavic BAMers, the national tensions that BAM was supposed to ameliorate in fact grew more divisive throughout the USSR.

6 // The Rails of Fraternal Cooperation

BAMers Abroad and Foreigners at Home

> Unfortunately, Komsomol BAM headquarters has just now learned,
> based on an unexplained and belated receipt of information from
> the Bureau of International Youth Tourism Sputnik, that certain
> youth selected to participate in the first Druzhba [Friendship] voy-
> age to Cuba were not the best representatives of BAMer youth. We
> have received no explanation from Sputnik regarding these deficient
> young people.
>
> Report of the Komsomol Central Committee, 1981

ANOTHER IMPETUS BEHIND BAM construction and its attendant propaganda campaign was the need to impress the Soviet Union's allies and
enemies, particularly the People's Republic of China, with the USSR's ability to undertake and complete this massive endeavor as an expression of Soviet geostrategic and military might. In culling labor from the youth of those
"fraternal nations" that were within the Soviet sphere of influence, the BAM
administration attempted to amass an additional workforce to supplement
the poorly trained and insufficiently motivated domestic BAMers. These

fraternal nations included Bulgaria, Cuba, Czechoslovakia, East Germany, Hungary, Mongolia, Poland, Romania, and Vietnam, which belonged to Comecon, the Soviet-led Council for Mutual Economic Assistance. Chinese youth were not invited to participate in the "project of the century." Former BAMer Nikolai V. Nikitin recalled working with the East Germans: "To tell the truth, we got along fairly well with the [East] Germans despite their poor command of Russian and their obvious displeasure at having to spend their summers in our mosquito-infested and sweltering camp. Their refusal to share their cigarettes with us really irked us, though."[1]

The administration used foreign labor throughout the BAM Zone to propagandize the railway among Soviet allies. The project's managers felt this accomplishment would serve as a catalyst in increasing trade between the European USSR and the Pacific Rim, particularly with Japan, and thus help to reduce the Soviet economy's dependence on trade with Western Europe and the United States.[2] To complete the ambitious goal of driving the nearly 2,500-mile railway across Eurasia within a decade, BAM officials made two fundamental decisions. First, they used the incentive of foreign travel, higher pay, and automobile vouchers in an attempt to encourage generally ineffectual domestic cadres to build the railway more quickly and efficiently. This incentive to work more diligently was for those workers considered "morally upstanding" and "pacesetting." Second, the BAM administrators employed ideological and practical inducements to attract international laborers, most of whom were already studying in the Soviet Union, to assist in the project's construction.[3]

Many BAMers traveled outside the USSR as ostensible ambassadors of Soviet achievements, to perpetuate the officially generated illusion of BAM as a showcase of international solidarity and cooperation. Based on findings in the archives, however, it is more likely that the approximately ten thousand BAMers who journeyed abroad actually damaged the reputations of the project in particular and the Soviet Union in general in the eyes of some of their hosts.[4] Rather than promoting BAM and Soviet state socialism, many BAMers abroad deflected attention from the project through their social, not only ideological, interactions with other young people. These BAMers gained personal knowledge of the world outside the Soviet Union, and upon their return home, they would relate their experiences to their comrades.

Non-Soviet BAMers labored on the project in a distinctly unequal capacity in comparison with their Soviet counterparts. Because of the unreliable nature of some domestic BAMers, railway administrators turned to these foreigners, most of whom were recruited from a number of socialist countries. In return for Soviet economic and political assistance, BAM leadership used gentle but persistent pressure to convince the heads of socialist nations to send their youth to BAM. Non-Soviet youth who worked on the railway were frequently surprised and even disgruntled at being segregated from their Soviet counterparts while toiling on low-prestige infrastructure construction assignments, many of which were located in the hinterlands of the BAM Zone.

To the state's considerable embarrassment, however, these international BAMers witnessed firsthand the railway's corruption, gross inefficiency, and colossal waste of resources. Later, these individuals would undoubtedly relate their experiences to those back home, as had the Soviet youth who had ventured abroad. Evidence suggests that the foreign BAMers' generally negative impressions of their time working on the project further damaged both their and their countrymen's opinions of the Soviet Union as a political and economic model worthy of emulation. This contributed to a loss of faith in Soviet-style state socialism. It might also have led to a widespread discrediting (and in some cases an outright rejection) of Soviet military and humanitarian assistance in a number of developing nations, particularly among Soviet "client states" in southern and eastern Africa.[5]

BAMers Abroad

Between 1974 and 1984, some BAMers traveled outside the USSR, on board special Druzhba (Friendship) and Zvezdnyi (Starlit) trains and also on cruises.[6] Under Komsomol control, the Druzhba and Zvezdnyi trains were managed not by high-level bureaucrats, but by middle-ranking and relatively young Komsomolers, most of whom were under thirty. Although the avowed purpose of the Druzhba and Zvezdnyi journeys was to use foreign travel as a reward for laborers who exceeded their production quotas, Komsomol BAM headquarters also expected that the recipients would propagandize the railway's accomplishments. While ostensibly engaging in "socialist fraternization" with the youth of the host nations, Soviet BAMers abroad participated in decidedly nondoctrinaire conversations and occasional drunken soirees that served the unintended function of casting the BAMers and the Soviet Union in a negative light.

In one example from the Western BAM Segment, railroaders who had exceeded their production norms by the greatest percentage were sent to East Germany in October 1975 on board the Zvezdnyi. This special agitational train operated from the BAM Zone administrative center of Tynda and various regional headquarters.[7] These 340 individuals were selected according to recommendations submitted to the project's leadership by their peers and supervisors. All potential travelers required the final approval of Moscow-based Sputnik, the Soviet Bureau of International Youth Tourism, and the Komsomol BAM construction headquarters in Tynda.[8] Nearly all of the participants had surpassed production norms that GlavBAMstroi had established with little or no understanding of the varying work conditions at the project's construction sites. Komsomol BAM chief Valentin Sushchevich remarked that the most outstanding of the chosen workers had surpassed their rail-laying and dormitory construction quotas by some 200 percent; he lauded the equal division of travel permits between BAMer men and women, and emphasized the fact that many of the most successful builders came from Moscow and Leningrad.[9] Yet Sushchevich also admitted to his superiors in Moscow that the influence of personal connections (*blat*) and a desire to impress officials in the center also played a role in deciding who got to journey abroad.

Problems during the voyages of the supposedly "pacesetting" BAMers arose almost immediately after their travels began. In fact, Sushchevich's deputy, Iurii Galmakov, felt compelled to apologize to Egon Krenz of the East German Union of Free Youth for some BAMers' behavior during their tours of the Lenin Museum in Leipzig and Frederick the Great's Sans Souci palace in Potsdam. Somewhat embarrassedly, Galmakov admitted to Krenz that Soviet youth had "defiled" the palace's gardens by frequent spitting and urinating in public. Galmakov also noted that certain unnamed travelers "violated social order" and "failed to adequately serve as agitators for the project" by neglecting to engage in a discussion of BAM with their socialist comrades. Instead of inspiring the East Germans to follow the Soviet example and undertake such a "grand exploit" as the BAM railway, the young travelers, Galmakov confessed, drank to excess and participated in "immoral behavior" (one guesses that this included sexual activity) with East German youth while visiting Berlin, Dresden, Leipzig, and Weimar.[10]

Writing in 1976, Sushchevich displayed a decidedly more negative attitude toward the BAMers abroad than he had in the previous year. The Komsomol BAM chief noted that those young people who had traveled to East

Germany and Hungary "violated social order" by "fraternizing with members of the opposite sex" in both nations.[11] In the same report, Sushchevich stated that several participants confessed to frequent intoxication during debriefings with their Komsomol chaperones, most of whom were ten to fifteen years their senior, after returning to the Soviet Union.[12] The generational dynamic is important, as archival documents reveal that the chaperones and the younger workers often did not interact socially. Instead, at the conclusion of a day's structured activities in a particular town or city, they divided themselves into separate groups, both of which apparently consumed large amounts of alcoholic beverages. Why might the older BAM representatives have "allowed" the younger cohort to socialize more or less freely with local youth? Undoubtedly this was due to the fact that the workers outnumbered their chaperones on an average of twenty to one.[13]

Other BAMers traveled to Cuba. According to a 1976 issue of the *BAM Builder*: "While traveling through the People's Republic of Cuba, young BAMers endeavored to strengthen the fraternal solidarity of the Cuban and Soviet peoples in the struggle against imperialism and reaction while promoting the dual concerns of democracy and social progress."[14] The behavior of those BAMers chosen to travel outside the Soviet Union did not improve in the 1980s. In 1981, Sushchevich's successor, Iurii Verbitskii, criticized the actions of some two hundred BAMers who had boarded the first Druzhba train to steam through Cuba. Verbitskii reported that bribe-accepting Sputnik functionaries permitted BAMers "who [are] not the best examples of 'pacesetting' young workers" to slip through the project's personnel selection system and to travel to the island. He went on to describe the BAMers' conduct in Cuba as "frequently impolite" and "unduly familiar" with the local population, noting the damage done to Soviet-Cuban relations by the BAMers' boorish behavior, specifically their complete lack of Spanish-language skills and general ignorance of Cuban culture. Verbitskii lamented the BAMers' ignorance of Cuban history after the 1959 popular revolution led by Fidel Castro and Ernesto "Che" Guevara in an indication of some official interest in the affairs of the USSR's closest ally in the Caribbean and Latin America.[15]

Another objective of the BAMer campaign abroad was to boost the general population's impression of the Soviet youth who were visiting their nation. In no country was this more obvious than in Hungary, whose population at the time possessed a fresh memory of the 1956 Soviet intervention.

In 1975, the Komsomol BAM apparatus arranged for fifty-six competition winners to meet Hungarian youth studying in the USSR, to listen to a series of lectures on the history of the Magyar people, and to view a number of films on Hungary's geography and culture in an effort to foster "international friendship" in preparation for their voyage to Hungary on board a Druzhba train the following year.[16] This particular group of BAMers, however, was not to travel to Hungary with a small number of overextended chaperones. In an attempt to put the best possible face on both the BAM project specifically and the Soviet people in general for the Hungarians, the Komsomol chose some thirty-three CPSU members to accompany the competition winners. These chaperones were chosen in part because they had helped to stage an exhibit of paintings by Hungarian artists in the BAM Zone towns of Severobaikalsk and Shushensk the previous year. These individuals were also selected to serve as a "stabilizing force" to prevent the competition winners from engaging in any further embarrassing behavior.[17]

BAM Deputy Chief Galmakov criticized Ivan Rekhlov, director of the Shushensk Portrait Gallery, for failing to publicize the Hungarian art exhibition, which led to the show's paltry attendance. Despite the presence of the dutiful Party members, the winners of the campaign fared no better than their fellow BAMers in creating a favorable impression of their project and their nation among the Hungarians. Writing in 1976, Sushchevich noted that many of those who traveled to Hungary were guilty of repeated "violations of production discipline and social order."[18] He also remarked with considerable alarm that a significant portion of those selected for travel had, in their haste to exceed production quotas and receive permission to travel outside the Soviet Union, contributed to "deficiencies in dormitory construction."[19]

Another ill-fated trip abroad consisted of a 1981 voyage by a mixed group of young Komsomolers and professional railroaders to Cuba, Vietnam, North Korea, and the Philippines on board a Druzhba steamer. The Komsomol intended this trip to cement ties between the Soviet Union and these (with the exception of the Philippines) socialist nations, each of which sold goods to the USSR at fixed prices.[20] In exchange for being hosted by the Cubans, BAMers would assist in the construction of the Havana-Santiago-de-Cuba railway while on the island; in Vietnam, the BAMers would also work with transportation in Hanoi and Ho Chi Minh City (commonly known as Saigon).[21] The promised assistance of the BAMers never materialized, however, as the Komsomol BAM headquarters blamed the Union of BAM

Transport Workers for creating a poorly organized itinerary and allowing "less than desirable elements" to participate in the trip.[22] Because of the organization's lax standards, the Komsomol apparatus was as much to blame, since it had the final say on which BAMers were allowed to leave the country. In another effort to combat the BAMers' glacial construction pace and their lax labor discipline, the project's Komsomol managers arranged for prize-winning laborers of such socialist competitions as the "I Am the Master of the Project" campaign to travel to a number of allied countries, including East Germany, Hungary, Poland, and Cuba.[23] This movement and similar competitions were plagued by the same problems of "undisciplined" BAM cadres who cast themselves, the project, and the USSR as a whole as much less doctrinaire and industrous than intended by Soviet officialdom. The campaign received the brunt of official criticism.

In 1983, Vladimir Shcherbin, head of the Komsomol BAM headquarters, singled out young BAMers who had traveled to Cuba and Hungary for the purpose of publicizing the railway and "providing an example of Soviet achievement in railway construction worthy of emulation."[24] Shcherbin castigated these individuals for failing to sufficiently foster a "sense of socialist competition" among their Cuban and Hungarian comrades by expressing more interest in imbibing local spirits than trumpeting their construction achievements. Furthermore, Shcherbin noted with great concern, as Sushchevich had earlier, that many participants in BAM promotion campaigns in both Cuba and Hungary displayed "irresponsibility" toward their socialist obligations as representatives of the project by failing to mention BAM whatsoever to their Cuban and Hungarian comrades.[25] Interestingly, Shcherbin placed the blame for the campaign's failure not with the Komsomol, but with his organization's convenient target, the USSR Ministry of Transportation's Union of BAM Transport Workers, which he hinted permitted known "violators of social order" to go abroad by accepting "favors" (that is, bribes) from competition participants. Shcherbin boldly accused the union of exaggerating descriptions of its members' accomplishments and withholding information of criminal wrongdoing by supposedly "outstanding" transport workers whom it had selected for the trips.

The need to strengthen trade with Japan occupied an important position in the regime's effort to legitimize the railway. At a 1974 meeting of Trade Unions Central Committee, E. F. Kozhevnikov, the USSR's minister of transport construction, stated that "credits from Japan" were necessary to ensure the project's on-time completion. In a secret document dated September 19, 1974, the Khabarovsk Krai Communist Party organization stated that "the second transcontinental way [that is, the BAM project] with its connection to the ocean will assist in the improvement of economic ties between the Soviet Union and the countries of the Pacific basin."[26]

Older BAM representatives, those over the Komsomol cutoff age of thirty-five, also ignored official expectations regarding their behavior while overseas. The Komsomol archive contains dozens of reports of high-level *apparatchiki* (a commonly used pejorative term for bureaucrats) who rewarded themselves with travel to nations located outside the "fraternal circle," shopped for goods that were in short supply at home, and obtained scarce building materials for their own work brigades. In 1981, and again in 1984, a "special group" of high-level railway administrators spent more than two weeks in Japan.[27] These individuals' purported purpose in visiting the island nation was to meet with "young Japanese socialists" to discuss Tokyo's stance on the disputed Northern Territories after the 1973 visit of Japanese Prime Minister Kakuei Tanaka to Moscow failed to resolve the long-standing territorial issue. Reports made after both groups' return from Japan, however, indicated that members of the BAM delegation ignored their official purpose. Instead, they purchased electronic equipment and discussed trading Soviet timber for Japanese tractors and cranes with representatives of well-known *keiretsu* while supposedly "bolstering fraternal relations with our Japanese Communist comrades."[28] These reports made no mention of any contact whatsoever between BAM officials and pro-Moscow Japanese Communists.

The intended purpose of the Druzhba train trips and cruises and the higher-level "special groups" was to propagandize BAM and to encourage platonic "socialist fraternization" with the youth of the host nations. But BAMers who participated in these journeys often engaged in unapproved activities, revealing the average BAMer's lack of ideological dedication. This cast the BAMers and the USSR in a different light than that desired by the state. For those young people who witnessed and participated in the BAMers' debaucheries, the "path to the future" did not lead to Communism, but to something far more desirable. Indeed, the opportunity to leave the Soviet Union, if only for a short time, was a prize for all BAMers and undoubtedly served as a motivational tool for those eager to see the outside world for themselves. The fact that most BAMers acted as typical young people and not as buttoned-down ambassadors of Marxism-Leninism came as a surprise or a disappointment to the dedicated Komsomol BAM officials who strove to enlist foreign support for BAM.[29]

Foreigners on the Railway

Approximately ten thousand non-Soviet youth labored on the BAM project between 1974 and 1984, and the administration worked hard to include them for both ideological and practical reasons.[30] The older generation of BAM officials remembered the efficient and cost-effective forced labor of German and Japanese prisoners of war who had toiled on the second BAM attempt from 1943 to 1953.[31] During the railway's heyday, the project's leadership assumed that foreign youth might be induced to help build BAM not through coercion, but with the promise that they would receive valuable hands-on training and education in their respective professions or academic disciplines while toiling on the railway. In its desperation to complete BAM within a decade, the project's Komsomol apparatus actively recruited foreigners who were already studying in the USSR as well as those young people not in the Soviet Union. In turn, it consciously risked discrediting the USSR in the foreigners' eyes by exposing them firsthand to the serious deficiencies of the project and the entire nation. The railway's leadership was well aware of this reality. By and large, foreigners' brigades toiled on projects of little or no prestige and were generally segregated from the Soviet detachments with which they were supposed to be cooperating. Although BAM propaganda ignored the fact that Soviet and foreign construction columns often worked apart from one another, the image of a "multinational" (*mezhdunarodnyi*) endeavor was largely a Russian language–only environment where the interaction between workers from supposedly "fraternal" socialist nations and the USSR was heavily curtailed by the state.

Generally speaking, foreign students enrolled at institutes and universities throughout the Soviet Union traveled to the BAM Zone during a *trudovoi semestr* (work semester) in which they were promised by the BAM Komsomol apparatus that they would help Soviet youth to build the railway. Foreign BAM brigades served a useful propagandistic purpose by providing palpable examples of the project's "international" composition, which the state employed as proof of the Soviet Union's equal treatment of all of the world's youth, regardless of ethnicity. Foreign BAMers represented a source of cheap labor, as they received modest stipends that were smaller than those of the native laborers. Unlike their Soviet counterparts, however, foreign BAMers could not leave the project without withdrawing from their respective host universities and leaving the USSR permanently. It is clear that foreign BAMers felt compelled to remain with the project for this reason.[32]

The image of BAM as a voluntary association of international youth appeared frequently in both the national and BAM Zone press, both of which often covered international youth working on the project. A typical example of national coverage of the railway was an April 1975 *Izvestiia* collection of foreign journalists' impressions of the project that included a series of highly complimentary articles by reporters from several Warsaw Pact and even some NATO nations, including Belgium, France, and West Germany, that encouraged workers from all over the world to join the "project of the century" in spirit if not in person. A particularly pertinent example was a contribution entitled "Mosty" (Bridges) by journalist Franz Keler of the East German weekly *Horizont* (Horizon). Keler claimed to "feel like a Soviet citizen" after viewing BAM's great achievements.[33] He pointed to the fact that East Germany should use the construction and labor organization models perfected by the BAMers as a blueprint for its own socialist future. This permutation of the international component of the BAM "myth" was indicative of the effort made by Soviet officialdom to involve all socialist nations (with the notable exception of the USSR's ideological rival, the People's Republic of China) in the project. Known as the era of détente, this was a time when the Soviet Union's leadership strove to improve relations with its other nemesis, the United States.[34]

Latin American BAMers

BAM leadership viewed Latin American and Caribbean youth as fertile sources of potential labor because of the close relationship between the Soviet Union and the emerging socialist governments of the region, particularly Cuba. BAM officials were encouraged by the seemingly inexorable spread of socialism among these peoples as evidence of the increasing popularity of Soviet- and Cuban-aided "peoples' fronts" in Argentina, Chile, and Nicaragua during the early 1970s.[35] To encourage Cubans already in the Soviet Union and those still in Cuba to take an interest in coming to the BAM Zone, project chief Valentin Sushchevich initiated a "mutual exchange program" between BAMers and laborers on Cuba's Havana-Santiago-de-Cuba Central Railway. Ostensibly this exchange would strengthen social and professional ties between railroaders of both nations. This railway, somewhat condescendingly labeled the "Cuban BAM" by BAM administrators, was designed with the help of Soviet railway professionals and would link the island's two major cities by rail for the first time.

In reality, however, the Soviet-Cuban "mutual exchange program" evolved into an elaborate facade that concealed a decidedly one-way transfer of young Cubans to the USSR in return for Soviet humanitarian and military assistance. The job of enticing the *Comité Nacional de la Unión de Jóvenes Comunistas* (the UJC, or the National Committee of the Union of Young Communists) to send its members to the BAM Zone fell to Deputy Director Vladimir Mukonin of the Komsomol BAM headquarters. As part of the effort to convince Havana to part with a substantial portion of its best young workers, Mukonin wrote in 1977 that the "pride of the Soviet people in BAM mirrors that of the Cuban nation in the Havana-Santiago-de-Cuba railway," and that despite obstacles in the process of completing both lines, BAM and the Cuban Central Railway would serve as the Komsomol and UJC's "gifts to their [respective] peoples."[36] Mukonin proposed an "exchange of party materials and personnel," requesting that the UJC send Cuban volunteers to help build BAM as part of a "socialist competition campaign" between the young people of each nation.[37]

In 1977 and 1978, José Esquina of the UJC agreed to arrange the details of a "socialist competition" between the builders of the Central Railway and BAM *after* members of his organization currently in Cuba and those already studying in the Soviet Union had been dispatched to the BAM Zone. Esquina's only stated condition for sending members of his organization to BAM was that representatives of the UJC's daily *Juventud Rebelde* (Rebellious youth) be allowed to accompany their comrades to cover "the BAMers' successful rail-laying methods."[38] Esquina also invited Soviet BAMers to the Eleventh World Festival of Youth and Students in Havana, which the UJC sponsored. The festival, which the Castro government named the "Festival of Anti-Imperialist Solidarity, Peace, and Friendship," was held in honor of the sixtieth anniversary of the October Revolution and in commemoration of the twenty-fifth anniversary of the July 1953 assault by young Cuban revolutionaries, including Castro himself, on the Moncada barracks in Santiago-de-Cuba.[39]

By attending the World Festival of Youth and Students, Esquina maintained that youth from "the birthplaces of José Martí and Vladimir Lenin" would strengthen the already close ties between the Soviet and Cuban peoples.[40] What he did not mention, however, was that his organization wanted the fifty-odd Soviet BAMers attending the festival to remain in Cuba when the event ended and help with the construction of the railway. Mukonin acquiesced to Esquina's recruitment tactic with the implicit understanding that the exchange of the labor of fifty of his workers for the skills of the several thousand Cubans who came to work on BAM served the purposes of both men.

Another result of the Mukonin-Esquina correspondence was a "Joint Soviet-Cuban Agreement on Socialist Competition between the Young Builders of the Baikal-Amur Railway and the Central Cuban Railway" in which both Leonid Brezhnev and Fidel Castro affirmed their nations' commitment to completing their respective railways.[41] UJC officials eventually sent more than ten thousand Cubans to BAM over a ten-year period, a time in which Soviet technical aid to Cuban railroaders laboring on the Havana-Santiago-de-Cuba line increased markedly. This spike in Soviet aid to the embryonic Cuban railway system can certainly be viewed as "compensation" for the use of so many young Cubans, some of whom did not return to their homeland for several years after their stints in the USSR on the BAM project. Approximately a quarter of the young Cubans who labored on BAM entered the Cuban army immediately upon their completion of duty in the BAM Zone. A substantial portion of this cohort served as military advisers in Angola. Once in southern Africa, many Cuban ex-BAMers served as "advisers" and assisted soldiers of the Marxist Popular Movement for the Liberation of Angola in their struggle against various Chinese- and U.S.-supported opposition groups.[42]

Cuba was not the only Latin American country to take note of the BAM project. The rise of a socialist opposition in Argentina—namely, the Montoneros guerrilla organization, against the United States–backed regime of Juan Domingo Perón—resulted in the propagandizing of BAM among Argentine youth. The primary promoter of the railway within Argentina, and outside the Soviet Union altogether, was writer Raúl Larra. Galina Mironova, an employee of the Molodaia gvardiia (Young Guard) publishing house, has discussed Larra in some detail. The author of some nineteen pro-socialist books and short stories translated by Molodaia gvardiia into Russian, Larra was well-known among Komsomolers, and his writings were distributed widely in the USSR during the 1970s and 1980s.[43] In 1982, Larra visited the tunnelers of BAMtonnelstroi and received a great deal of media coverage while spending time with Spanish-speaking BAMer brigades that summer.[44] During his stay, Larra penned *Siberian Symphony*, a novel that was published in Spanish by the Soviet foreign-language press Progress Publishers and simultaneously in Russian by Molodaia gvardiia. In this tedious work, Larra highlighted the labor of South American BAMers and gratefully acknowledged Soviet support of "liberation movements" in Nicaragua, El Salvador, and his native Argentina.

Officials at BAM headquarters designed a media campaign that would define *Siberian Symphony* as the archetypal example of BAM belletristic writing. Such a promotional effort would help to accomplish two propaganda goals. First, Soviet leaders of Latin American brigades encouraged returning Argentine BAMers to smuggle the novel in its original Spanish form into Argentina to propagandize the railway and encourage even more youths to volunteer on the BAM project. Second, in its Russian edition, *Siberian Symphony* provided a positive representation of the railway from a foreigner's perspective. Although the drive to introduce the book to Argentine and Soviet readers began auspiciously, BAM media officers soon abandoned the smuggling idea. Suspicious Argentine authorities had begun to routinely detain returning Argentine BAMers and confiscate copies of the novel. As for the Russian edition of Larra's book, some officials later admitted that unspecified "difficulties in translation" made *Siberian Symphony* too dry and didactic for time-challenged railway laborers.[45]

BAM officials used the USSR's burgeoning connections with other "fraternal" Latin American nations to recruit more "motivated volunteers" for the project. The victory of Chilean Marxist Salvador Allende in his country's September 1970 presidential election marked the beginning of a period of close interaction between the Komsomol and socialist Chilean youth organizations. After Allende's December 1972 visit with Brezhnev in Moscow, in which the new Chilean leader declared that Chile and the Soviet Union "enjoyed a newly strengthened relationship," the Komsomol began to send out feelers to the government in Santiago regarding its interest in the BAM project.[46]

The ties between Allende and Brezhnev proved to be short-lived, however. After right-wing strongman Augusto Pinochet ousted the Chilean president in September 1973, many young Chilean socialists were executed, exiled, or forced to flee their native land. Award-winning "Hero of Socialist Labor" and prominent BAMer Viktor Lakomov invited a number of surviving exiles to the BAM Zone for training in railway and building construction techniques. Lakomov was well-known within Chilean railroader and governmental circles for his multiple visits to Chile as a construction consultant between 1970 and 1973 and as a representative of what Allende himself once termed the "best qualities of Soviet-style socialism."[47] In exchange for housing and instructing the South American exiles, Lakomov and his deputies at the Komsomol BAM headquarters asked that the Chileans assist in building the railway. Lakomov also requested that they and the Argentine BAM veterans help promote the railway project upon their eventual return home.[48]

After their arrival in the BAM Zone in the summer of 1974, the dozens of Chilean exiles, under the supervision of their "sponsor" Lakomov, quickly discovered to their great surprise that they were not to work and learn alongside their Soviet rescuers as they had been promised. Rather, they were posted as carpenters, not railroaders, in a Spanish-speaking only brigade. The Chileans petitioned their new commander within Angarstroi for reassignment: "How can Hero of Socialist Labor Viktor Ivanovich Lakomov, one of the finest railway specialists in the Soviet Union, a man who helped the Chilean people build railways during the legitimate government of Salvador Allende, not allow us to return the favor he so graciously bestowed upon us? We are railroaders, not carpenters, and we wish to build the 'Second Trans-Siberian Railway' alongside our Soviet liberators. We ask this in the spirit of the Chilean and Soviet Communist parties."[49] To the Chileans' dismay, however, Lakomov divided their cohort and assigned them to housing construction brigades composed entirely of other Spanish speakers and supervised by Spanish-speaking Soviet citizens who were Slavs. Despite inquiring several times about the circumstances of their placement with other Latin Americans, the Chilean railroaders never received an explanation from Lakomov or anyone else from the Komsomol BAM headquarters in Tynda.[50]

What the Chileans and their fellow Latin Americans did not know was that the railway's leadership never intended to integrate them with Soviet collectives for fear that the native BAMers would paint a negative picture of "socialist life" in the USSR. Such candidness might temper the foreigners' enthusiasm for working diligently on the railway and supporting Soviet-style socialism in their home countries.[51] One motivation behind the leadership's importation of foreign labor was to convince these young people of the benefits of Soviet-style socialism by presenting BAM as a glorious example of socialism's ability to undertake and complete such immense and complex projects as BAM. Instead of bolstering the foreigners' concepts of the railway, the isolation of the Argentines, Chileans, and Cubans from their Soviet comrades fostered a sense of segregation and bewilderment among the Spanish-speaking BAMer population. This confusion and sense of isolation in turn spawned apathy and disillusionment toward the Soviet way of life.

Warsaw Pact BAMers

Students from the Warsaw Pact nations, and East Germany in particular, played an important and more publicized role in BAM construction. Accounts in the BAM Zone media tended to profile youth who echoed the official positivism regarding the project and allowed themselves to be photographed on the job.[52] In the summer of 1975, correspondent V. Popov of *Vostochno-Sibirskaia pravda* (East Siberian truth) described the dormitory-painting exploits of East Germans Heiner Seifert and Dieter Lindig, students at the Leningrad Polytechnic Institute who had volunteered to become BAMers.[53] Curiously, Popov's story does not contain interviews with Seifert and Lindig themselves; rather, it is written from a distant perspective in which the reader learns nothing about the two East Germans except that they painted one side of a five-story building in only one week's time. In this fashion, Popov's contribution differs markedly from profiles of Soviet BAMers, which invariably contained detailed descriptions of the workers themselves, including their hometowns, opinions of life in Siberia, and impressions of the project.[54] It is plausible that despite their success as painters, Seifert and Lindig voiced less-than-favorable impressions of BAM and their role on the project when interviewed by Popov. If that were the case, the journalist would have faced the prospect of not writing the article at all and risk condemnation from his superiors. Instead, Popov wrote a personality-free account focusing on the Germans' tasks instead of their opinions of BAM.

The BAM "hagiographer" Tatiana Tomina chose her subjects based on their nationality rather than on their importance or uniqueness as individuals. In the 1983 edition of *BAM—A Panorama of a Multinational Endeavor*, Tomina related the story of one Vladek Zaichek, a Czechoslovak Communist Party official and BAM veteran who met with the head of GlavBAMstroi. In her essay "Vladek Is Going to BAM Again," Tomina ignored the achievements of Zaichek and his brigade of Czechoslovak railroaders. Instead, she emphasized the sense of privilege and "deep honor" Zaichek felt after his "brotherly conversation" with the leader of the BAM hierarchy.[55]

The railway's administration also encouraged foreign BAMers who could write well in Russian to contribute articles to newspapers across the BAM Zone and elsewhere in the Soviet Union. Aspiring engineer Kristian Brückner, an East German, wrote in *Vechernii Kishinev* (Evening Kishinev), the newspaper of his "adopted hometown," that his experience in building the BAM settlement of Zvezdnyi alongside other foreigners has endowed him with "socialist fire" and strengthened his character despite the primitive living and working conditions at his team's worksite.[56] As with Popov's story, Brückner's submission defied the convention of the majority of BAM newspaper articles, but for different reasons. The fact that Brückner mentioned the harsh circumstances of daily life confronted by all BAMers is unusual. The genre of BAM worker profiling typically tended to marginalize the climatic and topographical impediments to BAM construction, but Brückner devoted an entire paragraph to describing the swarms of insects that bedevil him and his comrades. Other writers dismiss the insects as temporary annoyances that will soon be eliminated as part of the inevitable Promethean triumph of Soviet technology over nature. Brückner's article appeared not in a BAM Zone publication likely to be read by the workers themselves, but in a newspaper for the residents of Kishinev in the far-off Moldavian Soviet Socialist Republic. This piece never appeared in the BAM Zone or national press, probably because Brückner's frank description of his brigade's frustrations with Siberian mosquitoes and mud led the Komsomol leadership in Moscow to believe that such an article might serve to weaken the already fragile morale of the BAMer cadres, Brückner's expression of his "socialist fire" notwithstanding.

The impressions of East German Roland Grosse in the newspaper *Severnaia pravda* (Northern truth) confirmed that "no language barrier" existed between German, Mongolian, and Soviet youth within a Start brigade based at the BAM town of Udokan. Grosse, along with the other brigade members, learned to sing songs "about BAM, friendship, and peace" in Mongolian and German in addition to Russian.[57] According to the report, Grosse beamed when describing the "East Germany Day" held by the German contingent, and the Udokan authorities had promised Grosse's conationals and the Mongolians a tour of the Soviet Union cities after completion of their work.[58]

The impressions of those Soviet BAMers who worked with international brigades illustrates the fact that the use of any language besides Russian was frowned upon.

Despite such positive representations from Popov, Brückner, and Grosse, some who visited and worked on the BAM project did remark on the discontent and occasional disillusionment of non-Soviet BAMers. East Germans Haino Westfalia and Dieter Ostertag viewed the railway as a project that would help the Soviet Union to reach its "glorious Communist future" by expediting the flow of goods and raw materials between the eastern and western USSR.[59] But they were confused and disappointed that their assignments did not include any railway construction assignments. As with the Chileans, the East Germans did not lay track alongside their Soviet comrades as they had been promised, but installed plumbing as a part of a brigade of Czechoslovaks, Poles, and Hungarians in which Russian was the only lingua franca, albeit a decidedly weak one for many.

Another factor that compounded the foreigners' dissatisfaction was the communication problem within such multinational brigades composed of youth who spoke little or no Russian and whose native tongues were often unrelated to one another. This lack of mutual intelligibility resulted in the formation of national cliques that worked and socialized apart from those of other nationalities, Soviet or non-Soviet.[60] This differentiation by language among the supposedly "multinational" BAM youth revealed the fiction of a unified, linguistically homogenous labor force. A 1975 article by K. Privalov of *Moskovskii komsomolets* (Moscow Komsomoler), for example, describes the "bonds of socialist competition forged between Soviet and foreign BAMers," but also clearly states these groups worked and socialized in separate tent communities.[61]

The Komsomol archives show that BAM administrators were cognizant of and concerned about the foreign workers' less-than-rosy opinions of the BAM project. In a representative report to the Komsomol BAM construction headquarters, A. D. Kniazev of the agitational-propaganda train *Komsomolskaia pravda* (Komsomol truth) reported that "several dozen" students from a number of Warsaw Pact and developing nations working within a particular Vitiaz (Hero) detachment frequently complained to him about their current assignment. It consisted mainly of installing toilets and painting buildings in the newly founded settlements of Lena and Taiura in the summer of 1975.[62] When the foreigners expressed a strong desire to be transferred to a different worksite where they could actually lay rails, Kniazev was unable to accommodate them after explaining that "all construction billets [were] currently full."[63]

What Kniazev could not admit to his charges was that the foreign BAMers under his supervision were prohibited by the Komsomol from laboring on the railway itself due to official concerns that they would learn of its serious technical deficiencies and casual construction pace firsthand.[64] Kniazev also reported that other Soviet advisers working with the Vitiaz detachment reported their embarrassment at having to explain the lack of functional construction equipment and knowledgeable supervisors to their foreign guests, who in many instances knew more about their jobs than their bosses.[65] The exclusion of foreigners from meaningful assignments at a time when the railway needed as much skilled labor as possible not only impeded construction progress, but also further discredited BAM in the minds of many youth from abroad, all of whose primary knowledge and opinions of the Soviet Union derived from their experiences on the project. Consequently, the disillusionment of all BAMers, Soviet and non-Soviet, began well before the Gorbachev era, as other observers have argued, although this disenfranchisement was not publicized until the mid-1980s, by which time the railway had lost the nation's (and much of the world's) interest.[66]

International students enrolled at the Patrice Lumumba Peoples' Friendship University (*Universitet Druzhby Narodov imeni Patricia Lumumby*) in Moscow also contributed to the endeavor during their summers away from school as members of the International Student Construction Brigade, which was known colloquially as the "Friendship Brigade."[67] This group was a part of the eight thousand member and multinational "All-Union Thirtieth Anniversary of Victory Student Construction Brigade," whose members labored on summer projects across the Soviet Union from the early 1960s to late 1980s.[68] As with the Vítiaz detachment mentioned earlier, the Lumumba University students worked in an unequal capacity relative to their Soviet counterparts. Beginning with the "Friendship 1975" program, some three hundred students from Lumumba University undertook such disparate tasks as fire station construction, school renovation warehouses, sewage system installation, and dormitory erection. The Friendship Brigade served as a cheap and generally more motivated labor force than Soviet workers because of their stronger ideological commitment.[69]

It is important to note that BAM administrators split the hundreds of Lumumba University students who arrived each summer into two groups. The first cohort included foreign BAMers who possessed at least a modicum of Russian-language training; generally these were Bulgarians, Czechoslovaks, East Germans, Hungarians, Mongolians, and Poles. The foreign BAMers who lacked any Russian-language skills were sent to a separate location and given the dirtiest and most arduous assignments in Siberia's sweltering summer temperatures and amid clouds of insects; generally these were Africans, Latin Americans, and South and Southeast Asians. The archives do not reveal why those who could not speak Russian were segregated and given the most difficult tasks, but it is plausible that BAM headquarters, not knowing exactly what to do with these BAMers from the developing world, sent them to jobs that required the least amount of instruction and supervision.

Both BAM Zone and national media outlets strove to publicize members of the Friendship Brigade whose ideological profiles matched the state's image of the ideal BAMer as a committed socialist who was zealous in his or her desire to complete the railway. One such individual was Bolivian Gonsalo Alvarado, who was among the first wave of Lumumba University students to reach the BAM Zone in the summer of 1974. Alvarado's father, a prominent Bolivian Communist, was killed by "fascist bandits." Subsequently, Alvarado fled Bolivia to pursue an engineering education in the USSR.[70] Along with other Friendship Brigaders from Nigeria, Bangladesh, and India (which enjoyed increased Soviet support after fighting an inconclusive border war with the Soviet Union's ideological rival China in 1962), Alvarado's detachment labored to build structures along the Abakan-Taishet BAM segment at the project's western terminus. Journalist Iurii Petruk proclaimed their activities "increase[d] the technical knowledge of all people, not just Soviet citizens."[71] In reality, however, the topographical and geologic conditions of construction in the BAM Zone differed markedly from the environs of Alvarado's comrades. As a result, the skills they learned in Siberia would prove to be of little value back home. Dr. Michael Waganda, a Kenyan national and former student at the Patrice Lumumba Peoples' Friendship University in Moscow, has commented on this. Waganda, who lived in the Soviet Union during the BAM's heyday and studied with many foreigners who worked on the railway, recalled that his "friends from Africa, Asia, and Latin America" viewed their time spent working on the railway as "practically worthless."[72]

Another highly profiled member of the initial Lumumba brigade to visit BAM was Jean-Marie Manirako, a Rwandan physics student who worked with a Rovesnik (Contemporary) brigade. The brigade consisted of Lumumba students from Chile, Colombia, Argentina, and Ethiopia at the famous Bratsk hydroelectric station that was featured in the *Bratsk Station* poems of the well-known poet Evgenii Evtushenko.[73] In the same article in which he lionized the exploits of Gonsalo Alvarado's detachment, Petruk wrote that Manirako's BAM experience would allow him to return to Rwanda and assist with dam projects there. He explained that the Rwandan's initial image of Siberia as an inhospitable wasteland had been replaced with an understanding of the region's beauty and livability.[74]

K. Privalov of *Moskovskii komsomolets* noted in 1975 that such BAMers as a Sri Lankan Vitiaz member named Lalit Attanaiake adapted well to their new surroundings in the taiga. Attanaiake, who once believed that he would find Siberia eternally snowbound and inhospitable, later affirmed with his comrade Ramendra Kumar of India that "if there was a place like Siberia in our lands, we would certainly live there after finishing our work on BAM."[75] Soviet journalists enjoyed boasting that youth from developing nations quickly acclimatized to life in the BAM Zone and even preferred life in Siberia to that in their homelands. Either intentionally or unintentionally, they served to popularize the "un-internationalist" notion that existence in the Soviet Union was superior to that anywhere else.

In addition to luring foreign youth to join the BAM project with promises of a technical education, BAM administrators also courted foreign industrial magnates and political dignitaries from abroad in an effort to secure more laborers. For example, the bosses of Nizhneangarsktransstroi regularly invited Hungarian officials to visit the BAM Zone between 1974 and 1984 in a bid to form "sponsorship agreements" between the railway and Hungarian industries.[76] In reality though, BAMers used these relationships to acquire high-quality finished goods from Soviet client states for little or no cost and without Moscow's knowledge. This process was reflected in a 1977 visit to Severobaikalsk by a group of administrators from the Videoton electronics factory in Budapest. During this trip, BAM officials received a number of "gifts" in the form of record players, televisions, and other items from the Videoton representatives. Not completely placated, the Nizhneangarsktransstroi bosses requested that young workers from Videoton come to the BAM Zone the following summer for a "tour of the area," to "further strengthen fraternal relations and improve social contacts."[77] This was never intended to be a vacation, of course, as the young Hungarians were assigned to BAM construction soon after their arrival.

Records of similar visits by delegates, including the Soviet-controlled Committee of European Youth Organizations, reveal why the Hungarians from the Videoton factory and other visiting foreign groups agreed to what appears to be such an unequal relationship with their Soviet hosts. The BAM apparatus always provided the delegations' transportation to and from the BAM Zone free of charge, and not by rail, as one might expect, but by the much more expensive method of flight. Once in the area, BAM administrators treated their foreign guests to "complimentary production examples" (free samples) of foreign-made cigarettes, mineral water, and alcohol purchased by BAMers while overseas. These bribes included luxury food items that neither the foreigners nor their Soviet hosts could easily locate at home.[78] BAM officials made certain that visiting dignitaries collected "stipends" (various amounts of foreign currency), ostensibly for "the purchase of BAM souvenirs and books," but which in reality were nothing more than kickbacks.[79] In all, both the "production examples" and the "stipends," along with the "comradely company" of the project's young female secretaries, helped to ensure that the foreign dignitaries took home positive impressions of BAM that certainly helped to reduce their hesitation about sending their youth to help build another country's railway.

Although bribed foreign officials directed some "volunteers" to the railway, the project suffered from a constant shortage of qualified and motivated builders. Despite this deficiency, however, not all foreign students who wished to participate in the construction of BAM were allowed to do so. In 1974, East German high school student Kirsten Radtke wrote the Komsomol Central Committee in Moscow to express her desire to travel and possibly work in the BAM Zone. In an undated reply, administrator V. Aldokhin applauded Radtke's enthusiasm but informed the youngster that she had to wait two years and receive training in an occupation required by the project. Only then, Aldokhin stipulated, could Radtke apply to come to BAM as a member of an East German student construction brigade. Another letter, this one a November 1974 communication from a group of Dresden students, eagerly requested a copy of the Komsomol-published book *BAM—nachalo* (BAM —The beginning) and asked about the feasibility of working on the railway. "The Komsomol chose to ignore the Dresdeners' request due to a fictional 'shortage of BAM publications' [which it produced in the hundreds of thousands]," according to Galina Mironova.[80] Apparently, one BAM official could not confirm the "political reliability" of the East Germans (their membership status within the Komsomol-like Union of Free German Youth), and thus their attempt to join the railway was ended abruptly.

Two Czechoslovak students petitioned the Komsomol in 1978 to allow them and a small group of their classmates to work on the railway and tour the BAM Zone and other regions of the USSR. The Czechoslovaks stated that their classmates were interested in the "construction of BAM itself, but also in what kind of people are working there and what working conditions are like in the BAM Zone generally."[81] The youth organization curtly responded that "construction in areas approved for visitation ha[d] not yet begun," and in a blatant misrepresentation of fact remarked that "the Komsomol [could] not invite any foreign students to the region."[82] A 1983 request by twenty-eight Czechoslovak youth to travel to BAM at their own expense and work on the railway received no response from the Komsomol BAM headquarters.[83]

The BAM administration rejected dozens of other similar requests. Bulgarian students wrote the offices of the newspaper *BAM* in 1979 after hearing about the railway project. They had studied the project and composed a lecture entitled "BAM—The Project of the Century," which they delivered to a combined audience of more than five thousand people. After learning of the students' desire to see the BAM Zone for themselves, BAM chief Valentin Sushchevich chose not to respond directly and instead forwarded the letter to the Komsomol's sister organization in Bulgaria.[84] When asked to comment on his treatment of this and other requests by foreigners to visit and work on BAM, Sushchevich replied that "they [the young foreigners] were not serious in their desire to come to the BAM Zone . . . [and] . . . their requests to come to the Soviet Union were possibly motivated by 'external influences.'"[85] The term "external influences" indicates Sushchevich's suspicion that the West or other enemies of the USSR sought to place spies within the USSR with the ultimate objective of learning more about "the railway of the century." In fact, some former BAMers and non-BAMers contend that the United States, other unidentified "Western powers," and Israel secretly placed spies within the BAMer population to observe and even delay the project's progress.

The "Chinese Question"

The existence of a densely populated and, in the eyes of BAM's managers, threatening People's Republic of China loomed over the project from its inception. After a March 1969 border incident in which Soviet forces briefly occupied Zhenbao Island (known in Russian as Damanskii), an islet located within the Wusuli Jiang (Ussuri) River on the Chinese side of the USSR border, Sino-Soviet relations entered an especially chilly period.[86] This resulted in the Beijing government's proclamation that the Soviet encroachment at Zhenbao constituted an act of war.[87] With its geographic proximity to China, the BAM project played an important strategic and geopolitical role from 1974 to 1984 as an expression of Soviet military and economic might in Eastern Siberia and the Soviet Far East.[88] In representing China to the railway's laborers, BAM propagandists carefully avoided any semblance of provocation in relation to their southern neighbor. During 1976, a dozen high-ranking members of the Eastern Segment BAM headquarters delivered nearly two hundred lectures on Chinese history, language, and culture that BAMers were expected to attend.[89]

In 1978, BAMer members of Znanie (the All-Union Knowledge Society) gave a series of lectures on "Chinese foreign policy issues" and "Soviet positions on the Chinese question," which stressed a policy of peaceful coexistence between the two claimants to the Marxian legacy.[90] Inherent in both the presentations of the Eastern Segment administrators and the Znanie members was an understanding that China's large contingent of troops stationed along the Sino-Soviet border remained a palpable menace to Soviet economic and political interests in northern Asia. Consequently, the construction of BAM should be presented to the Chinese, who closely monitored activities in the BAM Zone, as a purely economically motivated endeavor rather than a military undertaking that could pose negative implications for Sino-Soviet relations.

A prominent example of the conciliatory rhetoric found in the state's characterization of China to the BAMer population was a 1978 speech given at the Third All-Union Conference of the Soviet-Chinese Friendship Society by BAMer Sergei A. Manoilenko. Treating the citizens of the People's Republic in a mostly benign fashion as "our friendly neighbors to the south," Manoilenko applauded the efforts of his BAMer comrades in "preserv[ing] the close, fraternal connections between the Soviet and Chinese peoples."[91] Nevertheless, he also acknowledged the Chinese debt to the Soviet people by reminding his audience that until the USSR's cultural and economic assistance was rejected by the "occasionally reckless Chinese government in Beijing," "generous" Soviet aid had helped China to develop a modern economic base through the sending of tourists, medical assistance, and industrial specialists after the 1949 Communist revolution. Manoilenko conspicuously failed to mention the Ussuri River incident specifically or the Sino-Soviet split generally. Instead, he stressed that "our working Chinese brothers" (whom Manoilenko differentiated from the government of the People's Republic) should not view BAM as a menace to their territorial integrity. He emphasized that the railway was an example of how Soviet-style "industrial socialism," rather than the agrarian-based Maoism favored in Beijing, would conquer the difficult topographical and geological conditions of Eastern Siberia.[92]

Internationalism Achieved?

The state's dual-pronged strategy to publicize BAM and recruit labor for the endeavor failed to achieve its intended goals. The railway's administration rewarded even haphazardly chosen substandard domestic workers with travel outside the Soviet Union. Many young BAMers shirked their officially mandated "social responsibilities" and instead used the opportunity of relaxed adult supervision to "eat, drink, and be merry" as many given such new freedoms often do. Rather than providing the world's socialist nations with shining examples of industrious and socially conscious young people, the "BAMer abroad" program had the reverse effect of either sullying or altering non-Soviet citizens' opinions of the project, and by extension, the USSR in general. The Soviet state, through the Komsomol and other official organizations, failed to employ BAMers who traveled abroad as ambassadors of Soviet achievements. This was due in no small part to the railroaders' less than admirable, but nevertheless completely understandable, behavior.

The lack of competent and dedicated Soviet BAMers compelled the project's supervisors to recall the efficient and cost-free labor of German and Japanese prisoners of war on the earlier BAM project with nostalgia. Viewing the young people within the Soviet Union's "fraternal circle of nations" and the Warsaw Pact as an economical and highly motivated pool of labor, the Komsomol strove to lure foreign students in the 1970s and 1980s to the BAM Zone. Its promise to the foreigners that their education would be enhanced by laying track alongside the USSR's BAMers, however, proved ultimately hollow. Most foreign BAMers never enjoyed the opportunity to toil alongside their Soviet comrades, and the project's administration was unable to shield them from the blatant inefficiency and waste on what the Komsomol and Communist Party of the Soviet Union had heralded as most important public works project of the Brezhnev years. Perhaps even more important, the government's utter inability to convince either foreign or Soviet BAMers of the railway's progressive nature and international flavor starkly pointed to the lack of dynamism and flexibility within the official propaganda machine that churned out the BAM myth during the era of "developed socialism." By the mid-1980s, the state's grasp on this component of the BAM "myth" slipped even further, as frustrated and apathetic BAMers from the Soviet Union and abroad returned home to tell family and friends about the dead ends that defined the "path to the future."

7 // Conclusion

Brezhnev's Folly in Perspective

Stalin, Khrushchev, and Brezhnev are flying together in an airplane. Suddenly, the Devil appears outside Brezhnev's window and begins to cut away at a wing with a saw until it is nearly split in half. Brezhnev sticks his head out of the door, speaks with Satan while the airplane is still in flight, and the Devil vanishes as quickly as he had appeared. With the airplane door still open, Brezhnev announces to the others that he has sent the Devil to work on BAM since he is such an efficient worker.

Popular BAM joke, circa 1980

COLONEL-GENERAL G. I. KOGATKO, the former head of BAM Zone Military Forces, wrote: "The history of BAM is not only one of a heroic accomplishment as many people have already written and said, but also of a serious martial undertaking. On the BAM everything happened, from the heroic and tragic, to the serious and amusing, to the happy and sad."[1] Although the world of the "project of the century" grew during BAM's decade of prominence, the "path to the future" itself did not lead to any concrete accomplishments in the industrial or social development of the USSR. Soviet officialdom was unable to contend with the wide array of unforeseen circumstances that resulted from such a massive undertaking. These included the genuine concern over damage to the local ecology voiced by a nascent conservation movement, the unintended consequences of allowing large numbers of unruly BAMers to travel abroad, the dissatisfaction of foreign workers toiling within the BAM Zone, the restiveness and occasionally criminal tendencies of the half-million-strong BAMer population, the isolation and disenfranchisement of BAMers from marginalized ethnic populations, and those women who felt underappreciated in their dual roles as workers and mothers. Each of these ultimately intractable tensions produced fault lines in the geology of BAMer society that, mirrored in the country at large, wrested apart the world's first self-proclaimed socialist state less than a decade after BAM's announced completion in 1984. As the *Moscow News* reported in 1993: "The 'Construction Project of the Century' has been forgotten."[2]

Despite the efforts of Soviet officialdom, the BAM project failed to achieve any of its stated goals. The railway's purported objective of providing an economic stimulus in Siberia and the Russian Far East was not realized. Although its supporters envisioned the project as a "laboratory of social development," in reality the railway was noteworthy for its highly sophisticated world of propaganda.[3] The project made few positive tangible contributions to the economic development of the Soviet Union. However, BAM did make a lasting impression on the country's social and cultural history. Many Soviet citizens thought of the project as the butt of popular jokes rather than the "project of the century." In its failure to live up to the high expectations forced upon it by the regime, the BAM project provides a blueprint for understanding the Brezhnev era. By repeating ad nauseam claims of BAM's economic, social, and cultural significance, the Komsomol, the Communist Party, and the Soviet government held an unwavering belief that the USSR's youth needed this message to avoid a loss of collective faith. Ironically, however, the realities of the railway helped to intensify such a loss of faith in the Soviet political and economic system in general.

The state had intended to excite Soviet youth about "building Communism" in Eastern Siberia and the Soviet Far East. In reality, many young BAMers came to the realization that the propaganda trope of the railway as an economic and social panacea was not realistic. Among those *bamovtsy* who lost their confidence in the project, some began to question the "command-administrative system" with its hyper-centralization and resistance to reform. While these concerns would find a partially sympathetic voice during the Gorbachev years, many former BAMers dissociated themselves from the now weakened "collective of workers and peasants," in spirit if not in body. Although the pace and direction of reform would be controlled from the top until the late 1980s, the behavior of many BAMers within the world of "developed socialism" revealed that such an inattentive approach to governance was doomed to failure.

The project's boosters in Moscow failed to acknowledge the gravity of organizing and motivating a young labor force while pushing to open Siberia's vast natural resources to exploitation. In their zeal to establish a secondary lifeline between the European USSR and the nation's eastern reaches in the event that the Trans-Siberian fell into the hands of the Chinese or another rapacious enemy, the railway's administrators incorrectly gauged the Soviet system's will to blaze the "path to the future." The experience of building BAM completed the disenchantment by the mid-1980s of the generational cohort of youths in their twenties and thirties, many of whom had participated directly in BAM or who socialized closely with BAM veterans. Rather than motivating them to support the status quo, BAM had the reverse effect. In 1984, the railway was complete in name only, while the reification of BAM as the "beacon to our Communist future" was the only real product of a decade's worth of intense human and material sacrifices. It was obvious to many that there was not much behind the myth, just as the Brezhnev era as a whole was more notable for its window dressing than any substantive accomplishments.

Those promoting the railway attempted to justify the project's great human and material cost to the populace by trumpeting BAM's ultimate goal: the attainment of Communism. This was encapsulated in such slogans as "Ahead to Tynda" and countless others that the state unfurled along the tracks of the "road to tomorrow." Oleg M. Lebedev, director of the Railway Forces Museum in the town of Shchelkovo outside Moscow, discussed these propagandistic epithets. As Lebedev and other former BAMers such as Valentin Sushchevich, the former Komsomol BAM headquarters chief, have stated, the regime intended that the railway's construction symbolize an attainable future.[4] The Siberian and Far Eastern expanses opened up by the railway lay beyond the strictures of "developed socialism," however. As the "path to the future," BAM would carry the Soviet people to the promised land of a Communist twenty-first century. The fiction of BAM as an attainable latter-day

Eden was perhaps the least nuanced and, ironically, the least attainable facet of the entire BAM propaganda campaign.

While official propaganda outlets proclaimed in 1984 that the BAMers had won their struggle against nature, the price of their Pyrrhic victory was severe damage to the BAM Zone's fragile ecosystem, most notably the pollution of cherished Lake Baikal. To be sure, *bamovtsy* who labored on the railway earned supplementary hardship pay and vouchers for new cars. Almost all of them left after their stints were over, however, and few saw any subsequent return for their efforts as the state refused to honor their vouchers with new automobiles, and the career advancement many BAMers anticipated after their tours of duty never materialized. BAM's agonizingly slow pace of construction and eventual failure to eclipse the Trans-Siberian Railway as a viable link between Siberia and the European USSR ensured that it would never equal the glory of past Soviet achievements. The final act in the railway's drama, the driving of the "golden spike" in September 1984, was a professed commemoration of the railway's completion, but in reality it served as an indication that official interest in the project had come to an end.[5] In an ironic twist, this ceremony closely resembled the Promontory, Utah, celebration that marked the completion of the American Trans-Continental Railroad in 1869. This Soviet version of the golden spike ceremony held over one hundred years later, however, revealed that BAM was far from finished, and this fact was patently obvious to anyone riding its poorly-ballasted rails. Indeed, this opinion was shared by nearly all of my BAM interviewees, with the notable (and understandable) exception of Valentin Sushchevich.

The BAM propaganda machine's usage of tropes and imagery specific to Soviet discourse of the 1970s and early 1980s resulted in the creation of a varied but ultimately inert body of propaganda. Although no one knew it at the time, the deluge of BAM media coverage from 1974 to 1984 would be the last such attempt in Soviet history to galvanize public opinion in favor of a massive building and investment program. As much as the building of the city of Magnitogorsk, the Turkestano-Siberian Railway, and the Dneprostroi hydroelectric dams had marked the Soviet physical and social landscape in the 1930s, the inculcation of the BAM "myth" mapped the topography of official cultural policy during the Brezhnev era.[6] This ethereal construction was the foremost accomplishment of the Brezhnev years.

The BAM experience was noteworthy for its lack of tangible accomplishments, of which there were almost none. The relation of the BAM message to society revealed Soviet officialdom's inadequacies as well as its utter lack of sensitivity to a growing number of latent social and cultural tensions in the country. The stagnation of BAM propaganda after its initial formulation indicated the ideological staidness that, by the early 1970s, had gripped the corpus of Soviet governance like some form of mental rigor mortis. While official representations of BAM remained stagnant, the real world around these representations did not. Perhaps this helps to explain the events of the Brezhnev era, a time during which the government refused to acknowledge reality to a greater degree than any regime before it in Soviet history. The unintended consequences of BAM set the stage for the final act in the drama of Soviet state socialism—namely, the events of the Gorbachev years. The state-sponsored propaganda machine that had created the official image of BAM and many other endeavors in the Soviet Union slowly ground to a halt by 1991, much as railway construction had done some ten years before.

With the driving of the "golden spike" in 1984, BAM moved from the front pages of official interest to the classified section of the USSR's propaganda industry. The project did return to the news in the late 1980s, when a scandal arose over the validity of the car vouchers that many BAMers had received from the government in recognition of their terms of service. When the Ministry of Railways and GlavBAMstroi announced in 1988 that they lacked the financial resources to honor the vouchers with actual automobiles, many former BAMers took to the streets in protest, which served as a test of Gorbachev's policy of *glasnost* (openness).[7] Although the authorities permitted the irate BAM veterans to demonstrate, the protests soon lost their vigor as the demonstrators realized that other, more pressing problems (such as the scarcity of quality finished goods and the ruble's diminishing purchasing power) required their attention.

Another social ramification of BAM includes the project's role in increasing the country's divorce rate, which by the 1980s had reached approximately 80 percent, according to some observers.[8] With many married men laboring on BAM, with their wives and children remaining at home to maintain valued apartment space, the loneliness of being far from one's spouse coupled with the temptation of working closely with young members of the opposite (and in some cases the same) sex proved too strong for many BAMers to resist. With the ease of divorce assured by Soviet law by the 1960s, the predictable outcome for many relationships involving a BAM worker was separation or divorce. Many interviewees for this book, especially the women, remarked: "My ex-husband/wife worked on BAM."[9]

BAMers' experiences and the acquaintances they made during their service served as a seedbed of entrepreneurship for many thirty-somethings in the post-Soviet period.[10] After returning from their tours of duty in the BAM Zone, many former BAMers maintained their friendship and networks for social and economic reasons. Others assumed the mantle of environmental protection in the project's earliest days; the issue of how to protect Lake Baikal's sensitive ecology became a national concern during the late 1980s.[11] In this way, BAM provided a positive influence on Soviet society, where it had failed so miserably in the realm of economic and cultural transformation.

After President Boris Yeltsin's violent clash with the state parliament in October 1993 nixed hope of a rapidly improving Russian economy, some officials and journalists in Moscow and the BAM Zone promoted the notion of the project as a potential savior of the Russian economy.[12] Interestingly, the Russian government declared BAM officially complete in 1991 after admitting that the Soviet claim that the railway became fully operational some seven years earlier was premature.[13] The accession of President Vladimir Putin witnessed a renewed official interest in infrastructure projects, and after a number of years, BAM was declared complete for the third time in 2001. However, the railway was actually completed on December 5, 2003, with the opening of the nearly ten-mile-long Severomuisk (North Muya) Tunnel, the longest tunnel in the Russian Federation, after a construction period of twenty-seven years.[14] BAM's efficiency is no longer plagued by an insufficient number of trains, which in the past had to contend with track damage caused by melting permafrost and a lack of capital to maintain rolling stock.[15]

Today, the former "path to the future" remains of far less interest to the general public, particularly outside of Siberia and the contemporary Russian Far East, and garners less official attention than it did during the Brezhnev years.[16] Although the railway is at last complete, many of those living in the BAM Zone have forsaken hope that the it will become economically viable in the near future. For now, the greatest legacy of the so-called "path to the future" is to serve as a reminder of the past for many of the half-million former BAMers and scores of other residents of the former Soviet Union.

NOTES

CHAPTER 1. Introduction: The Project of the Century

1. Brezhnev, "Pobeda stroitelei BAMa," 1.

2. Matvieva, "Respublika BAMa," 11.

3. In Russian, the railway is Baikalo-Amurskaia Magistral.

4. See Josephson, "Science and Technology as Panacea," 25–26.

5. Chichkanov, "Problemy i perspektivy dlia razvitiia proizvoditel'nykh silakh na Dal'nom Vostoke." See also Stites, "World Outlook and Inner Fears," 311.

6. Propaganda has had a long history in the Soviet Union and the contemporary Russian Federation. See Kenez, *Birth of the Propaganda State.*

7. One of the first characterizations of BAM as a product of the "era of stagnation" appears in Khatutsev, "Bum i BAM." Other discussions of BAM as a product of a stagnating system include Bovin, "Kurs na stabil'nost' porodil zastoi"; Matvieva, "Respublika BAMa"; and Mote, "BAM, Boom, Bust." For reflections on the political and social climate of the Brezhnev period and considerations of stagnation (*zastoi*), see Bialer and Gustafson, *Russia at the Crossroads*; Bushnell, *Moscow Graffiti*; Byrnes, *After Brezhnev*; Cohen, *An End to Silence* and *Rethinking the Soviet Experience*; Dobrenko, *Izbavlenie ot mirazhei*; Scanlan, *Marxism in the USSR*; and James P. Scanlan, *Technology, Culture, and Development: The Experience of the Soviet Model* (Armonk, N.Y.: M. E. Sharpe, 1992). One must note, however, that Moshe Lewin in *The Gorbachev Phenomenon* and Stephen Kotkin in *Armageddon Averted* disagree with the notion of *zastoi* expressed in some of the works cited here.

8. On the role of Russian railways as conduits of revolutionary sentiment during the revolutions of 1905 and 1917, respectively, see Reichman, *Railwaymen and Revolution* and Argenbright, "Russian Railroad System and the Founding of the Communist State."

9. See Kotkin, *Magnetic Mountain.*

10. John Scott, *Behind the Urals*, xii–xiii.

11. On the nature and development of earlier Soviet propaganda, see Kenez, *Birth of the Propaganda State.* Kenez focuses on the development of Soviet propaganda during the decade after the Bolshevik revolution and defines the "Soviet concept of propaganda," in which the purpose of propaganda is to convince and inculcate official doctrine through education rather than brainwashing. Kenez sees "one voice" running through Soviet journalism between 1917 and 1929; official coverage of BAM from 1974 to 1984 evidenced a similar monolithic and consistent perspective.

12. Regarding the Turkestano-Siberian Railway, see Payne, *Stalin's Railroad* and "Turksib." William K. Wolf's "Russia's Revolutionary Underground" looks at the power structures and conflicts behind the building of the Moscow metro system. The studies of Payne and Wolf provide an interesting contrast to this work on the BAM railway in that coercion was the main motivational tool for the directors of the Turkestano-Siberian Railway and Moscow subway, while BAM propagandists and supervisors attempted to instill pride in building socialism and a sense of civic duty to achieve results. On the literary campaign to promote and justify the canal's construction among the Soviet population, see Cynthia A.

Ruder, *Making History for Stalin: The Story of the Belomor Canal* (Gainesville: University Press of Florida, 1998).

13. On the construction of Dneprostroi, see Rassweiler, *Generation of Power*. I see a common theme between BAM media coverage and Rassweiler's work, which was undertaken in Ukraine. The Soviet government employed both Dneprostroi and BAM as unifying symbols designed to encourage productivity and support from all Soviet citizens, whether they were directly involved in those respective efforts or not. According to Rassweiler, the state believed that Dneprostroi would improve the economic potential of the Dnepr River region, although bureaucratic incompetence and labor disorganization ultimately weakened the effectiveness of the project. These problems intensified with BAM.

14. The Great Purges were a series of campaigns of political repression and persecution that were directed against the CPSU, ethnic minorities, the military, peasants, and others from October 1936 to November 1936. In Russian the CPSU is called the Kommunisticheskaia Partiia Sovetskogo Soiuza.

15. Martin McCauley, *Khrushchev and the Development of Soviet Agriculture: The Virgin Land Programme, 1953–1964* (New York: Holmes & Meier, 1976).

16. Karpikov, interview. See also *Metody bor'by s ledovymi zatrudneniiami na gidrostantsiiakh Sibiri* (Novosibirsk: Redaktsionno-izdatel'skii otdel Sibirskogo otdeleniia AN SSSR, 1965); Igor P. Butiagin, *Prochnost' l'da i ledianogo pokrova: Naturnye issledovaniia na rekakh Sibiri* (Novosibirsk: Nauka, Sibirskoe otdelenie, 1966); and Peterson, *Troubled Lands*.

17. See Robert G. Darst, "Environmentalism in the USSR: Opposition to the River Diversion Projects," *Soviet Economy* 4, no. 3 (1988): 223–52; and Weiner, *Little Corner of Freedom*, 339, 414–28.

18. On the importance of the Trans-Siberian Railway in the political and military history of late imperial Russia, see Marks, *Road to Power*.

19. On the two earlier BAM projects, see Elant'seva, "BAM: Nauchno-tekhnicheskoe obespechenie stroitel'stva v 30-e gody," "BAM: Pervoe desiatiletie," "Iz istorii stroitel'stva zhelezhnoi dorogi Komsomolsk-Sovetskaia Gavan' (1943–45 gg.)," "Kto i kak stroil BAM v 30-e gody?," *Obrechennaia doroga*, "Periodicheskaia pechat' BAMlaga," and *Stroitel'stvo no. 500 NKVD SSSR*.

20. Known in the West as "the Gulag," the USSR's penal system of labor camps was called Glavnoe upravleniie ispravitel'no-trudovykh lagerei i kolonii (Chief Directorate of Corrective Labor Camps and Colonies).

21. Bovin, "Kurs na stabil'nost' porodil zastoi," 98.

22. See Shelia Fitzpatrick, "Stalin and the Making of a New Elite, 1928–1939," *Slavic Review* 38, no. 3 (September 1979): 377–402.

23. The Komsomol, or Kommunisticheskii Soiuz Molodezhi in Russian, was the All-Union Leninist Communist Youth League.

24. The idea of BAM as the successor to and superior than the Trans-Siberian Railway quickly gained currency within the Soviet Union and among some foreign journalists. See Aganbegian, "BAM—mashtab ekonomiki sotsializma"; Bogatko, *Vtoroi put' k okeanu*; Connoly, "Second Trans-Siberian Railway"; "Final Rails Laid on Key Line to Open Up Siberian Riches"; and Shinkarev, *Vtoroi Transsib*. An excellent overview of the role of Eastern Siberia and the Far East in the course of Russian history is Stephan, *Russian Far East*.

25. Ibragimova, "Doroga v zavtra"; and Shniper, "V granitsakh obozrimogo budushchego."

26. Within the contemporary Russian Federation, the BAM Zone includes (moving from west to east) areas in Krasnoyarsk Krai, Irkutsk Oblast, the Buriat Republic, Zabaikalsk Krai, Amur Oblast, and Khabarovsk Krai.

27. "Taiga" refers to a belt of subarctic coniferous forest dominated by spruce and fir trees that lies between the Arctic and the continental climatic zones of Asian Russia. It includes significant areas of permafrost.

28. The term "big science project," coined by the historian of science Paul Josephson, describes Soviet achievements in such fields as nuclear science, space exploration, computer technology, and biomedicine. See Josephson, "Science and Technology as Panacea," and *Totalitarian Science and Technology.* A concise examination of the Soviet penchant for "techno-hubris" and its influence on the utopian casting of such large-scale undertakings as BAM is in Josephson, "Atomic-Powered Communism." Such rosy treatments of the project's economic and social potential include Adzhiev, *BAM i promyshlennye kompleksy Vostoka SSSR;* Andreev and Sungorkin, "Novosel na BAMe"; Anikin, "BAM: Stroika veka, trassa muzhestva"; "BAM—doroga skvoz' stoletiia"; Fedin, *BAM—kuznitsa komsomol'skogo kharaktera;* Gorbunov, "'Materik budushchego'"; Khodza, *Zvonkoe slovo BAM;* Kultysheva, "Nas sdruzhila magistral'"; Mankov'skii, *BAM stroiat molodye;* Matafonov, "Otkryvaiutsia bol'shie vozmozhnosti"; Mozhin and Savel'ev, "Magistral' i khoziaistvennaia garmoniia"; Nedeshev et al., *BAM i osvoenie Zabaikalia;* Raksha, *An Unusual Journey;* A. Sergeev, "BAM—zheleznodorozhnaia magistral' pervoi kategorii"; Sobolev, *Zona Baikalo-Amurskoi magistrali;* Sushchevich, "Trudovaia i obshchestvenno-politicheskaia aktivnost' stroitelei Baikalo-Amurskoi zheleznodorozhnoi magistrali, 1974–1984 gg."; Tenetov, "K vostoku ot Baikala"; and Vikulov, *BAM i mineral'nye resursy severa Buriatii.*

29. Conn, "Cooperation in Space." The scholar Phyllis Conn has revealed that such political and social trends as de-Stalinization, Khrushchev's "thaw," and bureaucratization weighed heavily on the Soviet space program's effort to surpass the United States.

30. Mote, "Baykal-Amur Railway"; and Aganbegian, *Economic Challenge of Perestroika,* 71.

31. One reason for this is that the pertinent military archives in Russia were closed at the time I conducted the primary research for this project.

32. Ward, "Selling the 'Project of the Century'", 77n6.

33. Argudiaeva, *Trud i byt molodezhi BAMa,* 9; and Belkin and Sheregi, *Formirovanie naseleniia v zone BAM,* 41.

34. Argudiaeva, *Trud i byt molodezhi BAMa,* 24; and Belkin and Sheregi, *Formirovanie naseleniia v zone BAM,* 44.

35. Nikitin, interview and Shtikov, interview.

36. "Po tselinnoi traditsii," 1.

37. Karpikov, interview.

CHAPTER 2. Prometheanism versus Conservationism on the Railway

Epigraph: Brezhnev, "Pobeda stroitelei BAMa," 1.

1. This chapter employs newly available archival materials to examine the debate that ultimately emerged between the center and BAM-based administrative units within the Komsomol and Communist Party apparatuses over the need to protect the ecosystem of the BAM Zone.

2. Regarding the unique geographic and ecological characteristics of the BAM Zone, see Minakir, *Russian Far East*, 3–9; and Pryde and Mote, "Environmental Constraints and Biosphere Protection in the Soviet Far East," 53. Two comparative perspectives on the role of nature protection in the context of recent U.S. history are Marx, *Machine in the Garden*, and Brick and Cawley, *Wolf in the Garden*.

3. Weiner, *Little Corner of Freedom*, 16. In an earlier study, Weiner looks closely at the history of the Soviet conservation movement from the 1920s to the 1930s. See Weiner, *Models of Nature*.

4. Josephson, "Science and Technology as Panacea," 51.

5. See Ianitskii, *Ekologicheskoe dvizhenie v Rossii* and *Ekologiia, demokratiia, molodezh'*. See also Feshbach and Friendly, *Ecocide in the USSR*.

6. Kenez, *Birth of the Propaganda State*.

7. Shinkarev, "BAM: Takie oni, pervoprokhodtsy," 6.

8. Vtorushin, "Promyshlennaia zona BAMa," 2; Molchanov, "Ot Baikala do Amura," 1, 3; and Anikin, "BAM: Stroika veka, trassa muzhestva," 2.

9. Molchanov, "Ot Baikala do Amura," 1, 3; and Anikin, "BAM: Stroika veka, trassa muzhestva," 2.

10. Bogatko, "Put' k okeanu," 3; B. Prokhorov, "Utro bol'shoi stroiki," 1; and "BAM—stroika vsenarodnaia," *Pravda*, 1.

11. Bogatko, "Put' k okeanu," 3.

12. Suturin, "Udarnaia Komsomol'skaia," 2; and N. Petrov, "Daesh' BAM!" 1.

13. On the role of helicopters in BAM construction, see Nazarov, *Vertolety na Baikalo-Amurskoi magistrali*.

14. Iankovskii, "Taezhnyi desant," 2.

15. Ermolaev et al., "Ot Baikala do Amura," 2, emphasis mine.

16. See Suturin, "Udarnaia Komsomol'skaia," 2; Isakov, "Sibir' vstrechaet stroitelei BAMa," 1; Iankovskii, "Put' v Zvezdnyi," 3; Letov, "K severu ot BAMa," 1; and "Fevral'sk vstrechaet passazhirskii," 1.

17. B. Prokhorov, "Utro bol'shoi stroiki," 2.

18. Kazmin, "Sebe i potomkam—2. Tyly giganta," 2.

19. Molodiakov, "Ekspress," 4; and Orlov, "Otkryto dvizhenie," 1.

20. Kleva, "Svoi pered sboikoi," 1.

21. See Josephson, "Science and Technology as Panacea," 40.

22. Komarov, *Unichtozhenie prirody*. This work appeared in an English edition as *The Destruction of Nature in the Soviet Union* (White Plains, N.Y.: M. E. Sharpe, 1980).

23. Komarov, *Unichtozhenie prirody*, 191.

24. Karpikov, interview.

25. Ibid.; Nikitin, interview; and Shtikov, interview.

26. State Archive of the Russian Federation, Moscow (GA RF), f. A-259, op. 46, ed. khr. 5430, d. 9-5-74, ll. 5–22.

27. Kasischke, interview.

28. Resolution number 561 of the USSR Council of Ministers and the CPSU Central Committee, dated July 8, 1974. Resolution 455 of the RSFSR Council of Ministers, dated August 7, 1974. GA RF, f. A-259, op. 46, ed. khr. 4461, d. 10-9-214, ll. 10–23.

29. Russian State Archive of Social-Political History, Moscow (RGASPI), f. 1-M, op. 61, d. 372, ll. 10–20.

30. Nikitin, interview.

31. Russian State Archive of Contemporary History, Moscow (RGANI), f. 89, per. 35, dok. 8, l. 1; and Ianitskii, *Ekologicheskoe dvizhenie v Rossii*, 30.

32. See ZumBrunnen, "Lake Baikal Controversy."

33. RGANI, f. 89, per. 35, dok. 8, l. 1.

34. RGASPI, f. 1-M, op. 61, d. 255, l. 157; and RGANI, f. 89, per. 35, dok. 8, l. 1, respectively.

35. RGANI, f. 89, per. 35, dok. 8, l. 5.

36. See Koptyug and Uppenbrink, *Sustainable Development of the Lake Baikal Region*.

37. RGANI, f. 89, per. 35, dok. 8, l. 5.

38. RGANI, f. 89, per. 35, dok. 8, l. 5. On the difficulties surrounding the construction of the North Muisk Tunnel, see Dienes, "Economic and Strategic Position of the Soviet Far East," 281.

39. See Kazmin and Starukhin, "Tonneli," 2; Shinkarev, "BAM: Takie oni, pervoprokhodtsy," 6; and Sagers, "News Notes," 148–49.

40. RGANI, f. 89, per. 35, dok. 8, l. 5.

41. Karpikov, interview.

42. RGANI, f. 89, per. 35, dok. 8, l. 5.

43. RGANI, f. 89, per. 35, dok. 8, l. 1.

44. Sushchevich, interviews.

45. Nikitin, interview.

46. Maksimova, "Na poklon k dikoi prirode?," 3.

47. Resolution number 530, dated June 15, 1966, was named "A Position on the Collective Members of the All-Russian Protection of Nature Society." RGASPI, f. 27-M, op. 1, d. 90, l. 46.

48. GA RF, f. A-404, op. 1, d. 2173, l. 6.

49. Weiner, 16; GA RF, f. A-404, op. 1, d. 2166, l. 1 and d. 2172, l. 1; and RGASPI, f. 1-M, op. 61, d. 255, l. 14.

50. RGASPI, f. 27-M, op. 1, d. 90, l. 61.

51. RGASPI, f. 1-M, op. 36, d. 442, ll. 2–7; RGASPI, f. 1-M, op. 61, d. 255, ll. 13–14; and RGASPI, f. 1-M, op. 65, d. 30, ll. 14, 73.

52. RGASPI, f. 1-M, op. 61, d. 372, ll. 110–11.

53. RGASPI, f. 27-M, op. 1, d. 32, l. 7.

54. RGASPI, f. 27-M, op. 1, d. 226, ll. 118–19; and RGASPI, f. 1-M, op. 61, d. 255, l. 9.

55. RGASPI, f. 1-M, op. 61, d. 255, l. 9. See also Helgeson, "Population and Labour Force." Soviet sociological studies of the BAMer population include Argudiaeva, *Trud i byt molodezhi BAMa*; Belkin and Sheregi, *Formirovanie naseleniia v zone BAM*; Starin, *Sotsialisticheskoe sorevnovanie stroitelei BAMa, 1974–1984 gg.*; Sushchevich, "Trudovaia i obshchestvenno-politicheskaia aktivnost' stroitelei Baikalo-Amurskoi zheleznodorozhnoi magistrali"; and Zhelezko, *Sotsial'no-demograficheskie problemy v zone BAMa*.

56. Z. Apresian to Iurii Verbitskii in RGASPI, f. 27-M, op. 1, d. 287, l. 2. Mustafin, "Kak poladit' s prirodoi."

57. Verbitskii to Z. Apresian in RGASPI, f. 27-M, op. 1, d. 287, l. 2.

58. RGASPI, f. 27-M, op. 1, d. 287, ll. 3–4.

59. Mustafin in RGASPI, f. 27-M, op. 1, d. 287, l. 13.

60. Verbitskii in RGASPI, f. 27-M, op. 1, d. 287, l. 7.

61. RGASPI, f. 27-M, op. 1, d. 221, l. 84; and RGASPI, f. 27-M, op. 1, d. 231, ll. 6–11.

62. RGASPI, f. 27-M, op. 1, d. 231, l. 6; and RGASPI, f. 27-M, op. 1, d. 125, l. 27.

63. RGASPI, f. 27-M, op. 1, d. 237, l. 48.

64. RGASPI, f. 1-M, op. 65, d. 30, l. 73; and RGASPI, f. 1-M, op. 65, d. 85, l. 41.

65. The December 1977 statement is in RGASPI, f. 27-M, op. 1, d. 120, ll. 63–64.

66. RGASPI, f. 27-M, op. 1, d. 104, l. 85.

67. The anonymous Spotlighter's comment is in RGASPI, f. 27-M, op. 1, d. 90, l. 41.

68. The broadside is found in RGASPI, f. 27-M, op. 1, d. 37, l. 32.

69. The Spotlight bulletin published in the Amur Oblast Party organ *Avangard* is in RGASPI, f. 27-M, op. 1, d. 90, l. 48; and RGASPI, f. 27-M, op. 1, d. 37, l. 18.

70. RGASPI, f. 27-M, op. 1, d. 37, l. 18.

71. RGASPI, f. 27-M, op. 1, d. 90, l. 48.

72. RGASPI, f. 27-M, op. 1, d. 125, l. 27.

73. The 1977 report is in RGASPI, f. 27-M, op. 1, d. 111, ll. 12–13.

74. Sushchevich, interviews.

75. RGASPI, f. 27-M, op. 1, d. 111, l. 45.

76. RGASPI, f. 27-M, op. 1, d. 111, l. 45.

77. See Sushchevich, "Trudovaia i obshchestvenno-politicheskaia aktivnost' stroitelei Baikalo-Amurskoi zheleznodorozhnoi magistrali," 19.

78. The Galmakov essay is in RGASPI, f. 27-M, op. 1, d. 125, l. 25.

79. RGASPI, f. 27-M, op. 1, d. 125, ll. 25–26.

80. RGASPI, f. 27-M, op. 1, d. 125, l. 26.

81. Ibid., f. 27-M, op. 1, d. 125, l. 26; RGASPI, f. 1-M, op. 61, d. 372, l. 10; and RGASPI, f. 27-M, op. 1, d. 90, l. 67b.

82. The A. Grigorev material is in GA RF, f. A-404, op. 1, d. 2152, ll. 13–14.

83. GA RF, f. A-404, op. 1, d. 2152, ll. 13–14.

84. The Khromchenko report is in RGASPI, f. 27-M, op. 1, d. 90, l. 47.

85. RGASPI, f. 27-M, op. 1, d. 90, l. 48.

86. RGASPI, f. 27-M, op. 1, d. 287, l. 6.

87. Valkov and the conference is in RGASPI, f. 27-M, op. 1, d. 287, l. 6.; and RGASPI, f. 1-M, op. 61, d. 255, l. 60.

88. Tkach, "V interesakh pokolenii," 3.

89. Morozov in RGASPI, f. 27-M, op. 1, d. 267, l. 54.

90. RGASPI, f. 27-M, op. 1, d. 267, l. 54.

91. RGASPI, f. 27-M, op. 1, d. 267, l. 54.

92. Morozov, "Nash dom—priroda," 4.

93. Ibid.

94. "Okhrana prirody—tekhnicheskie reshenia," 3.

95. Archives of the Union of Railway Transport Workers are found in GA RF, f. R-5474, op. 20, d. 8199, l. 10.

96. RGASPI, f. 27-M, op. 1, d. 124, ll. 24–37.

97. RGASPI, f. 27-M, op. 1, d. 124, ll. 29–32.

98. Ermolaev and Gaeva's 1975 declaration is in RGASPI, f. 27-M, op. 1, d. 37, ll. 8–9.

99. RGASPI, f. 27-M, op. 1, d. 37, l. 13.

100. Stebel'kov, "I eto nashe delo," 3.

101. See Josephson, *New Atlantis Revisited*.

102. RGASPI, f. 1-M, op. 31, d. 993, l. 58.

103. For more on the relationship between the native Siberian peoples and late Soviet-era "gigantomaniac" construction endeavors, including BAM, see Slezkine, *Arctic Mirrors,* 337–85. The highly disruptive impact of BAM construction on the Buriat and Evenk peoples, the two largest aboriginal groups in the BAM Zone, has yet to be examined seriously by scholars. For the official Soviet position on native Siberians and their relationship with BAM and other large-scale development projects in the region, see Boiko, Eremin, and Beloshapkin, *BAM i narody Severa.*

104. On the rich history of the Buriat people, see Humphrey, "Buryats." Concerning the dynamic between the indigenous peoples of the BAM Zone and the project, see Slezkine, *Arctic Mirrors,* and "From Savages to Citizens." See also Boiko, "Osobennosti sotsial'nogo upravleniia razvitiem narodov Severa v sviazi so stroitel'stvom BAMa" and *Sotsial'noe razvitie narodov Nizhnego Amura,* as well as Boiko, Eremin, and Beloshapkin, *BAM i narody Severa.*

105. RGASPI, f. 1-M, op. 31, d. 993, l. 58.

106. See Bubiakin, *Idut poezda v Iakutiiu.*

107. RGASPI, f. 27-M, op. 1, d. 90, ll. 10–17.

108. RGASPI, f. 1-M, op. 61, d. 255, ll. 3, 15.

109. The uproar over the pollution of Lake Baikal from the Baikalsk pulp operation that erupted during the late 1980s is summarized in Weiner, *Little Corner of Freedom,* 429–39.

110. See Rezun, *Science, Technology, and Ecopolitics in the USSR;* and Weiner, "Environmental Issues in Eastern Europe and Eurasia."

111. Lysenko's comments are in RGASPI, f. 1-M, op. 36, d. 442, l. 2.

112. RGASPI, f. 1-M, op. 61, d. 255, ll. 6–7.

113. RGASPI, f. 1-M, op. 36, d. 442, l. 2; and RGASPI, f. 1-M, op. 61, d. 255, ll. 6–7.

114. RGASPI, f. 1-M, op. 36, d. 442, l. 4.

115. Regarding the tourism potential of the BAM Zone, see Vasil'ev, *Turistskie marshruty Zapadnogo BAMa.*

116. Andreeva, "Rabota, v kotoroi net melochei," 2.

117. "Okhrana prirody—zabota obshchaia," 1.

118. Ibid.

119. Ibid. Regarding the difficulties associated with the timber and fishing industries in the BAM Zone, see Barr, "Forest and Fishing Industries," 117, 153.

120. "Okhrana prirody—zabota obshchaia," 1.

121. Cherepanova, "Okhrana vod—nasha obiazannost'," 4.

122. Lavrinenko, "Stroim kharaktery," 1.

123. For a Western perspective on the South Iakut territorial production complex, see Mote, "South Yakutian Territorial Production Complex" and "Baykal-Amur Railway," 84–87. A Soviet overview of the territorial production complexes is Dobrovol'skii, Koshelev, and Khanaev, *Toplivno-energeticheskii kompleks zony BAMa.*

124. Vozin, "Iuzhno-Iakutskii TPK," 4.

125. "Okhrana prirody—zabota obshchaia," 1; and "Okhrana prirody—tekhnicheskie resheniia," 3.

CHAPTER 3. Crime and Corruption in BAM Society

Epigraph: This 1976 Resolution of the Komsomol Central Committee appears in RGASPI, f. M-1, op. 35, d. 633, l. 1.

1. This CPSU report is in Irkutsk Oblast Center of Contemporary History Documents, Irkutsk (TsDNI IO), f. 127, op. 97, d. 38, ll. 7–8.

2. Poleshak's comments are in RGASPI, f. M-27, op. 1, d. 35, l. 36.

3. Fedin, "BAM—simvol trudovoi doblesti," 2.

4. Pilkington, *Russia's Youth and Its Culture*, 95. Sociologist Hilary Pilkington's discussion of the Komsomol's weighty responsibility to produce "reconstructors of communism," whose duty was to promote "developed socialism," reflects the often overwhelming challenges faced by those who came to BAM for patriotic and ideological reasons. Although Pilkington focuses on Soviet youth of the mid-1980s and beyond, her observations regarding the apathy and palpable resistance of those who labored on such signature projects as BAM ring true for the 1974–84 period as well.

5. Raskin, *Entsiklopediia khuliganstvuiushchego ortodoksa*, 67. References to the extent and popularity of BAM-based humor can be found in several post-Soviet BAM retrospectives, most notably Kogatko, *Doroga, kotoruiu ne vybirali.* Although the contributors to this work by Kogatko are unanimous in their sentiment that a resurrected BAM could serve as an economic savior for a beleaguered Russia, they also agree that humorous impressions of BAM as illustrated by this collection revealed many Soviet citizens' lack of seriousness and contempt for the "road to the future." Sushchevich, interviews.

6. Kudriavtsev, *Preduprezhdenie prestupnosti nesovershennoletnykh.*

7. Other Brezhnev-era studies on youth crime, hooliganism, and theft include Kuznetsova, *Prestuplenie i prestupnost*; Minkovskii, "Osnovnye etapy razvitiia sovetskoi sistemy mer bor'by s prestupnost'iu nesovershennoletnykh"; *Alkogolizm—put' k prestupleniiu*; and Tanasevich, *Preduprezhdenie khishchenii sotsialisticheskogo imushchestva.*

8. Some representative studies that attempted to restore purpose and intentionality to such social categories as youth and the unemployed, which earlier scholarship had labeled as prone to criminal activity, include Neuberger, *Hooliganism*; Thurston, *Liberal City, Conservative State*; Thompson, *Whigs and Hunters*; Hobsbawm, *Uncommon People* and *Primitive Rebels*; and Foucault, *Discipline and Punish.*

9. Regarding the issue of how to treat sources that cover such a culturally and socially specific phenomenon as crime in the Soviet Union, I have concluded that the vast majority of data on BAM Zone crime is "accurate." A helpful, if now dated, Western survey of Soviet criminology during the late 1960s is Connor, *Deviance in Soviet Society.* Scholar Walter D. Connor traces Soviet approaches to deviance and concludes the state's reporting of rates of alcoholism, juvenile delinquency, and petty crimes (such as theft of state property) increased markedly after Stalin's death in 1953. He also speculates that the nation's absolute crime rate also rose by arguing that law enforcement agencies, crippled by a combination of institutional staidness and corruption within the Ministry of Internal Affairs, grew increasingly tolerant of nonpolitical crimes in the post-Stalin years. Karamyshev's 1979 letter to Sushchevich is cited in RGASPI, f. 27-M, op. 1, d. 221, l. 101.

10. Zhelezko, "Stroiteli Baikalo-Amurskoi magistrali—obekt sotsiologicheskogo issledovaniia," 104; and Starin, *Sotsialisticheskoe sorevnovanie stroitelei BAMa, 1974–1984 gg.*, 42.

11. Iankovskii, "Taezhnyi desant," 2.

12. RGASPI, f. 1-M, op. 2, d. 85, l. 21. Regarding the numerous "Communist morality" campaigns that the Komsomol instituted outside of the BAM Zone, see Riordan, "Komsomol."

13. On the workers' stress resulting from primitive living conditions, see, for example,

GA RF, f. A-501, op. 1, d. 7799, l. 66; RGASPI, f. 1-M, op. 45, d. 288, l. 35; RGASPI, f. 1-M, op. 65, d. 5, l. 163; RGASPI, f. 27-M, op. 1, d. 168, l. 57–58; and RGASPI, f. 27-M, op. 1, d. 58, l. 5.

14. On this point, see Chalidze, *Criminal Russia*. Valery Chalidze, a prominent polymer physicist and Soviet dissident, cofounded the Moscow Human Rights Committee with Andrei Sakharov and Andrei Tverdokhlebov and coedited the *tamizdat* (dissident publications produced outside the USSR) journal *Chronicle of Human Rights in the USSR* from 1973 to 1982, after the Soviet government had refused to grant him permission to return to the Soviet Union after a trip abroad. See also Connor, *Deviance in Soviet Society*, 10–11.

15. Nikitin, interview; Argudiaeva, *Trud i byt molodezhi BAMa*; Belkin and Sheregi, *Formirovanie naseleniia v zone BAM*; Kostiuk, Traskunova, and Konstantinovskii, *Molodezh Sibiri*; Medvedeva, *Trudovaia i politicheskaia aktivnost*; Zhelezko, *Sotsialno-demograficheskie problemy v zone BAMa* and "Stroiteli Baikalo-Amurskoi magistrali—obekt sotsiologicheskogo issledovaniia," 104.

16. Regarding Brezhnev's fanciful conception of the BAM project, see Aksiutin, *L. I. Brezhnev*; Leonid I. Brezhnev, *Pages from His Life* (Oxford: Pergamon Press, 1982); and Brezhnev, "Pobeda stroitelei BAMa," 1.

17. The April 1975 report from Central BAM Segment Headquarters is in RGASPI, f. 1-M, op. 65, d. 30, l. 1.

18. RGASPI, f. 1-M, op. 65, d. 30, ll. 16, 20; and Connor, *Deviance in Soviet Society*, 10–11.

19. The October 1975 report is in RGASPI, f. 1-M, op. 65, d. 30, ll. 16, 20.

20. The information on the BAMer settlement of Urgal comes from RGASPI, f. 27-M, op. 1, d. 168, ll. 52–54.

21. The 1975 handbook is cited in RGASPI, f. 27-M, op. 1, d. 22, l. 50.

22. RGASPI, f. 27-M, op. 1, d. 22, ll. 50–51.

23. RGASPI, f. 27-M, op. 1, d. 128, l. 68.

24. RGASPI, f. 27-M, op. 1, d. 128, ll. 68–70.

25. Sushchevich, interviews.

26 *Sambo* is a term derived from the Russian phrase *samozashchita bez oruzhiia* (self-defense without weapons) and referring to an internationally recognized martial art whose techniques are based on the Japanese forms of judo and jujitsu.

27. The oath is cited in RGASPI, f. 27-M, op. 1, d. 45, l. 108.

28. The "I Am the Master of the Project" campaign is cited in RGASPI, f. 27-M, op. 1, d. 221, l. 101. See also Friedrich Kuebart, "The Political Socialisation of Schoolchildren," in Jim Riordan, ed., *Soviet Youth Culture* (Bloomington: Indiana University Press, 1989), 103–21. Kuebart examines the methods of social control employed by the state in the classroom and in particular the rituals created by officialdom to foster a sense of inclusiveness among the youth of the USSR.

29. RGASPI, f. 27-M, op. 1, d. 192, ll. 142–43; and RGASPI, f. 27-M, op. 1, d. 206, ll. 1–2.

30. Sushchevich, interview.

31. Crime rates as cited in RGASPI, f. 27-M, op. 1, d. 144, l. 3.

32. RGASPI, f. 27-M, op. 1, d. 144, ll. 6–7.

33. RGASPI, f. 27-M, op. 1, d. 144, ll. 6–7.

34. On schoolchildren publicly refusing to join the organization, see RGASPI, f. 27-M, op. 1, d. 110, l. 61.

35. GA RF, f. A-501, op. 1, d. 7799, l. 39; and RGASPI, f. 27-M, op. 1, d. 110, l. 84.

36. For the account of Kolesnikov's encounter with this "drunken hooligan," see RGASPI, f. 27-M, op. 1, d. 79, l. 84.

37. Khakhanov, "On pogib na postu," 4.

38. See Sergeyev, *Wild East*, 73–74; and Connor, *Deviance in Soviet Society*, 39–42. The temperance movement was not a new phenomenon in the Soviet Union. For more on this, see Transchel, *Under the Influence.*

39. This Kosei bulletin is in GA RF, f. A-501, op. 1, d. 7799, l. 66; and Connor, *Deviance in Soviet Society*, 44.

40. The report delivered to the RSFSR Council of Ministers by GlavBAMstroi is in RGASPI, f. 1-M, op. 31, d. 888, ll. 131–32; and RGASPI, f. 27-M, op. 1, d. 108, ll. 76–79.

41. GOREM stands for *golovnoi remontno-vosstanovitel'nyi poezd*, or chief repair and restoration train. GOREM-21 was a division of GlavBAMstroi.

42. The investigating commission is mentioned in RGASPI, f. 1-M, op. 45, d. 288, ll. 35–37.

43. On the SKTB, see Starin, *Sotsialisticheskoe sorevnovanie stroitelei BAMa*, 145–47.

44. A "sleeper" is a piece of timber, stone, or metal that lies perpendicular to the rails and holds them in place.

45. The comments of the investigating Komsomol official are in RGASPI, f. 27-M, op. 1, d. 108, ll. 76–79.

46. The Safonov incident is mentioned in RGASPI, f. 27-M, op. 1, d. 149, l. 55.

47. The Miachislavovich story is in RGASPI, f. 27-M, op. 1, d. 206, ll. 14–15.

48. Korneliuk are Gridtsev are in RGASPI, f. 1-M, op. 45, d. 288, l. 49.

49. Terekhin is mentioned in RGASPI, f. 1-M, op. 45, d. 288, l. 49.

50. The "discipline days" are mentioned in RGASPI, f. 1-M, op. 45, d. 288, l. 49.

51. The "Anti-Drunkenness and Alcoholism Commission" is in ibid., l. 57. Curiously, not a single archival document I encountered specified the actual details of the alcohol sales guidelines.

52. The Commission to Combat Drunkenness and Alcoholism is in RGASPI, f. 27-M, op. 1, d. 168, ll. 57–58.

53. The 1975 report is in RGASPI, f. 27-M, op. 1, d. 35, l. 38.

54. The misbehaviors of these three members of the Riazan Komsomoler brigade are detailed in RGASPI, f. M-27, op. 1, d. 30, ll. 32–34.

55. Davydchik's experience is in RGASPI, f. 27-M, op. 1, d. 35, l. 37.

56. "Prichina nechast'ia—khalatnost'," 4.

57. Barichko, "Ogniu—zaslon!" 4.

58. The story of the drunken locomotive engineer is in TsDNI IO, f. 127, op. 97, d. 38, ll. 7–8.

59. Natoka, "P'ianstvo—prichina bed," 4; and Nikitin, interview.

60. The secret Komsomol report on sexual crimes committed by its workers in 1978 is in RGASPI, f. 27-M, op. 1, d. 168, ll. 46–49, 50–58, 64–69; and Pilkington, *Russia's Youth and Its Culture*, 163.

61. Gromov's story is in RGASPI, f. M-27, op. 1, d. 30, ll. 42–44; RGASPI, f. 27-M, op. 1, d. 198, ll. 25–27; and RGASPI, f. 27-M, op. 1, d. 243, l. 40.

62. See Riordan, "Komsomol," 30.

63. See Adzhiev, *BAM i promyshlennye kompleksy Vostoka SSSR*; Berezovskii, "Kontury kompleksa," 2; Dobrovol'skii, Koshelev, and Khanaev, *Toplivno-energeticheskii kompleks zony BAMa*; and Kozlovskii, "Syp'evye kompleksy BAMa," 2.

64. Kazakov as quoted in Medvedeva, *Trudovaia i politicheskaia aktivnost'*, 88, 90.

65. Kazakov as mentioned in RGASPI, f. 1-M, op. 65, d. 8, ll. 28–31.

66. Medvedeva, 90.

67. See, for example, RGASPI, f. 27-M, op. 1, d. 9, ll. 36–39; RGASPI, f. 27-M, op. 1, d. 42, ll. 1–2; and RGASPI, f. 27-M, op. 1, d. 33, l. 19.

68. The disappearance of materials involving members of the SMP-585 is in RGASPI, f. 27-M, op. 1, d. 74, l. 121.

69. Galmakov's letter and experience is detailed in RGASPI f. 1-M, op. 81, d. 112, ll. 65–66; and Sushchevich, interviews.

70. Efimov's thievery scheme is mentioned in RGASPI, f. 1-M, op. 81, d. 285, ll. 3–4.

71. RGASPI, f. 27-M, op. 1, d. 202, ll. 1–2; and RGASPI, f. 27-M, op. 1, d. 207, ll. 41–42.

72. Shtikov, interview.

73. Details of this 1979 investigation are in RGASPI, f. 1-M, op. 81, d. 285, l. 9.

74. Nikitin, interview.

75. RGASPI, f. 27-M, op. 1, d. 185, ll. 81–82.

76. Chalidze, *Criminal Russia*, 188–96.

77. Skorobogatov, "Etazhi taezhnogo ansamblia dlia velikoi stroiki veka," 4.

78. RGASPI, f. 27-M, op. 1, d. 185, ll. 81–82.

79. This 1975 letter of condemnation is in RGASPI, f. 27-M, op. 1, d. 35, l. 36.

80. See Meney, *La Kleptocratie*, 121–69; and Davidow, *Third Soviet Generation*, 40–43.

81. See Pilkington, *Russia's Youth and Its Culture*, 99.

82. These Verbitskii details are in RGASPI, f. 27-M, op. 1, d. 264, ll. 1–2.

83. Ibid., ll. 3–7.

84. Ibid., ll. 14–18.

85. Ibid., ll. 20–21.

86. The open letter is found in RGASPI, f. 27-M, op. 1, d. 185, ll. 147–48.

87. Compare this with Davidow, *Third Soviet Generation*, 15–56. The journalist and lifelong Communist, Russian émigré Mike Davidow ignores the area's climatic conditions in his discussion of the Siberian landscape and instead chooses to note that "[BAM] will make the taiga an ally because it views its severe nature not as an enemy but as a potential friend" (Davidow, *Third Soviet Generation*, 17).

88. TsDNI IO, f. 127, op. 100, d. 143, l. 8.

89. See Mote, "BAM after the Fanfare."

90. See Brooks, *Thank You, Comrade Stalin*, 245. The historian Jeffrey Brooks has discussed the lack of "postwar dynamism," both social and economic, that increasingly plagued the Soviet Union until the arrival of Mikhail Gorbachev.

91. Beginning in the mid-1990s, the sentiment that a refurbished BAM could serve to ameliorate Russia's financial woes was echoed by several post-Soviet commentators, most notably the Yeltsin-era prime minister Viktor Chernomyrdin, the Putin-era speaker of the state Duma Gennadi Seleznev, and the former minister of foreign affairs and former prime minister Evgenii Primakov. See Chernomyrdin, "O pervoocherdnykh merakh," 5; Seleznev, "Postanovlenie Gosudarstvennoi Dumy," 1; Primakov, *Postanovlenie Pravitel'stva Rossiiskoi Federatsii ot 19 ianvaria 1999 g. No. 69*; Baliev, "U BAMa—vtoroe dykhanie," 5; Moshenko, *BAM—budushchee Rossii*; Mukonin, "VKSh-BAM"; Nikiforova and Sharov, "BAM i tablitsa Mendeleeva," 1–2; and Sushchevich, "Nas mnogo, veterany!" 2.

92. See Sergeyev, *Wild East*, 73–74.

CHAPTER 4. Working Alone: Women on the Railway

1. Jo Peers, "Workers by Hand and Womb: Soviet Women and the Demographic Crisis," in *Soviet Sisterhood: British Feminists on Women in the USSR,* edited by Barbara Holland (London: Fourth Estate, 1985), 117.

2. Argudiaeva, *Trud i byt molodezhi BAMa,* 24.

3. The sociologist Vladimir Shlapentokh, in his *Love, Marriage, and Friendship* (pages 171–211), examines this growing self-consciousness and attendant resentment among Soviet women of men's higher pay and social status. See also Baranskaia, *A Week Like Any Other,* and Gray, *Soviet Women.*

4. A similar struggle by Southern U.S. women during the 1870s and 1880s is examined in Edwards, *Gendered Strife and Confusion.* See also Wood, *Baba and the Comrade.*

5. Dymova, "Nesluchainyi vybor," 4.

6. Regarding the treatment of the women's question in Bolshevik, feminist, and populist circles both before and after the 1917 revolution, see Glickman, *Russian Factory Women,* 219–241, 272; Gorsuch, "Soviet Youth and the Politics of Popular Culture during NEP," and "A Woman Is Not a Man"; Richard Stites, *Equality, Freedom, and Justice: Women and Men in the Russian Revolution, 1917–1930* (Jerusalem: Hebrew University, 1988) and *The Women's Liberation Movement in Russia: Feminism, Nihilism, and Bolshevism, 1860–1930* (Princeton, N.J.: Princeton University Press, 1978); and Wood, *Baba and the Comrade,* 13–39.

7. See Robert H. McNeal, *Bride of the Revolution: Krupskaya and Lenin* (Ann Arbor: University of Michigan Press, 1972); and T. N. Kuznetsova and E. P. Podvigina, eds., *O Nadezhde Krupskoi: Vospominaniia, ocherki, stat'i sovremennikov* (Moscow: Izdatel'stvo politicheskoi literatury, 1988).

8. See B. V. Sokolov, *Armand i Krupskaia: Zhenshchiny vozhdia* (Smolensk: Rusich, 1999).

9. See I. F. Armand, *Stat'i, rechi, pis'ma* (Moscow: Politizdat, 1975); and R. C. Elwood, *Inessa Armand: Revolutionary and Feminist* (Cambridge: Cambridge University Press, 1992).

10. Buckley, "Soviet Interpretations of the Woman Question," 25; and Engel and Posadskaya-Vanderbeck, *Revolution of Their Own,* 25.

11. This phenomenon is examined in Goldman, *Women, the State, and Revolution,* 296–343.

12. Buckley, "Soviet Interpretations of the Woman Question," 39.

13. On the role of Soviet women during World War II, see John Alexander Armstrong, *The Soviet Partisans in World War II* (Madison: University of Wisconsin Press, 1964); G. Astafiev, *Devushka iz Kashina* (Moscow: Moskovskii rabochii, 1974); Cottam, *Defending Leningrad* and *On the Road to Stalingrad;* Kazimiera J. Cottam, ed. and trans., *Soviet Airwomen in Combat in World War II* (New York: Military Affairs/Aerospace Historian, 1983), *The Golden-Tressed Soldier* (New York: Military Affairs/Aerospace Historian, 1983), and *Women in Air War: The Eastern Front of World War II* (New York: Legas, 1997); Engel and Posadskaya-Vanderbeck, *Revolution of Their Own,* 13–14; Elena Skriabina, *Siege and Survival: The Odyssey of a Leningrader,* translated and edited by Norman Luxenburg (Carbondale: Southern Illinois University Press, 1971), and *After Leningrad: From the Caucasus to the Rhine, August 9, 1942–March 25, 1945: A Diary of Survival during World War II,* translated and edited by Norman Luxenburg (Carbondale: Southern Illinois University Press, 1978); Nina Kosterina, *The Diary of Nina Kosterina,* translated by Mirra Ginsburg (New

York: Avon, 1970); and Zoia M. Smirnova-Medvedeva, *Opalennaia iunost'* (Moscow: Voenizdat, 1967).

14. Bil'shai, *Reshenie zhenskogo voprosa v SSSR*, 255.

15. Barbara Holland and Teresa McKevitt, "Maternity Care in the Soviet Union," in Holland, *Soviet Sisterhood*, 152.

16. This atmosphere of private discussion and debate, which covered a range of topics that were forbidden in public, is discussed in Alexeyeva and Goldberg, *Thaw Generation*.

17. Buckley, "Soviet Interpretations of the Woman Question," 40. Regarding the impact of industrial development on societal expectations of women as caregivers and workers throughout Europe, see Tilly and Scott, *Women, Work, and Family*, 63–88.

18. Elena Zubkova, *Russia after the War: Hopes, Illusions, and Disappointments, 1945–1957* (Armonk, N.Y.: M. E. Sharpe, 1998), 151–63.

19. Bridger, "Young Women and Perestroika," 179; and Pilkington, "Russia and the Former Soviet Republics."

20. Buckley, "Soviet Interpretations of the Woman Question," 49; and Lapidus, *Women in Soviet Society*, 246.

21. On the treatment of the "double burden" in sociological and demographic circles, see Danilova et al., *Sovetskie zhenshchiny*; Kharchev and Golod, *Professional'naia rabota zhenshchin i sem'ia*; Krylova et al., *Sovetskaia zhenshchina—trud, materinstvo, sem'ia*; Novikova, *Zhenshchina v razvitom sotsialisticheskom obshchestve*; and Savinova, "Zhenshchina v sovetskom obshchestve." See, for example, Gurko, "Vliianie dobrachnogo povedeniia na stabil'nost' molodoi sem'i"; and Khripkova and Kolesov, *Devochka—podrostok—devushka*.

22. This demographic information is in RGASPI, f. 1-M, op. 65, d. 267, ll. 2–5.

23. Aganbegian, "BAM—mashtab ekonomiki sotsializma"; Nikitin, interview; and Uspenskii, "V promyshlennoi zone BAMa."

24. See Peers, "Workers by Hand and Womb," 116, 142–43; Buckley, "Soviet Interpretations of the Woman Question," 49; and Lapidus, *Women in Soviet Society*, 246.

25. Pilkington, "Russia and the Former Soviet Republics," 205.

26. On all-female formations, see Argudiaeva, *Trud i byt molodezhi BAMa*, 50. The statement is from *Baikalo-Amurskaia magistral'—panorama vsenarodnoi stroiki*, 1st edition, 13.

27. See, for example, Fokin, "Schastlivaia Eva Dudash i ee druz'ia," 2; Kolesova and Sungorkin, "Pomidor-gastroler," 2; "Po tselinnoi traditsii," 1; Riabova, Bashinova, and Tugutov, "Vypalo nam stroit' put' zheleznyi," 2; Serezdinova, "Khorosheet rodnaia Sibir'"; Timakov and Baroian, "I mediki stroiat BAM," 3; and Volina, "Obyknovennaia romantika," 3.

28. Musalitin, "Vladilena Danilova i ee brigada," 2.

29. Pobozhii, "Pervoprokhodtsy," 2; and Fokin, "Skaz o trasse," 2.

30. Pobozhii, "Pervoprokhodtsy," 2.

31. Fokin, "Skaz o trasse," 2.

32. Sechkovskii, "Devushki trassy," 3.

33. Ibid.

34. Zbrueva's story is in RGASPI, f. 27-M, op. 1, d. 92, l. 45.

35. Vasina's story is in RGASPI, f. 27-M, op. 1, d. 96, l. 10.

36. Churaeva's profile is in ibid., l. 12.

37. Raspopova's story is in RGASPI f. 1-M, op. 34, d. 1007, ll. 157–58.

38. The poster is mentioned in RGASPI, f. 1-M, op. 65, d. 267, l. 6.

39. Komarova and Gruzdova are in ibid., l. 8.

40. Ibid.

41. O. Vasil'ev, "V brigade Liudmily Sergeevoi," 2.

42. Ibid.

43. Monina and Lavrova are in "S prazdnikom!" 3.

44. Ibid.

45. This "journal" may or may not have been written by the cited author; see Niskovskikh, "A na dushe spokoino i svetlo," 3.

46. Ignatenko, "Tochka prilozheniia," 3.

47. Ibid.

48. Argudiaeva, *Trud i byt molodezhi BAMa*, 24; and Belkin and Sheregi, *Formirovanie naseleniia v zone BAM*, 44.

49. "Zhenshchiny vsesoiuznoi udarnoi," 3.

50. Fokin, "Schastlivaia Eva Dudash i ee druz'ia," 2.

51. Gribkova is introduced in "Svoe mesto v zhizni," 2.

52. Ibid.

53. Murashova is in Chudnovskii, "Schast'e sluzhit' liudam," 3.

54. Basova is quoted in Dymova, "Nesluchainyi vybor," 4.

55. Ibid.

56. Golovnina is described in Kozenko, "Voploshchenie mechty," 2.

57. Kokhan, "Na ravnykh," 7.

58. Shinkarev, "BAM: Takie oni, pervoprokhodtsy," 6.

59. Ibid.

60. Isakov, "Tyly stroiki," 2; and Iankovskii, "Put' v Zvezdnyi," 3.

61. Mironova, interview.

62. See especially Orlov, *Druz'ia moi, tonnel'shchiki* and *Baikalo-Amurskaia magistral'—panorama vsenarodnoi stroiki*, 1st edition, 1975, 94.

63. Panchenko is mentioned in Solntseva, "Galina Panchenko—prodavets," 3.

64. Ibid.

65. Mironova, interview.

66. *Baikalo-Amurskaia magistral'—panorama vsenarodnoi stroiki*, 1st edition, 1975, 94.

67. This and other "request letters" cited are in RGASPI, f. 1-M, op. 45, d. 277, ll. 35.

68. Ibid.

69. Ibid., ll. 36–37.

70. Ibid., ll. 35–37.

71. Ibid.

72. Mironova, interview.

73. The *chastushka* is from Raskin, *Entsiklopediia khuliganstvuiushchego ortodoksa*, 67.

74. Mironova, interview; and Nikitin, interview.

75. Carrère d'Encausse, *Decline of an Empire*, 115.

76. A. Prokhorov, "Konflikt svoego i chuzhogo v sovetskoi kul'ture 70-kh godov (na primere vizual'nykh reprezentatsii zhenshchin v zhurnale 'Ogonek')," 375–81. A perspective on women's resistance to official economic and cultural policies in Communist Poland that provides an interesting contrast to Soviet reproductive and familial directives is Kenney, "Gender of Resistance in Communist Poland."

77. RGASPI, f. 27-M, op. 1, d. 216, l. 31; RGASPI, f. 1-M, op. 65, d. 85, l. 18; and RGASPI, f. 6-M, op. 17, d. 539, l. 61.

78. Mironova, interview.

79. Argudiaeva, *Trud i byt molodezhi BAMa*, 24.

80. This estimate is based on my survey of BAM coverage in the national and local media, which peaked in the late 1970s and began to decline as the project neared its announced completion in the fall of 1984.

81. Order of Lenin recipients mentioned in RGASPI, f. 6- M, op. 17, d. 539, l. 20.

82. Ibid., l. 47.

83. RGASPI, f. 6-M, op. 18, d. 403, ll. 53, 56, 61.

84. Doronin's story is in RGASPI, f. 6- M, op. 17, d. 539, l. 61.

85. Sushchevich, interviews.

86. Nikitin, interview; and Shtikov, interview.

87. RGASPI, f. 27-M, op. 1, d. 16, l. 11.

88. These statistics are in ibid.

89. RGASPI, f. 27-M, op. 1, d. 216, l. 31.

90. Data on unemployed women in Buriat ASSR is from RGASPI, f. 27-M, op. 1, d. 16, l. 11.

91. On the "heroes of socialist labor" see RGASPI, f. 27-M, op. 1, d. 316, l. 63.

92. RGASPI, f. 27-M, op. 1, d. 321, ll. 18, 25–6, 29, 31, 48, 53.

93. On dorm residents Rostovshchikova and Serebriakova see RGASPI, f. 27-M, op. 1, d. 77, l. 51.

94. Ibid.

95. Sushchevich's comments on Denisova are in RGASPI, f. 27-M, op. 1, d. 22, ll. 65–66.

96. Ibid., l. 66.

97. Sushchevich, interviews.

98. The letter-writing campaign is in RGASPI, f. 27-M, op. 1, d. 320, ll. 97–100.

99. Kultysheva, "Nas sdruzhila magistral'," 1.

100. Sushchevich, interviews.

101. Ibid.

102. Osokina, "Stroka oplachena sud'boiu," 6.

103. Mironova, interview; and Shtikov, interview.

104. RGASPI, f. 27-M, op. 1, d. 320, ll. 97–100.

105. Mironova, interview.

106. Mironova, interview; and Nikitin, interview.

107. The September 1984 meeting is mentioned in RGASPI, f. 27-M, op. 1, d. 320, l. 20.

108. Sushchevich, interviews.

109. Ibid.

110. RGASPI, f. 27-M, op. 1, d. 320, ll. 8, 9–14.

111. The Komsomol's announcement is mentioned in ibid., l. 15.

112. Ibid., l. 20.

113. Ibid., l. 22.

CHAPTER 5. National Differentiation and Marginalization on the Railway

Epigraph: This report from the Komsomol BAM construction headquarters is found in RGASPI, f. 27-M, op. 1, d. 309, ll. 39–40.

1. Sushchevich, interviews.

2. Kagarlitsky, *Thinking Reed,* 216–37.

3. Teresa Rakowska-Harmstone was one of the first Western observers to note the Brezhnev regime's concern with the potentially destructive results of state-sponsored Great Russian nationalism. See Rakowska-Harmstone, "Dialectics of Nationalism in the USSR," 392.

4. Hollinger, "How Wide the Circle of the 'We'?"

5. I have derived the label "the genetic school" from the writings of political scientist John A. Armstrong, who wrote a number of studies on the origins of nationalism, most notably *Nations before Nationalism.* Armstrong states that "the principal lesson . . . to be derived from consideration of the temporal variations of nationalism is that . . . nationalism must be approached *genetically* [*sic*]." See Armstrong, "Autonomy of Ethnic Identity," 30. Horowitz, "How to Begin Thinking Comparatively."

6. Armstrong, "Autonomy of Ethnic Identity," 25.

7. Seminal studies that conceive of the nation and nationalism as artificially created rather than as organic phenomena include Anderson, *Imagined Communities;* Bhabha, *Nation and Narration;* Breuilly, *Nationalism and the State;* Deutsch, *Nationalism and Social Communication;* Deutsch and Foltz, *Nation-Building;* Hobsbawm and Ranger, *Invention of Tradition;* A. Smith, *Myths and Memories of the Nation* and *National Identity.* In particular, the sociologist Anthony Smith has devoted his career to mining the depths of the "problem of national identity," which he presents as a decidedly unnatural idea that is shaped by ever-changing interpretations of class, language, and religion. See also Suny, *Revenge of the Past,* 6–11.

8. Doak, "What Is a Nation and Who Belongs?"

9. Suny, *Revenge of the Past,* 18–19.

10. Carrère d'Encausse, *Decline of an Empire,* 13.

11. Suny, *Revenge of the Past.*

12. Hélène Carrère d'Encausse, "When the 'Prison of Peoples' Was Opened," in Denber, *Soviet Nationality Reader,* 91.

13. Minogue and Williams, "Ethnic Conflict in the Soviet Union."

14. A. Smith, "Ethnic Identity and Territorial Nationalism in Comparative Perspective," 59.

15. See Terry Martin, *Affirmative Action Empire: Nations and Nationalism in the Soviet Union, 1923–1939* (Ithaca, N.Y.: Cornell University Press, 2001); and Slezkine, "USSR as a Communal Apartment," 418–19.

16. Carrère d'Encausse, *Nationality Question in the Soviet Union and Russia,* 16–17; and Hirsch, "Soviet Union as a Work-in-Progress."

17. Carrère d'Encausse, "When the 'Prison of Peoples' Was Opened," 89.

18. See Elantseva, "Periodicheskaia pechat' BAMlaga," 167–75, and *Stroitelstvo no. 500 NKVD SSSR;* "Deported Nation Appeals to President Mikoyan"; Robert Conquest, *The Nation Killers: The Soviet Deportation of Nationalities* (London: Macmillan, 1970); and A. M. Nekrich, *The Punished Peoples: The Deportation and Fate of Soviet Minorities at the End of the Second World War* (New York: Norton, 1978).

19. Alexeyeva and Goldberg, *Thaw Generation.*

20. *XXII s"ezd Kommunisticheskoi Partii Sovetskogo Soiuza,* 216. See also G. Smith, "Nationalities Policy from Lenin to Gorbachev"; and William J. Tompson, *Khrushchev: A Political Life* (New York: St. Martin's Griffin, 1997), 237–38.

21. Carrère d'Encausse, "When the 'Prison of Peoples' Was Opened," 94–95.

22. Motyl, *Sovietology, Rationality, Nationality*, 95.

23. Tishkov, *Ethnicity, Nationalism, and Conflict*, 39. Although the historian Valerii Tishkov has classified many non-Russian elites as "peripheral," he notes that Party members within such groups enjoyed growing levels of prestige and influence in Brezhnev's USSR. On the remarkable stability of elites within Brezhnev's generational cohort, see Fowkes, *Disintegration of the Soviet Union*, 100; and Suny, *Revenge of the Past*, 119.

24. Fowkes, *Disintegration of the Soviet Union*, 95–99.

25. Rakowska-Harmstone, "Dialectics of Nationalism in the USSR," 395.

26. Ibid.; and Carrère d'Encausse, *Decline of an Empire*, 58–70.

27. See Jeremy R. Azrael, ed., *Soviet Nationality Policies and Practices* (New York: Praeger, 1978).

28. Regarding the dangers inherent in promoting Russian nationalism within a majority non-Russian USSR, see Martin, *Affirmative Action Empire*; and Andrei Amalrik, *Will the Soviet Union Survive until 1984?* (New York: Harper & Row, 1970), 38.

29. Brass, "Language and National Identity in the Soviet Union and India," 116.

30. Statistics on the railway's leadership are in GA RF, f. R-5474, op. 20, d. 8199, l. 121; and RGASPI, f. 1-M, op. 61, d. 278, ll. 1–3.

31. Carrère d'Encausse, *Decline of an Empire*, 138–39.

32. See Rakowska-Harmstone, "Dialectics of Nationalism in the USSR," 402.

33. Fowkes, *Disintegration of the Soviet Union*, 93; and Suny, *Revenge of the Past*, 123.

34. Carrère d'Encausse, *Decline of an Empire*, 212–13.

35. Fowkes, *Disintegration of the Soviet Union*, 91.

36. Ibid.

37. Ethnic minorities in special detachments are mentioned in RGASPI, f. 6-M, op. 17, d. 539, l. 1.

38. Ibid.

39. RGASPI, f. 6-M, op. 17, d. 539, l. 3. Horowitz, "How to Begin Thinking Comparatively," 16; and Sushchevich, interview, April 19, 2000.

40. RGASPI, f. 6-M, op. 17, d. 539, l. 3.

41. Tiazhelnikov is mentioned in ibid., l. 16.

42. Tokareva, interviews. At the time of the interview, Tokareva served as head of the reading room at the Russian State Archive of Social and Political History in Moscow.

43. Mote, "Baykal-Amur Railway"; and Voronov and Smirnov, "Zakreplenie molodezhi v zone BAMa," 17.

44. RGASPI, f. 27-M, op. 1, d. 279, l. 51. See also Vardys, "Lithuanians."

45. RGASPI f. 27-M, op. 1, d. 279, l. 52; and Kionka, "Estonians."

46. See Belkin and Sheregi, *Formirovanie naseleniia v zone BAM*; Medvedeva, *Trudovaia i politicheskaia aktivnost*; and Zhelezko, *Sotsial'no-demograficheskie problemy v zone BAMa*.

47. Sukhanov, "BAM stroit vsia strana." Representative examples of the "unification" theme during the Brezhnev era include Bagramov, *Natsional'nyi vopros v bor'be idei*; Ivanov and Kaprytin, *Internatsional'naia gordost' narodov sotsialisticheskogo sodruzhestva*; Liubarskii, *Rozhdenie velikogo soiuza*; Ten, *Rukovodstvo KPSS protsessom*; Tsamerian, *Teoreticheskie problemy obrazovaniia* and *Natsional'nye otnosheniia v SSSR*; Zelenchuk and Guboglo, *Natsional'noe i internatsional'noe v sovetskom obraze zhizni*; and Zhitov et al., *Velikaia sila druzhby narodov*.

48. Serdiuk is in GA RF, f. R-5474, op. 20, d. 8199, l. 47.

49. Nasrullaev is in RGASPI, f. 27-M, op. 1, d. 96, l. 5.

50. Ibid.

51. Kaskapov is in RGASPI, f. 1-M, op. 65, d. 30, l. 151.

52. The documentary is mentioned in RGASPI, f. 27-M, op. 1, d. 96, l. 16.

53. The "pacesetting" work is found in RGASPI, f. 27-M, op. 1, d. 54, l. 11.

54. Shinkarev, "BAM: Takie oni, pervoprokhodtsy," 6.

55. Evtushenko as quoted in Fadeev, *BAM: Zolotoe zveno*, 18.

56. Drannikov, "Daesh' Baikal, daesh' Amur!" 1; and Isakov, "Tyly stroiki," 2.

57. Iankovskii, "Put' v Zvezdnyi," 3.

58. "BAM—stroika vsenarodnaia," 1.

59. Bostrukhov, "Golovnoi uchastok magistrali," 1.

60. Leimanis is profiled in RGASPI, f. 27-M, op. 1, d. 30, ll. 57–64.

61. Titomir's story is in RGASPI, f. 27-M, op. 1, d. 96, l. 4.

62. Emelianov, "Paren' iz Khashuri," 3.

63. "ArmBAMstroi: Ukrepliaem pozitsii," 3.

64. Zhuravlev, "Prinimai, BAM, Iakutian!" 2–3.

65. Zhuravlev, "Postoiannaia propiska Iakutian-BAM," 3.

66. Fedina, "Bamovtsy iz odnogo sela," 4.

67. See Robert Weinberg, *Stalin's Forgotten Zion—Birobidzhan and the Making of a Soviet Jewish Homeland: An Illustrated History, 1928–1996* (Berkeley: University of California Press, 1998); and Rakowska-Harmstone, "Dialectics of Nationalism in the USSR," 406.

68. These "For Participation in BAM Construction" awards are detailed in RGASPI, f. 27-M, op. 1, d. 321, ll. 18, 25, 26, 30, 43, 52, 62, 63.

69. These figures are from RGASPI, f. 27-M, op. 1, d. 62, l. 28.

70. Filippov is in RGASPI, f. 1-M, op. 61, d. 278, l. 27; and ibid., l. 22.

71. Ibid., l. 28.

72. These housing details are in ibid.

73. This yearlong evaluation on BAMer formations that originated from the Caucasus is in ibid., l. 8.

74. On the BAMer detachments from the Caucasus and Eastern Siberia, see ibid., l. 10.

75. Ibid.

76. On the project slowdown, see RGASPI, f. 1-M, op. 81, d. 283, l. 54.

77. Verbitskii's comments are in RGASPI, f. 27-M, op. 1, d. 140, l. 16.

78. RGASPI, f. 27-M, op. 1, d. 150, l. 53.

79. On the composition of the workforce in Iakut ASSR towns, see ibid.

80. Boiko, Eremin, and Beloshapkin, *BAM i narody Severa*, 34, 52.

81. This statistical data for 1978 is in RGASPI, f. 27-M, op. 1, d. 182, l. 14.

82. This AzerbaidzhanstroiBAM story is in ibid., ll. 14–15.

83. Verbitskii's comments are in RGASPI, f. 27-M, op. 1, d. 213, ll. 12–13.

84. The 1983 communiqué is in RGASPI, f. 27-M, op. 1, d. 293, l. 9.

85. Sushchevich's comments are in RGASPI, f. 27-M, op. 1, d. 278, ll. 83–84.

86. The Komsomol report is in RGASPI, f. 27-M, op. 1, d. 279, l. 31.

87. The February 1982 bulletin is in RGASPI, f. 27-M, op. 1, d. 292, l. 18.

88. This 1975 dispatch is in RGASPI, f. 27-M, op. 1, d. 62, l. 69.

89. Sushchevich, interviews.

90. Tokareva, interviews.

91. Nikitin, interview; and Shtikov, interview.

92. RGASPI, f. 6-M, op. 17, d. 539, l. 20.

93. Ibid.

94. RGASPI f. 27-M, op. 1, d. 150, l. 73; and Kavunenko, *Chervonyi pozd,* 154–57.

95. RGASPI, f. 27-M, op. 1, d. 82, ll. 62–64.

96. This information on locally generated "sponsorship" funds is in RGASPI, f. 1-M, op. 61, d. 278, l. 22.

97. Ibid.

98. Ibid., l. 26.

99. The 1976 letter is in RGASPI, f. 1-M, op. 64, d. 139, l. 9–14.

100. Prikhodko's brigade is mentioned in RGASPI, f. 1-M, op. 65, d. 30, l. 141.

101. Kaminskaia, *BAM—doroga druzhby.*

102. Ibid., 7.

103. Mass disturbances among soldiers and urban workers during the Brezhnev years are discussed in V. A. Kozlov, *Massovye besporiadki v SSSR pri Khrushcheve i Brezhneve (1953–nachalo 1980-kh gg.)* (Novosibirsk: Sibirskii khronograf, 1999).

104. Details of the failed bribery attempt are in RGASPI, f. 27-M, op. 1, d. 282, l. 48.

105. Cushman, "Ritual and the Sacralization of the Secular," 110; and Voronov and Smirnov, "Zakreplenie molodezhi v zone BAMa," 17.

106. The thirty-one unaccounted for Dagestanis are mentioned in RGASPI, f. 27-M, op. 1, d. 62, l. 103.

107. The story of the two Azeris is in ibid., ll. 110–12.

108. The three detained Armenians are mentioned in RGASPI, f. 27-M, op. 1, d. 74, ll. 28–30.

109. This "ethnically motivated disturbance" is in RGASPI, f. 27-M, op. 1, d. 77, l. 50.

110. This "series of unfortunate events" is detatiled in ibid., l. 51.

CHAPTER 6. The Rails of Fraternal Cooperation: BAMers Abroad and Foreigners at Home

Epigraph: This 1981 Report of the Komsomol Central Committee is in RGASPI, f. 1-M, op. 65, d. 438a, l. 29.

1. Nikitin, interview.

2. RGASPI, f. 27-M, op. 1, d. 279, l. 6.

3. For a standard explanation of the ideological precepts behind Soviet relations with developing countries both inside and outside the so-called circle of fraternal nations (a commonly used term describing an array of mostly socialist countries in Eastern Europe, Africa, Asia, and Central and South America), see Ponomarev, "Aktual'nye problemy"; and Ulianovskii, "Nekotorye voprosy." The theorists B. Ponomarev and R. Ulianovskii stated that the developing nations of Latin America, Africa, Asia, and the Caribbean count on the Soviet Union's assistance in throwing off the dual yokes of capitalism and colonialism. Furthermore, they declared that the USSR would assist all developing nations in rejecting foreign intervention through the granting of economic and military assistance.

4. These findings are specifically in the Komsomol repository in Russian State Archive of Social-Political History, Moscow (RGASPI).

5. The southern African nations of Angola and Mozambique (both Portuguese colonies

from the 1890s until 1974) and the eastern African nation of Ethiopia (under titular Italian control between 1895 and 1939) are representative examples of former Soviet "client states." While in the middle of several divisive conflicts during the 1970s and 1980s, these countries began to question the viability and practicality of Marxism-Leninism as a reputable developmental paradigm for postcolonial Africa. See Remnek, "Soviet Policy in the Horn of Africa."

6. On BAMers' travel outside the USSR, see RGASPI, f. 27-M, op. 1, d. 299, l. 9.

7. On the Zvezdnyi train, see RGASPI, f. 1-M, op. 65, d. 28, ll. 34–5.

8. On the final approval necessary for BAMer travelers, see RGASPI, f. 27-M, op. 1, d. 39, ll. 2, 16.

9. Sushchevich in ibid., l. 16.

10. Galmakov's comments are in RGASPI, f. 27-M, op. 1, d. 77, l. 82–85; and RGASPI, f. 27-M, op. 1, d. 74, ll. 33–34.

11. Sushchevich in ibid., ll. 82–83.

12. Ibid.

13. Ibid.

14. On the BAMers' Cuba trip, see Vezbakh, "Miting druzhby i solidarnosti," 4.

15. Verbitskii's comments are in RGASPI, f. 1-M, op. 65, d. 438a, l. 29.

16. The competition was known as the "First Year of the Tenth Five-Year Plan: A Pacesetting Finish." RGASPI, f. 27-M, op. 1, d. 105, l. 165; RGASPI, f. 1-M, op. 65, d. 28, l. 123; and RGASPI, f. 27-M, op. 1, d. 100, ll. 17, 79, 81.

17. On the trip to Hungary, see RGASPI, f. 27-M, op. 1, d. 74, ll. 62–63; and RGASPI, f. 27-M, op. 1, d. 77, ll. 3–4.

18. Sushchevich is in RGASPI, f. 27-M, op. 1, d. 105, l. 165.

19. Sushchevich's remarks are in RGASPI, f. 27-M, op. 1, d. 32, ll. 1–2.

20. Soviet ties with Vietnam were especially close after the Southeast Asian nation's invasion of Kampuchea/Cambodia in 1978 and China's retaliatory attack on Vietnam the following year, which the Vietnamese viewed as an assault on their national sovereignty and an aggressive strike of Sinoization. See Pike, "USSR and Vietnam." Furthermore, both Cuba and Vietnam served as members of the Soviet-controlled Council for Mutual Economic Assistance (CMEA) and were recipients of generous economic assistance from the USSR. See Thakur and Thayer, *Soviet Relations with India and Vietnam,* 3, 5, 13.

21. RGASPI, f. 27-M, op. 1, d. 252, ll. 21–22.

22. RGASPI, f. 27-M, op. 1. d. 253, ll. 122, 124.

23. On the "I Am the Master of the Project" campaign, see RGASPI, f. 27-M, op. 1, d. 300, l. 22.

24. Shcherbin is in ibid. and RGASPI, f. 27-M, op. 1, d. 299, l. 10.

25. Ibid.

26. This secret document is in GA RF, f. R-5474, op. 20, d. 8199, l. 124.

27. For a detailed discussion of the "Northern Territories" controversy, see Hara, *Japanese-Soviet/Russian Relations since 1945,* 13–33 and 113–50. After World War II, the Soviet Union and Japan began a fruitless process of negotiating ownership of the three southernmost islands in the Kuriles chain—Etorofu, Kunashiri, and Shikotan—and a group of islets known as the Habomais, which were seized by the Red Army in 1945.

28. The Japanese term *keiretsu* describes such large, family-owned monopolies as Mitsubishi, Sony, or Sumitomo that play a strong economic and political role in the oligarchical

system some Western observers have called "Japan, Inc." On "bolstering fraternal relations with our Japanese communist comrades," see RGASPI, f. 27-M, op. 1, d. 253, l. 123; and RGASPI, f. 27-M, op. 1, d. 332, l. 10.

29. Shtikov, interview.

30. On the "approximately ten thousand non-Soviet youth," see Smirnova, "Internatsional'nyi studencheskii otriad na BAMe," 4. Ponomarev, "Aktual'nye problemy," 37–71; and Ul'ianovskii, "Nekotorye voprosy," 109–19.

31. On forced labor during the BAM attempt from 1943 to 1953, see Elant'seva, "Iz istorii stroitel'stva zheleznoi dorogi," 90–100.

32. Nikitin, interview; and Shtikov, interview.

33. Keler, "Mosty," 3.

34. Colton, *Dilemma of Reform*, 196.

35. Regarding the official optimism in Moscow and Havana in the early to mid-1970s on the growing appeal of socialist ideas among the peoples living within an area that the USSR once considered to be firmly within the United States's sphere of influence, see V. Alekseev, "Problemy BAMa v burzhuaznoi istoriografii," 2; Donaldson, *Soviet Union in the Third World*; Gelman, *Soviet Union in the Third World*; Gouré and Rothenberg, *Soviet Penetration of Latin America*; Lowenthal, "Soviet 'Counterimperialism'"; and Menon, *Soviet Power and the Third World*.

36. Mukonin's comments are in RGASPI, f. 27-M, op. 1, d. 123, l. 71.

37. Ibid., ll. 71–72; and RGASPI, f. 27-M, op. 1, d. 138, ll. 158–60.

38. Esquina's conditions are in RGASPI, f. 27-M, op. 1, d. 160, ll. 1–14.

39. The U.S.-supported and authoritarian leader Fulgencio Batista (1902–75) dominated Cuban politics from 1933 until Castro's populist "26th of July" movement overthrew Batista's regime in January 1959. See Miller, *Soviet Relations with Latin America*, 43–44.

40. Esquina in RGASPI, f. 27-M, op. 1, d. 160, ll. 1–14.

41. On the joint competition, see RGASPI, f. 27-M, op. 1, d. 116, ll. 21–22.

42. Soviet contacts with Cuba increased throughout the 1970s, due in large part to the joint Soviet-Cuban intervention in Angola in 1975 and 1976, when Cuban and Soviet "advisers" assisted soldiers of the Marxist Movimento Popular de Libertacao de Angola (MPLA, or the Popular Movement for the Liberation of Angola) who were fighting against the Chinese-supported Frente Nacional de Libertacao de Angola (FNLA, or the Angolan Liberation National Front) and the U.S.-sponsored Uniao Nacional para a Independencia Total de Angola (UNITA, or the National Union for the Total Independence of Angola). See Klinghoffer, "Soviet Union and Angola." Cuba and the Soviet Union also supported the socialist regime of Colonel Mengistu Haile Mariam during their joint 1977–78 intervention in Ethiopia. See Remnek, "Soviet Policy in the Horn of Africa."

43. Mironova, interview.

44. Shestak, "'Sibirskaia simfonia' Raulia Larra," 4. Also, BAMtonnelstroi was responsible for all tunnel construction along the railway's path and was subordinate to GlavBAMstroi, itself a division of the USSR Ministry of Transport Construction that was responsible for overseeing and completing all BAM-related rail and building construction.

45. Comments on *Siberian Symphony* are from Sushchevich, interview, April 19, 2000.

46. Regarding the relationship between Allende and Brezhnev between 1970 and 1973, see Miller, *Soviet Relations with Latin America*, 141.

47. Lakomov's story is in RGASPI, f. 27-M, op. 1, d. 170, ll. 6–7.

48. Ibid., l. 7.

49. Angarstroi was a division of GlavBAMstroi responsible for overseeing and completing all BAM-related rail and building construction along the portion of the railway running along the Angara River in the Irkutsk region. The Chileans' petition to their commander is in RGASPI, f. 5474-R, op. 20, d. 8199, l. 83.

50. RGASPI, f. 27-M, op. 1, d. 170, ll. 6–7.

51. Nikitin, interview. In Peru, Maoism was making headway in the form of the Shining Path insurgents and represented an area of concern for Soviet strategists regarding the USSR's relationship with Chile.

52. Elant'seva, "Mesto foto-kinodokumentov v osveshchenii istorii stroitel'stva BAMa."

53. Seifert and Lindig are described in Popov, "Iz 42 stran," 2.

54. See, for example, Andreev and Sungorkin, "Novosel na BAMe," 2; Arokhorov, "Na dalekom 167-m," 3; Bobrovskii, "Ul'kan prinimaet gostei," 4; Iakovlev, "Trassa," 2; Serezdinova, "Khorosheet rodnaia Sibir'," 2; and Volina, "Obyknovennaia romantika," 3.

55. Tomina, "Vladek snova edet na BAM." See also Tomina, "Pesnia—Tozhe oruzhie."

56. Brückner, "Trudovoi semestr na BAMe," 1.

57. Smirnova, "Internatsional'nyi studencheskii otriad na BAMe," 4.

58. Ibid.

59. Westfalia and Ostertag are mentioned in Kolesova, "Magistral' druzhby."

60. Nikitin, interview.

61. Privalov, "Byla by v Indii Sibir'," 1.

62. Kniazev's report is in RGASPI, f. 27-M, op. 1, d. 82, ll. 15–16.

63. Ibid., l. 15.

64. Ibid., l. 16.

65. Ibid.

66. Pilkington, for instance, has noted that both Communist Party and Komsomol observers reported that Soviet BAMers also remarked at the primitive level of their housing conditions, but that this phenomenon began only after Gorbachev's rise to power in 1985. See Pilkington, *Russia's Youth and Its Culture*, 99.

67. Established in 1960, the Patrice Lumumba Peoples' Friendship University was named for Patrice Emergy Lumumba (1925–61), a prominent African socialist and first prime minister of the Republic of the Congo. Lumumba was assassinated with the collusion of the Congo's former Belgian colonial masters and, some scholars maintain, the United States. After a U.S.-supported military coup led by Colonel Mobutu Sese Seko in 1970, Congo became the Republic of Zaire and was under Mobutu's strict control until his displacement in May 1997 by rebel forces under the leadership of Laurent Kabila. Now known as the Democratic Republic of the Congo, this resource-rich nation continues to endure political instability as Kabila himself was overthrown in early 2001.

68. The "thirtieth anniversary of victory" is a reference to the 1945 Soviet victory in World War II.

69. On the Friendship Brigade, see "Interotriad—BAMu," 1; and RGASPI, f. 1-M, op. 39, d. 555, ll. 5–17.

70. Gonsalo Alvarado is mentioned in Petruk, "Tri kontinenta na BAMe," 2.

71. Ibid.

72. Waganda, interviews.

73. See Evgenii A. Evtushenko, *Bratskaia GES: Stikhi i poema* (Moscow: Sovetskii pisatel', 1967).

74. Petruk, "Tri kontinenta na BAMe," 2.

75. Attanaiake's comments are in Privalov, "Byla by v Indii Sibir'," 1.

76. Nizhneangarsktransstroi was a BAM construction subdivision based in the settlement of Severobaikalsk and organizationally similar to Angarstroi.

77. The Videoton electronics factory anecdote is in RGASPI, f. 27-M, op. 1, d. 128, l. 36.

78. On these bribes, see RGASPI, f. 27-M, op. 1, d. 279, ll. 140–41.

79. Ibid., l. 141.

80. Radtke's 1974 letter to the Komsomol Central Committee is in RGASPI, f. 1-M, op. 45, d. 297, ll. 41, 43, 135, 137. The November 1974 communication from a group of Dresden students is mentioned in Mironova, interview.

81. The Czechoslovak petition from 1978 is in RGASPI, f. 27-M, op. 1, d. 207, l. 7.

82. The Komsomol's response is in ibid., l. 8.

83. This 1983 request by twenty-eight Czechoslovaks is in RGASPI, f. 27-M, op. 1, d. 300, l. 64.

84. RGASPI, f. 27-M, op. 1, d. 207, ll. 13–14.

85. Sushchevich, interview, April 19, 2000.

86. For the Chinese reaction to Wusuli Jiang/Ussuri River incident, see "Clumsy Anti-China Farce Staged by Soviet Revisionist Clique," and "Soviet Revisionism Is U.S. Imperialism's No. 1 Accomplice."

87. On the Zhenbao incident, see "Viewpoints on the Possibility of a Soviet-Chinese War."

88. RGASPI, f. 27-M, op. 1, d. 104, l. 78.

89. Regarding the lectures on Chinese history, language, and culture, see RGASPI, f. 27-M, op. 1, d. 150, l. 56.

90. The lecture series by BAMer members of Znanie are mentioned in RGASPI, f. 27-M, op. 1, d. 183, l. 49.

91. Manoilenko's speech is mentioned in ibid., ll. 49–52.

92. Ibid.

CHAPTER 7. Conclusion: Brezhnev's Folly in Perspective

Epigraph: Popular BAM joke, circa 1980.

1. Kogatko, "Mify i real'nost'," 5.

2. Matvieva, "Respublika BAMa," 11.

3. Loktev and Orlov, "My stroim BAM, BAM stroit nas," 14.

4. Lebedev and Sushchevich, interviews.

5. See Shchegolev, "Poezd do stantsii Kuanda," 2; "Etot samyi schastlivyi den'!" 1; Kokhan, "Na ravnykh," 7; and "Prazdnik v Kuande," 1, 3.

6. Rassweiler, *Generation of Power.*

7. Perevedentsev, "Kuda idet doroga?"; Quinn-Judge, "Pragmatists and Pioneers Near the End of the Line"; Mote, "BAM, Boom, Bust"; and Sushchevich, "Nas mnogo, veterany!"

8. On the divorce rate, see Shlapentokh, *Love, Marriage, and Friendship,* 171–211.

9. Mironova, interview.

10. Ivanov, "BAM nachnet zhit' na mednye den'gi," 4.

11. See Ianitskii, *Ekologicheskoe dvizhenie v Rossii* and *Ekologiia, demokratiia, molodezh'.*

12. Granberg and Kuleshov, *Region BAM.*

13. See Chernomyrdin, "O pervoocherdnykh merakh," 5; Seleznev, "Postanovlenie Gosudarstvennoi Dumy," 1; and Primakov, *Postanovlenie Pravitel'stva Rossiiskoi Federatsii ot 19 ianvaria 1999 g. No. 69.*

14. "Russians Finally Complete BAM."

15. Lebedev, interview; and Yates and Zvegintzov, "Winnowing the Truth from Dubious Information."

16. Ivanov, "BAM nachnet zhit' na mednye den'gi," 4; Quinn-Judge, "Pragmatists and Pioneers Near the End of the Line," 25–27; Selivanov, "Plokhoe nasledstvo ili budushchee Rossii?" 1; and Specter, "Siberian Railroad," 7.

SELECTED BIBLIOGRAPHY

PRIMARY SOURCES

Archives and Library Repositories

Central Scientific-Technical Library of Russian Railway Transport, Moscow
Institute for Information on Social Sciences of the Russian Academy of Sciences
Irkutsk Oblast Center of Contemporary History Documents, Irkutsk (TsDNI IO)
- f. 127   Perechen' voprosov obkoma KPSS Irkutskoi oblasti
- f. 185   Perechen' voprosov, rassmotrennykh na zasedanii sekretariataIrkutskogo obkoma VLKSM (1969–92 gg.)
Museum of Railway Forces Library, Shchelkovo
Russian State Archive of Contemporary History, Moscow (RGANI)
- f. 5   Apparat TsK KPSS, 1952–84 gg.
- f. 89   Dokumenty, predstavlennym v Konstitutsionnyi sud RossiiskoiFederatsii po "delu KPSS"
Russian State Archive of the Economy, Moscow (RGAE)
- f. 364   Tsentral'nyi nauchno-issledovatel'skii institut informatsii,tekhniko-ekonomicheskikh issledovaniia i propagandazheleznodorozhnogo transporta (TsNIITEI) MPS SSSR i egopredshestvenniki, 1931–91
- f. 544   Komissiia po zapovednikam i okhrane prirody i laboratoriiaokhrany prirody, 1951–79
Russian State Archive of Social-Political History, Moscow (RGASPI)
- f. 1-M   Tsentral'nyi Komitet (TsK) VLKSM (1918–91 gg.)
- f. 6-M   Vsesoiuznye s"ezdy VLKSM (1918–91 gg.)
- f. 17-M   Tsentral'nyi Shtab studencheskikh otriadov TsK VLKSM
- f. 27-M   Shtab TsK VLKSM na stroitel'stve BAM
Russian State Library, Moscow
State Archive of the Russian Federation, Moscow (GA RF)
- f. A-259   Sovet ministrov RSFSR (Sovmin RSFSR), 1917–91
- f. A-262   Gosudarstvennyi planovyi komitet RSFSR (Gosplan RSFSR), 1925–90
- f. A-385   Verkhovnyi Sovet RSFSR, 1937–90
- f. A-404   Vserossiiskoe obshchestvo okhrany prirody (VOOP)
- f. A-410   Ministerstvo torgovli RSFSR (1924–91) i ego predshestvenniki,1924–91
- f. A-411   Ministerstvo finansov RSFSR (Minfin RSFSR), 1917–91
- f. A-501   Ministerstvo kul'tury RSFSR, 1953–91
- f. A-533   Gosudarstvennyi komitet Soveta Ministrov RSFSR po delamstroitel'stva (Gosstroi RSFSR), 1959–90
- f. A-546   Komitet po kinematorgrafii pri Sovete Ministrov RSFSR (Goskino RSFSR), 1963–88
- f. R-5474 Tsentral'nye komitety professional'nykh soiuzov rabochikh zheleznodorozhnogo transporta, 1919–
- f. R-9613 Redaktsii i izdatel'stva profsoiuznykh gazet, 1920–

Interviews

Buldakov, Vladimir P. (member of the Russian Academy of Sciences Institute of History). Interview by author. March 19, 1998. Moscow.

Karpikov, Aleksandr V. (geologist at Irkutsk State Technical University). Interview by author. May 8–10, 2000. Irkutsk.

Kasischke, Eric S. (researcher with the Environmental Research Institute of Michigan and associate professor of geography at the University of Maryland at College Park). Interview by author. October 22, 1997. Durham, N.C.

Kozlov, Vladimir A. (assistant director of the State Archive of the Russian Federation). Interview by author. March 26, 1998. Moscow.

Lebedev, Oleg M. (director of the Railway Forces Museum). Interview by author. April 3, 2000. Shchelkovo.

Mironova, Galina (editor at the *Molodaia gvardiia* publishing house). Interview by author. December 2, 1999. Mytishchi.

Nikitin, Nikolai V. (former BAMer and student at the Tomsk Polytechnic Institute). Interview by author. April 19, 2000. Moscow.

Shtikov, Nikolai N. (Irkutsk Pedagogical Institute, former BAM Zone resident). Interview by author. May 7, 2000. Irkutsk.

Sushchevich, Valentin A. (BAM Society founder). Interview by author. October 4, 1999, and April 19, 2000. Russian Youth Organizations Headquarters, Moscow.

Tokareva, Galina M. (head of the reading room at the Russian State Archive of Social and Political History). Interview by author. September 17, 1999, and May 5, 2000. Moscow.

Waganda, Michael (former student at Patrice Lumumba Peoples' Friendship University). Interview by author. October 15, 1999, and March 9, 2000. Moscow.

Newspaper and Journal Articles

Adzhiev, Murad E. "Ekonomiko-geograficheskie problemy BAM." *Priroda* 8 (August 1975): 3–11.

Aganbegian, Abel. "BAM—mashtab ekonomiki sotsializma." *Kommunist* 15 (October 1985): 34–45.

Alekseev, A. I. "Po marshrutam Baikalo-Amurskoi magistrali." *Voprosy istorii* 9 (1976): 112–22.

Alekseev, V. "Problemy BAMa v burzhuaznoi istoriografii." *BAM*, July 13, 1984, 2.

Andreev, N., and V. Sungorkin. "Novosel na BAMe." *Komsomolskaia pravda*, June 4, 1980, 2.

Andreeva, T. "Khozraschet bez rascheta." *Amurskii komsomolets*, November 27, 1974, 2.

———. "Kogda v tovarishchakh soglas'ia net." *Amurskii komsomolets*, July 31, 1974, 2.

———. "Rabota, v kotoroi net melochei." *Amurskii komsomolets*, December 10, 1975, 2.

———, and V. Fronin. "So Zlobinym, po-Zlobinski!" *Komsomolskaia pravda*, June 28, 1975, 2.

Anikin, N. "BAM: Stroika veka, trassa muzhestva." *Gudok*, July 28, 1974, 2.

Antoshkin, Evgenii. "Ust'-Kut—Zvezdnyi." *Molodaia gvardiia* 5 (May 1976): 30–34.

"ArmBAMstroi: Ukrepliaem pozitsii." *Stroitel' BAM*, October 2, 1975, 3.

Arokhorov, S. "Na dalekom 167-m." *Gudok*, June 18, 1974, 3.

Arov, B. "Kamen' lezhachii sdaetsia." *Iuzhnaia pravda*, August 29, 1982, 3.

Azhenov, M. S. "Razvitie sotsial'noi struktury Kazakhstana v usloviiakh sotsializma." *Voprosy filosofii* 8 (1980): 44–51.

Baliev, Aleksei. "U BAMa—vtoroe dykhanie." *Rossiiskaia gazeta*, July 1, 1997, 5.

"BAM—doroga mira." *Izvestiia*, April 12, 1975, 3.

"BAM—doroga skvoz' stoletiia." *Izvestiia*, May 6, 1978, 5.

"BAM: Do vstrechi 100 kilometrov." *Pravda*, July 10, 1984, 1, 3.

"BAM: God rabochoi biografii." *Izvestiia*, January 2, 1982, 1.

"BAM: Peremeny na trasse." *Gudok*, September 5, 1975, 3.

"BAM prodolzhaetsia." *Izvestiia*, November 5, 1984, 2.

"BAM—stroika vsenarodnaia." *Gudok*, August 8, 1974, 1.

"BAM—stroika vsenarodnaia." *Pravda*, August 7, 1974, 1.

"BAM stroit vsia strana." *Pravda*, January 29, 1976, 1.

Barichko, V. "Ogniu—zaslon! Legche predupredit'." *BAM*, November 2, 1983, 4.

Basin, E. "BAM—skoro pusk." *Pravda*, November 1, 1989, 1–2.

Bauer, V. "GTO na BAM." *Gudok*, July 11, 1974, 4.

Berezovskii, V. "Kontury kompleksa." *Izvestiia*, January 22, 1976, 2.

Bobrovskii, A. "Ul'kan prinimaet gostei." *Komsomol'skoe znamia*, October 7, 1975, 4.

Bogatko, Sergei. "Energiia dlia BAMa—1. Vysokoe napriazhenie." *Pravda*, October 10, 1982, 2.

———. "Energiia dlia BAMa—2. Zeia, Bureia." *Pravda*, October 11, 1982, 2.

———. "Po krasnomu punktiru." *Pravda*, January 28, 1979, 3.

———. "Put' k okeanu: Tam, gde proidet Baikalo-Amurskaia magistral'. 1. Zakoldovannaia Chara." *Pravda*, May 18, 1974, 3.

———. "Put' k okeanu: Tam, gde proidet Baikalo-Amurskaia magistral'. 2. Broskom-na sever!" *Pravda*, May 19, 1974, 2.

———. "S otkloneniem." *Pravda*, October 25, 1983, 2.

Bondarenko, V. "Platsdarm na trasse." *Gudok*, July 14, 1974, 2.

———. "Shirokii shag pervoprokhodtsev." *Gudok*, September 4, 1974, 3.

Borodin, O. "Pochemu den'gi dlia Baikalo-Amurskoi magistrali ne budut." *Izvestiia*, January 24, 1987, 1.

Bostrukhov, E. "Golovnoi uchastok magistrali." *Izvestiia*, September 3, 1975, 1.

Brezhnev, Leonid I. "Pobeda stroitelei BAMa." *Izvestiia*, May 22, 1975, 1.

Brobkin, V. "Budet li krasivnim Neriungri?" *Pravda*, April 10, 1981, 3.

Brückner, Kristian. "Trudovoi semestr na BAMe." *Vechernii Kishinev*, October 6, 1975, 1.

Cherepanova, P. "Okhrane prirody—neoslabnoe vnimanie." *BAM*, February 12, 1982, 4.

———. "Okhrana vod—nasha obiazannost'." *BAM*, February 4, 1983, 4.

Chernomyrdin, V. "O pervoocherdnykh merakh po stimulirovaniiu ekonomicheskogo razvitiia zony Baikalo-Amurskoi zheleznodorozhnoi magistrali." *Rossiiskaia gazeta*, July 1, 1997, 5.

Chichkanov, V. "Problemy i perspektivy dlia razvitiia proizvoditel'nykh silakh na Dal'nom Vostoke." *Kommunist* 16 (November 1985): 93–103.

Chiriaev, G. I. "BAM i Iakutiia." *Ekonomicheskaia gazeta* 32 (August 1974): 5.

Chudnovskii, O. "Schast'e sluzhit' liudam." *BAM*, July 30, 1982, 3.

"Clumsy Anti-China Farce Staged by Soviet Revisionist Clique." *Peking Review* 12 (March 21, 1969): 11–12.

Connoly, Violet. "The Second Trans-Siberian Railway." *Asian Affairs* 62, no. 1 (1975): 23–29.

Danielov, S. "Sushchestvennye 'melochi'." *Tikhookeanskaia zvezda,* August 11, 1975, 2.

Davydenko, V. "S alymi bantami na grudi." *Amurskaia pravda,* April 18, 1976, 2.

Degtiarev, V. "Donbass-BAMu." *Pravda,* May 23, 1975, 2.

Derevianko, A. P., and E. V. Ermakova. "Stroitel'stvo Baikalo-Amurskoi zheleznodorozh-noi magistrali: Istorigrafiia problemy." *Istoriia SSSR* 1 (January–February 1987): 123–36.

"Dlia tekh, kto stroit BAM." *Izvestiia,* August 13, 1975, 1.

Dmitriev, V. "Obzhivaia dalekie kraia." *Pravda,* October 21, 1979, 3.

Doak, Kevin M. "What Is a Nation and Who Belongs? National Narratives and the Ethnic Imagination in Twentieth-century Japan." *American Historical Review* 102, no. 2 (April 1997): 283–309.

Donchenko, I. "Nam morozy ne strashny." *Rabochee slovo,* November 16, 1974, 1.

Drannikov, V. "Daesh' Baikal, daesh' Amur!" *Gudok,* April 27, 1974, 1, 3.

Druzenko, Anatolii. "Chelovek v taige." *Izvestiia,* August 24, 1984, 2.

———. "Defitsit . . . ot izbytka." *Izvestiia,* August 31, 1984, 2.

———. "Magistral' i pashnia." *Izvestiia,* August 3, 1984, 2.

———. "Ot Baikala do Amura prolozhiki magistral'!" *Izvestiia,* September 30, 1984, 1–2.

———. "Shefy i shefstvo." *Izvestiia,* July 13, 1984, 2.

———. "Skala bez znaka kachestva." *Izvestiia,* September 7, 1984, 2.

———. "S tochki zreniia zakazchika." *Izvestiia,* August 17, 1984, 2.

Druzhenko, A., and B. Reznik. "Na BAMe." *Izvestiia,* August 21, 1987, 2.

"Dvizhenie otkryto." *Pravda,* November 5, 1980, 1.

"Dvoe na proseke." *Izvestiia,* April 14, 1977, 2.

Dvornikov, E. "Tam, gde Leny razbeg: S bloknotom po strane." *Pravda,* September 4, 1975, 1.

Dymova, M. "Nesluchainyi vybor." *BAM,* July 30, 1982, 4.

"Edem my, druz'ia, v dal'nie kraia!" *Izvestiia,* April 30, 1974, 1, 6.

Elantseva, Olga P. "BAM: Pervoie desiatiletie." *Otechestvennaia istoriia* 6 (November–December 1994): 89–103.

———. "Iz istorii stroitel'stva zhelezhnoi dorogi Komsomol'sk-Sovetskaia Gavan' (1943–45 gg.)." *Otechestvennye arkhivy* 3 (1995): 90–100.

———. "Kto i kak stroil BAM v 30-e gody?" *Otechestvennye arkhivy* 5 (1992): 71–81.

———. "Periodicheskaia pechat' BAMlaga." *Otechestvennaia istoriia* 4 (July–August 1993): 167–75.

Emelianov, A. "Paren' iz Khashuri." *Stroitel' BAM,* September 18, 1975, 3.

Ermolaev, V. "Led i plamen'." *Pravda,* February 3, 1978, 6.

———. "Zhivaia voda Baikala." *Pravda,* October 8, 1978, 3.

———, and Iu. Kaz'min. "Na vtorykh putiakh." *Pravda,* November 10, 1978, 2.

Ermolaev, V., Iu. Kaz'min, and A. Starukhin. "Chetyre goda spustia." *Pravda,* July 3, 1978, 2.

———. "Podnimaiutsia goroda." *Pravda,* July 5, 1978, 3.

Ermolaev, V., et al. "Glavnoe-put'! 3. Eshche raz o tylakh." *Pravda,* May 8, 1979, 2.

———. "Glavnoe-put'! 1. Piat' let spustia." *Pravda,* May 5, 1979, 2.

———. "Glavnoe-put'! 2. Mosty i tonneli." *Pravda,* May 7, 1979, 2.

———. "Ot Baikala do Amura. 1. Poezda idut po raspisaniiu." *Pravda,* January 3, 1981, 2.

———. "Ot Baikala do Amura. 2. Skvoz' gory i taigu." *Pravda,* January 5, 1981, 2.

———. "Ot Baikala do Amura. 3. Riadom s mashstral'iu." *Pravda,* January 6, 1981, 2.

"Etot samyi schastlivyi den'!" *Izvestiia,* October 1, 1984, 1.

Ezhelev, A., and V. Sukhachevskii. "Vse reshali sekundy." *Izvestiia*, August 27, 1984, 6.

Fedin, Vasilii M. "BAM—simvol trudovoi doblesti." *Komsomol'skaia zhizn'* 8 (April 1975): 2–8.

Fedina, S. "Bamovtsy iz odnogo sela." *BAM*, September 12, 1979, 4.

"Fevralsk vstrechaet passazhirskii." *Izvestiia*, September 21, 1983, 1.

"Final Rails Laid on Key Line to Open Up Siberian Riches." *New York Times*, September 30, 1984, 16.

Fokin, Iurii. "BAM: Ot Ust-Kuta do Kunermy." *Gudok*, April 5, 8, and 9, 1975, 2.

———. "Most cherez Lenu." *Gudok*, June 10, 1975, 2.

———. "Schastlivaia Eva Dudash i ee druz'ia." *Gudok*, July 27, 1975, 2.

———. "Skaz o trasse." *Gudok*, May 1, 1975, 2.

Gagina, T., V. Skalon, and F. Shtilmark. "Beregite taigu!" *Izvestiia*, December 18, 1974, 3.

Gomboev, A. "Belye ptitsy Muiskoi doliny." *Molodezh Buriatii*, December 18, 1982, 2.

Gorbunov, V. "'Materik budushchego'." *Pravda*, June 13, 1984, 2.

Gorin, I. "I vnov' prodolzhaetsia BAM." *Sovesednik* 20 (1985): 8–9.

Gorsuch, Anne E. "Soviet Youth and the Politics of Popular Culture during NEP." *Social History* 17 (May 1992): 189–201.

———. "A Woman Is Not a Man: The Culture of Gender and Generation in Soviet Russia, 1921–1928." *Slavic Review* 55, no. 3 (Fall 1996): 636–60.

Guber, Aleksandr. "Pervoprokhodets—eto professiia?" *Izvestiia*, December 11, 1983, 2.

Gulkevich, A. "Ia—khoziain stroiki. Zelenogradskie uroki." *Amurskii komsomolets*, December 25, 1975, 2.

Gureev, G., B. Stepyko, and V. Ilin. "Kazhdyi den'—udarnyi!" *Gudok*, September 18, 1974, 1.

Gurko, T. A. "Vliianie dobrachnogo povedeniia na stabil'nost' molodoi sem'i." *Sotsiologicheskie issledovaniia* 2 (1982): 88–93.

Hirsch, Francine. "The Soviet Union as a Work-in-Progress: Ethnographers and the Category *Nationality* in the 1926, 1937, and 1939 Censuses." *Slavic Review* 56, no. 2 (Summer 1997): 251–78.

Hollinger, David A. "How Wide the Circle of the 'We'? American Intellectuals and the Problem of Ethnos since World War II." *American Historical Review* 98, no. 2 (April 1993): 317–37.

Iakovlev, Aleksandr. "Trassa: Pis'ma, dnevniki, zapiski nashego sovremennika." *Komsomolskaia pravda*, December 2, 1975, 2.

Iankovskii, A. "Pervaia vesna." *Gudok*, June 6, 1974, 2.

———. "Poezd idet na vostok." *Gudok*, April 30, 1974, 4.

———. "Put' v Zvezdnyi." *Gudok*, June 16, 1974, 3.

———. "Taezhnyi desant." *Gudok*, June 4, 1974, 2.

———, and V. Kurkov. "Solntsu i vetru navstrechu." *Gudok*, May 1, 1974, 4.

Iastrebtsov, G. "Kilometr za kilometrom." *Pravda*, May 24, 1983, 3.

Ibragimova, Z. "Doroga v zavtra." *Ekonomika i organizatsiia promyshlennogo proizvodstva* 2 (March–April 1976): 55–72.

"Idet ugol' Iakutii!" *Izvestiia*, October 27, 1978, 1.

Ignatenko, A. "Tochka prilozheniia." *Baikalo-Amurskaia magistral'*, March 28, 1975, 3.

"Interotriad—BAMu." *Amurskii komsomolets*, July 9, 1975, 1.

Isakov, G. "Sibir' vstrechaet stroitelei BAMa." *Gudok*, May 7, 1974, 1.

———. "Tyly stroiki." *Gudok,* June 11, 1974, 2.

Ishechkin, V. "Elektronnyi dvoinik magistrali." *Gudok,* August 13, 1974, 2.

Ivanchenko, Aleksandr. "Zoloto dlia BAMa." *Novyi mir* 4 (April 1984): 55–111.

Ivanov, Nikolai. "BAM nachnet zhit' na mednye den'gi." *Kommersant,* March 4, 2000, 4.

Josephson, Paul R. "Atomic-Powered Communism: Nuclear Culture in the Postwar USSR." *Slavic Review* 55, no. 2 (Summer 1996): 297–324.

Kadzhaia, Valerii. "Poselok na trasse." *Iunost* 4 (1977): 91–95.

Kalinichev, V. "Taezhnye kilometry BAMa." *Izvestiia,* May 18, 1977, 2.

Kampeev, E. "Vsesoiuznyi agitpokhod na prostorakh Leny." *Leninskie maiaki,* July 31, 1975, 1.

Kapeliushnyi, L. "Diplomy na vyrost?" *Izvestiia,* January 7, 1982, 3.

Kazmin, Iurii. "Dlinnye kilometry—1. Tri goda spustia." *Pravda,* July 13, 1977, 2.

———. "Dlinnye kilometry—2. Ot peredovoi do tyla." *Pravda,* July 14, 1977, 2.

———. "Sebe i potomkam—1. Brosok v taigu." *Pravda,* September 24, 1974, 2.

———. "Sebe i potomkam—2. Tyly giganta." *Pravda,* September 25, 1974, 2.

———. "Sebe i potomkam—3. Arteriia zhizni." *Pravda,* September 27, 1974, 2.

———. "Vremia nabirat' skorost'—1. Glavnoe-'tselevye zadachi'." *Pravda,* September 5, 1976, 2.

———. "Vremia nabirat' skorost'—2. Rezervy upravleniia." *Pravda,* September 7, 1976, 2.

———, and A. Starukhin. "Tonneli." *Pravda,* December 10, 1979, 2.

———, and G. Petrov. "Vremia nabirat' skorost'. 3. BAM—kliuch k sokrovishcham." *Pravda,* September 8, 1976, 2.

———, and Z. Kliuchikov. "Put' otkryt." *Pravda,* December 29, 1979, 1.

———, Z. Kliuchikov, and G. Petrov. "Dlinnye kilometry. 3. Na 'stykakh' berega i moria." *Pravda,* July 16, 1977, 2.

Kedrov, K. "Baikalo-Amurskaia magistral'." *Ekonomicheskaia gazeta* 24 (June 1974): 9.

Keler, Franz. "Mosty." *Izvestiia,* April 12, 1975, 3.

Kenney, Padraic. "The Gender of Resistance in Communist Poland." *American Historical Review* 104, no. 2 (April 1999): 399–425.

Khakhanov, G. "On pogib na postu." *BAM,* December 10, 1980, 4.

Khaliulin, M. et al. "BAM: Pervyi shag." *Gudok,* January 1, 1975, 2.

Khatutsev, V. "Bum i BAM: Pochemu molodaia magistral' ne rabotaet v polniu silu." *Pravda,* June 11, 1987, 2.

Khodii, V. "Tam, gde drozhit zemlia." *Pravda,* September 26, 1975, 3.

Kin, A., and A. Kleva. "Avtodoroga vdol' BAMa." *Izvestiia,* August 30, 1983, 1.

"Kinoletopis' trudovogo podviga." *Gudok,* August 25, 1974, 4.

Kleva, A. "Svoi pered sboikoi." *Izvestiia,* March 12, 1984, 1.

Kokhan, E. "Na ravnykh." *Zolotoe zveno,* October 1, 1984, 7.

Kolesova, S., and V. Sungorkin. "Pomidor-gastroler." *Komsomolskaia pravda,* November 16, 1977, 2.

Konovalov, B. "Strategiia osvoeniia severa." *Izvestiia,* September 23, 1984, 2.

Kozenko, A. "Ot Urgala do Komsomol'ska-na-Amure: Tol'ko po-udarnomu." *BAM,* October 31, 1980, 4.

———. "Voploshchenie mechty." *BAM,* September 8, 1982, 2.

Kozlovskii, E. "Syp'evye kompleksy BAMa." *Pravda,* November 15, 1978, 2.

Kramer, Mark. "Declassified Materials from CPSU Central Committee Plenums: Sources, Context, Highlights." *Cahiers du Monde russe* 40, nos. 1–2 (January–June 1999): 271–306.

Krivoi, A. "Kuba—BAM." *BAM,* June 30, 1982, 4.

Kulikov, V. I. "Istoricheskii opyt partii po rukovodstvu massovym osvoeniem tseliny i sovremennost'." *Voprosy istorii KPSS* 4 (1984): 108–18.

Kultysheva, Tatiana. "Nas sdruzhila magistral'." *Sovetskaia Rossiia,* May 5, 1984, 1.

Kurkov, V., V. Narinskii, and A. Nakhimovskii. "Trassa zovet molodykh." *Gudok,* May 18, 1974, 2.

Kuznetsov, V. "Rel'sy v taige." *Pravda,* January 4, 1977, 1.

Lapin, S. "Obespechit' nadezhnuiu zashchitu." *BAM,* November 12, 1982, 4.

Lavrinenko, V. "Stroim kharaktery." *Amurskii komsomolets,* January 27, 1978, 1.

"Leningradtsy—nashi gosti: Na Lenskom meridiane." *Leninskii kommunist,* July 15, 1975, 1.

Letov, V. "K severu ot BAMa." *Izvestiia,* November 13, 1979, 1.

———. "Poezd idet k okeanu." *Izvestiia,* July 1, 1979, 2.

Loginov, A. "BAM: rabotat' po-Zlobinski." *Gudok,* July 5, 1975, 2.

———. "Oni prishli!" *Zabaikal'skii rabochii,* May 22, 1975, 2.

———. "Sorevnovaniiu—sravnimost'." *Gudok,* September 17, 1976, 2.

———. "Studencheskie milliony." *Gudok,* October 2, 1975, 2.

Loktev, V., and V. Orlov. "My stroim BAM, BAM stroit nas." *Komsomol'skaia zhizn'* 21 (November 1974): 14–16.

Lowenthal, Richard. "Soviet 'Counterimperialism'." *Problems of Communism* 25 (November–December 1976): 52–63.

Maksimova, L. "Na poklon k dikoi prirode?" *Amurskii komsomolets,* April 12, 1981, 3.

Manukha, A. "Stroiteli verny svoemu slovu." *Gudok,* October 5, 1975, 1.

Matafonov, M. I. "Otkryvaiutsia bol'shie vozmozhnosti." *Izvestiia,* September 30, 1984, 2.

Matafonov, V., and L. Kozelskii. "Na BAM—priamymi marshrutami." *Gudok,* December 9, 1975, 2.

Matvieva, Elena. "Respublika BAMa." *Moskovskie novosti,* December 8, 1993, 11.

Minkovskii, G. M. "Osnovnye etapy razvitiia sovetskoi sistemy mer bor'by s prestupnost'iu nesovershennoletnykh." *Voprosy bor'by s prestupnost'iu* 6 (1967): 37–74.

Molchanov, V. "Ot Baikala do Amura." *Pravda,* July 25, 1974, 1, 3.

Molodiakov, V. "Ekspress: Moskva-BAM." *Gudok,* September 26, 1974, 4.

Molokov, Iurii. "Severnaia nadbavka." *Izvestiia,* February 11, 1981, 2.

Mokhortov, K. V. "BAM nabiraet tempy." *Pravda,* February 11, 1975, 2.

———. "Magistral' druzhby." *Dal'nii vostok* 12 (1982): 115–22.

Morozov, N. "Nash dom—priroda." *BAM,* April 24, 1981, 4.

Moskalev, P., and V. Dmitrienko. "Nauchnyi fundament magistrali." *Gudok,* July 2, 1974, 2.

Mote, Victor L. "BAM, Boom, Bust: Analysis of a Railway's Past, Present, and Future." *Soviet Geography* 31, no. 5 (May 1990): 321–33.

Mozhin, V. P., and V. K. Savelev. "Magistral' i khoziaistvennaia garmoniia." *Ekonomika i organizatsiia promyshlennogo proizvodstva* 2 (March–April 1976): 36–45.

Musalitin, Boris. "Adres srochnogo gruza: BAM. Krepet sodruzhestvo stroitelei i truzhenikov stal'nykh magistralei." *Gudok,* July 23, 1974, 2.

———. "Ritmy udarnoi stroiki." *Gudok,* July 10, 1974, 2.

———. "Vladilena Danilova i ee brigada." *Gudok,* July 12, 1974, 2.

Mustafin, Iamil. "Kak poladit' s prirodoi?" *Molodoi kommunist* 9 (May–October 1982): 59–66.

"My—s BAMa." *Izvestiia,* March 8, 1975, 4.

"My tvoi, magistral', komissary." *Komsomolskaia pravda,* March 25, 1981, 2.

"Nashi dela i dumy s toboi, tovarishch s"ezd!" *Avangard,* February 26, 1976, 2.

Natoka, V. "P'ianstvo—prichina bed." *BAM,* September 2, 1983, 4.

"New Rail Project Dramatizes Soviet Power." *New York Times,* March 9, 1978, 1, 14.

Nikiforova, Valentina, and Ivan Sharov. "BAM i tablitsa Mendeleeva: K nesmetnym bogatst-vam Sibiri i Dal'nego Vostoka vedet legendarnaia doroga." *Pravda,* April 9, 1999, 1–2.

Niskovskikh, Iurii. "A na dushe spokoino i svetlo." *Na smenu,* October 8, 1975, 3.

North, R. N. "The Soviet Far East: New Center of Attention in the USSR." *Pacific Affairs* 51 (1978): 195–215.

"Okhrana prirody—tekhnicheskie reshenia." *BAM,* August 28, 1981, 3.

"Okhrana prirody—zabota obshchaia." *BAM,* January 16, 1981, 1.

"Oknami k Baikalu." *Gudok,* June 12, 1976, 2.

Oleinik, Boris. "Magistral'." Translated by Iurii Denisov. *Molodaia gvardiia* 11 (November 1981): 7.

Orlov, Valerii. "Goroda u magistrali." *Pravda,* March 31, 1984, 3.

———. "Granitnymi koridorami." *Pravda,* December 23, 1983, 2.

———. "Otkryto dvizhenie." *Pravda,* September 29, 1982, 1.

———. "Poezd idet na vostok." *Pravda,* June 30, 1980, and December 1 and 31, 1981, 1.

———. "Riadom s trassoi." *Pravda,* April 9, 1982, 3.

———. "Tonnel'shchiki ne podvedut." *Pravda,* February 28, 1983, 3.

———. "V teni slavy." *Pravda,* November 3, 1983, 3.

———, and G. Iastrebtsov. "U zdeshnikh mest surovaia krasa." *Pravda,* August 30, 1982, 2.

Osipov, I. "Na 'podstupakh' k magistrali." *Gudok,* August 7, 1974, 2.

Osokina, N. "Stroka oplachena sud'boiu." *Sovesednik* 7 (April 1984): 6.

Ovsiannikova, A. "BAM u kostra." *Novyi mir* 12 (December 1977): 198.

Pastukhov, S. "Glavnyi most BAMa v stroiu." *Pravda,* September 27, 1975, 1.

Pekarskii, S. "Baikalo-Amurskaia magistral': Liudi, opyt, problemy." *Kommunist* 7 (May 1977): 47–56.

Perevedentsev, Viktor. "Kuda idet doroga?" *Sovetskaia kul'tura,* October 11, 1988, 3.

Petrov, B. "Na shliupkakh po Lene." *Znamia oktiabria,* July 29, 1975, 1.

Petrov, G. "Nauchnyi fundament BAMa." *Pravda,* September 30, 1975, 2.

Petrov, N. "Daesh' BAM!: Moskva torzhestvenno provodila udarnyi komsomol'skii otriad stroitelei Baikalo-Amurskoi zheleznodorozhnoi magistrali." *Gudok,* April 30, 1974, 1.

Petruk, Iurii. "Tri kontinenta na BAMe." *Moskovskii komsomolets,* January 24, 1975, 2.

Pinneker, E. "Kladovye tepla." *Izvestiia,* November 14, 1978, 2.

Pobozhii, A. "Pervoprokhodtsy." *Gudok,* August 11, 1974, 2.

Podgaev, G. "Kak zhivetsia na BAMe." *Izvestiia,* October 18, 1975, 3.

Polansky, Patricia. "The Russians and Soviets in Asia." *International Library Review* 14 (1982): 217–62.

Ponomarev, B. "Aktual'nye problemy teorii mirovogo revoliutsionnogo protsessa." *Kommunist* 15 (October 1971): 37–71.

Popov, V. "Iz 42 stran." *Vostochno-Sibirskaia pravda,* August 15, 1975, 2.

"Po tselinnoi traditsii." *Pravda,* January 23, 1984, 1.

"Prazdnik v Kuande." *Izvestiia,* October 2, 1984, 1, 3.

"Prebyvanie tovarishcha L. I. Brezhneva v Irkutske." *Izvestiia,* April 4, 1978, 1.

Precoda, Norman. "Winds of Change Blow in Siberia . . . as Viewed from Within." *Environmental Review* 3 (Fall 1978): 2–19.

"Prichina nechast'ia—khalatnost'." *BAM,* January 13, 1982, 4.

Primakov, E. *Postanovlenie Pravitel'stva Rossiiskoi Federatsii ot 19 ianvaria 1999 g. No. 69. Voprosy khoziaistvennogo osvoeniia zony Baikalo-Amurskoi zheleznodorozhnoi magistrali.* Moscow: Respublika, 1999.

Privalov, K. "Byla by v Indii Sibir." *Moskovskii komsomolets,* August 21, 1975, 1.

Prokhorov, B. "BAM: Domashnie zaboty." *Izvestiia,* November 25, 1975, 2.

———. "Utro bol'shoi stroiki." *Izvestiia,* May 8, 1974, 1.

Prokhorov, V. "Profsoiuzy—stroiteliam BAM." *Trud,* August 1, 1974, 13.

Quinn-Judge, Sophie. "Pragmatists and Pioneers Near the End of the Line." *Far Eastern Economic Review* 141, no. 31 (August 4, 1988): 25–27.

Rakowska-Harmstone, Teresa. "The Dialectics of Nationalism in the USSR." *Problems of Communism* 23, no. 3 (May–June 1974): 1–22.

"Raw North Makes Some Wives Pine for Moscow." *New York Times,* March 9, 1978, 14.

"Rech' tovarishcha L. D. Kazakova." *Pravda,* March 4, 1976, 4.

Reznik, B. "Bystrye rel'sy BAMa." *Izvestiia,* November 3, 1982, 1.

Riabova, O., L. Bashinova, and O. Tugutov. "Vypalo nam stroit' put' zheleznyi." *Molodezh' Buriatii,* May 1, 1975, 2.

Riazanov, V. "Kontrasty." *Gudok,* August 16, 1975, 3.

Rotenfeld, B. "Goriachie budni." *Gudok,* August 20, 1974, 3.

"Russians Finally Complete BAM." *International Railway Journal* 44, no. 1 (January 2004).

Sagers, Matthew J. "Baikal-Amur Railway (BAM) Approaching Completion." *Soviet Geography* 30, no. 10 (December 1989): 772–73.

———. "News Notes: Controversial Bypass Constructed through North Muya Range on the Baikal-Amur Railway (BAM)." *Soviet Geography* 31, no. 2 (February 1990): 148–49.

Sandalov, V., et al. "Kto reshit problemy?" *Amurskii komsomolets,* March 23, 1975, 2–3.

Sarkisian, A. "V peredi—BAM!" *Komsomolskaia pravda,* September 18, 1975, 2.

Savinova, L. N. "Zhenshchina v sovetskom obshchestve." *Seriia "Istoriia"* no. 4 (1979): 3–62.

Savostin, Nikolai. "BAM." *Novyi mir* 1 (January 1977): 135–37.

Sechkovskii, Marek. "Devushki trassy." *Izvestiia,* April 12, 1975, 3.

Seleznev, G. "Postanovlenie Gosudarstvennoi Dumy o 25-letii nachala stroitel'stva Baikalo-Amurskoi zheleznodorozhnoi magistrali." *Komsomolskaia pravda,* April 22, 1999, 1.

Selivanov, Sergei. "Plokhoe nasledstvo ili budushchee Rossii? BAM ne zakroiut, nesmotria na to, chto magistral' prinosit odni ubytki." *Izvestiia,* June 3, 1999, 1.

Semenov, M. "Pamiatnye vstrechi." *Gudok,* August 18, 1974, 3.

Seredkin, A. "Sberech' prirodu na BAMe." *Komsomolets Zabaikalia,* May 26, 1976, 2–3.

Serezdinova, Valentina. "Khorosheet rodnaia Sibir'." *Izvestiia,* November 6, 1975, 2.

Sergeev, A. "BAM—zheleznodorozhnaia magistral' pervoi kategorii." *Ekonomicheskaia gazeta* 30 (July 1974): 17.

Sergeev, B. "BAM—stroika veka." *Molodaia gvardiia* 10 (October 1975): 319–20.

Seseikin, V. "Budni trassy." *Gudok,* August 10, 1974, 2.

———. "Problemy stanovleniia." *Gudok,* May 29, 1974, 2.

———. "Tam, za Lenoi-rekoi. Na trasse Baikalo-Amurskoi magistrali gotoviatsia k priemu vsesoiuznogo udarnogo komsomol'skogo stroitel'nogo otriada." *Gudok,* May 1, 1974, 4.

Shchegolev, A. "Poezd do stantsii Kuanda." *Sovetskaia Rossiia,* August 1, 1984, 2.

Shestak, I. M. "'Sibirskaia simfonia' Raulia Larra." *BAM,* July 23, 1982, 4.

Shinkarev, Leonid. "BAM—doroga mira." *Izvestiia,* April 12, 1975, 1.

————. "BAM: Idet pervyi poezd." *Izvestiia,* December 25, 1975, 1.

————. "BAM: Pervye kilometry." *Izvestiia,* June 2, 1974, 1, 4.

————. "BAM: Podymakhiny iz podymakhina." *Izvestiia,* August 25, 1974, 4.

————. "BAM: Prichal'naia stenka." *Izvestiia,* September 25, 1974, 4.

————. "BAM: Takie oni, pervoprokhodtsy." *Izvestiia,* June 11, 1974, 6.

————. "BAM: Vitimskii khod." *Izvestiia,* July 23, 1974, 6.

————. "Bereg iuzhnoi Iakutii." *Izvestiia,* September 9, 1975, 6, and September 15, 1975, 5.

————. "I pochta." *Izvestiia,* November 25, 1975, 2.

————. "Most cherez Lenu." *Izvestiia,* September 24, 1975, 1.

————. "Poezd idet po Iakutii." *Izvestiia,* October 30, 1977, 1.

"Shiritsia sorevnovanie stroitelei Baikalo-Amurskoi." *Gudok,* September 28, 1974, 1.

Shmyganovskii, V. "Morskie vorota BAMa." *Izvestiia,* December 27, 1975, 4.

Shniper, R. I. "V granitsakh obozrimogo budushchego." *Ekonomika i organizatsiia promyshlennogo proizvodstva* 2 (March–April 1976): 22–35.

Shobogorov, P. "BAM toropit geologov." *Izvestiia,* June 8, 1978, 2.

Sinkevich, N. "Doveriaia opytu s mekalke." *Gudok,* June 28, 1974, 2.

Skorobogatov, A. "Etazhi taezhnogo ansamblia dlia velikoi stroiki veka." *Gudok,* April 17, 1976, 4.

————. "Nosite na zdorov'e! Spetsodezhda dlia stroitelei Baikalo-Amurskoi magistrali." *Gudok,* June 6, 1974, 4.

Slezkine, Yuri. "From Savages to Citizens: The Cultural Revolution in the Soviet Far North, 1928–1938." *Slavic Review* 51, no. 1 (Spring 1992): 52–76.

————. "The USSR as a Communal Apartment, or How a Socialist State Promoted Ethnic Particularism." *Slavic Review* 53, no. 2 (Summer 1994): 414–52.

Smirnova, N. "Internatsional'nyi studencheskii otriad na BAMe." *Severnaia pravda,* August 25, 1984, 4.

Solntseva, V. "Galina Panchenko—prodavets." *Baikalo-Amurskaia magistral',* December 16, 1977, 3.

Sosnov, I. "Magistral' veka." *Izvestiia,* March 15, 1980, 2.

"Soviet Revisionism Is U.S. Imperialism's No. 1 Accomplice." *Peking Review* 12 (March 21, 1969): 25–26.

"Sozdadim letopis' vsenarodnoi stroiki." *Gudok,* August 30, 1974, 3.

Specter, Michael. "A Siberian Railroad, from Hero to Disaster." *New York Times,* August 15, 1994, 7.

"S prazdnikom!" *Baikalo-Amurskaia magistral',* March 5, 1976, 3.

Starukhin, A. "Kak 'urezali' gorod." *Pravda,* October 13, 1978, 3.

————. "Zdravstvui, Baikal!" *Pravda,* October 30, 1979, 1.

Stebel'kov, V. "I eto nashe delo." *Avangard,* March 3, 1981, 3.

Stroganov, A. "Novaia stranitsa." *Gudok,* January 31, 1975, 2.

"Stroika nachinaetsia s 'bol'shoi zemli'." *Gudok,* May 30, 1974, 2.

"Stroit BAM vsia strana." *Pravda,* April 8, 1975, 1.

"Stroitel'stvu BAMa—udarnye tempy." *Pravda,* June 8, 1984, 2.

Sungorkin, V. "Stan' chasovym prirody." *Komsomolskaia pravda,* January 7, 1979, 2–3.

Surkov, V., and V. Botvinikov. "Baikalo-Amurskaia magistral': Mineral'nyi kompleks." *Izvestiia,* September 19, 1976, 2.

Sushchevich, Valentin A. "Nas mnogo, veterany!" *BAM,* August 3, 1990, 2.

Suturin, A. "Udarnaia Komsomolskaia: U istokov Baikalo-Amurskoi magistrali." *Gudok,* April 25, 1974, 1, 2, 4.

"Sviaz' nalazhivaetsia." *Pravda,* December 5, 1976, 2.

"Svoe mesto v zhizni." *BAM,* January 16, 1981, 2.

Tatarnikov, A. "Mosty druzhby." *Gudok,* November 18, 1975, 2.

Tenetov, P. "K vostoku ot Baikala." *Izvestiia,* January 22, 1976, 2.

Timakov, V., and O. Baroian. "I mediki stroiat BAM." *Pravda,* June 29, 1976, 3.

Tiurina, E. A., and V. V. Tsaplin. "Iz istorii osvoeniia tselinnykh i zhelezhnykh zemel', 1954–56 gg." *Voprosy istorii* 4 (1979): 110–22.

Tkach, I. "V interesakh pokolenii." *BAM,* July 6, 1984, 3.

"Torgovlia na trasse." *Gudok,* August 8, 1974, 2.

Troshin, A. "Stranitsa pervaia." *Gudok,* August 16, 1974, 4.

Ulianovskii, R. "Nekotorye voprosy nekapitalisticheskogo razvitiia osvobodivshikhsia stran." *Kommunist* 1 (January 1966): 109–19.

Uriumtsev, O. "BAM vstrechaet marafon." *Sovetskaia molodezh',* October 5, 1982, 2.

Usoltsev, A. "Chelovek na BAMe." *Sovetskaia Rossiia* 6, January 8, 1981, 2.

Usov, N. "Schast'e—eto mir." *BAM,* September 22, 1982, 1, 3.

Uspenskii, Vladimir. "V promyshlennoi zone BAMa." *Novyi mir* 2 (February 1981) and 3 (March 1981): 183–95.

Uzorov, M. "Na vakhte Mostootriad No. 43." *Avangard,* February 26, 1976, 2.

Vasilev, O. "V brigade Liudmily Sergeevoi." *BAM,* March 5, 1982, 2.

Verbitskaia, O. M. "Planovoe sel'skokhoziaistvennoe pereselenie v RSFSR v 1946–1958 go-dakh." *Voprosy istorii* 12 (1986): 13–26.

Vezbakh, V. "Miting druzhby i solidarnosti." *Stroitel' BAM,* August 5, 1976, 4.

"Vizit druzhby." *Baikalo-Amurskaia magistral',* October 15, 1976, 1.

Volina, E. "Obyknovennaia romantika." *Gudok,* August 17, 1974, 3.

Volokitin, V. "Sosny u magistrali: Stali predmetom osoboi zaboty komsomol'skikh postov po okhrane prirody, vsekh uchastnikov dvizheniia 'Ia—khoziain stroiki'." *Amurskii komso-molets,* April 12, 1981, 2.

Voronov, V. V., and I. P. Smirnov. "Zakreplenie molodezhi v zone BAMa." *Sotsiologicheskie issledovaniia* 2 (1982): 16–21.

Vostrukhov, E. "Golovnoi uchastok magistrali." *Izvestiia,* September 3, 1975, 1.

Vozin, V. "Iuzhno-Iakutskii TPK: Priroda budet sokhranena." *BAM,* March 25, 1983, 4.

"V Politbiuro TsK KPSS." *Pravda,* March 23, 1984, 1.

"V Politbiuro TsK KPSS." *Pravda,* July 6, 1984, 1.

"V puti!" *Komsomolskaia pravda,* September 28, 1975, 1.

"Vstrecha tovarishcha L. I. Brezhneva so stroiteliami BAMa." *Izvestiia,* April 5, 1978, 1.

Vtorushin, S. "Promyshlennaia zona BAMa." *Pravda,* July 7, 1980, 2.

———, et al. "Sel'skii tsekh BAMa." 1. Riadom s magistral'iu." *Pravda,* September 6, 1981, 2.

———. "Sel'skii tsekh BAMa." 2. 'Tylovye rezervy.'" *Pravda,* September 7, 1981, 2.

Ward, Christopher J. "BAMing It Up: Wanderings around Moscow and Lake Baikal." *Inflections* 5 (December 2000): 3.

———. "Selling the 'Project of the Century': Perceptions of the Baikal-Amur Railway (BAM) in the Soviet Press, 1974–1984." *Canadian Slavonic Papers* 43 (March 2001): 75–95.

Weiner, Douglas R. "Environmental Issues in Eastern Europe and Eurasia: A Look at Recent Scholarship." *NewsNet: The Newsletter of the AAASS* 40 (September 2000): 1–8.

"XXV s"ezdu KPSS—dostoinuiu vstrechu!" *Gudok,* September 6, 1975, 1.

Yates, Athol, and Nicholas Zvegintzov. "Winnowing the Truth from Dubious Information: The Lessons Learned in Writing a Book on a Closed Zone of the Former Soviet Union." *Slovo* 12 (2000): 185–204.

Zhelezko, Sergei N. "Stroiteli Baikalo-Amurskoi magistrali—ob"ekt sotsiologichesko-goissledovaniia." *Sotsiologicheskie issledovaniia* 3 (1976): 104.

"Zhenshchiny vsesoiuznoi udarnoi." *Pobeda,* March 8, 1975, 3.

Zhigailov, Iu. "Put' poezdam otkryt." *Pravda,* February 21, 1981, 6.

Zhunin, I. "Shiritsia front rabot." *Gudok,* March 4, 1975, 1.

Zhuravlev, Vladimir. "Postoiannaia propiska Iakutian-BAM." *Molodezh' Iakutii,* August 10, 1974, 3.

———. "Prinimai, BAM, Iakutian!" *Molodezh' Iakutii,* May 28, 1974, 2–3.

SECONDARY SOURCES

Books

Abdullaev, Iurii N. *BAM—stroika vsenarodnaia, stroika molodezhnaia: V pomoshch' propagandistam, lektoram i komsomol'skomu aktivu.* Tashkent: Uzbekistan, 1976.

Adzhiev, Murad E. *BAM i promyshlennye kompleksy Vostoka SSSR.* Moscow: Znanie, 1978.

Aganbegian, Abel. *The Economic Challenge of Perestroika.* Translated by Pauline M. Tiffen. Bloomington: Indiana University Press, 1988.

———, A. A. Kin, and V. P. Mozhin, eds. *BAM: Stroitel'stvo, khoziaistvennoe osvoenie.* Moscow: Ekonomika, 1984.

Aizenberg, Efim. *Baikalo-Amurskaia magistral': Problemy, pervoochered. Zadachi, perspektivy.* Moscow: Znanie, 1979.

Alekseev, A. I. *Khozhdenie ot Baikala do Amura.* Moscow: Molodaia gvardiia, 1976.

Alexeyeva, Ludmila, and Paul Goldberg. *The Thaw Generation: Coming of Age in the Post-Stalin Era.* Boston: Little, Brown and Company, 1990.

Alkogolizm—put' k prestupleniiu. Moscow: Iuridicheskaia literatura, 1966.

Anderson, Benedict R. *Imagined Communities: Reflections on the Origin and Spread of Nationalism.* 2d ed. London: Verso, 1991.

Antropov, Petr I. *Do vstrechi na BAMe.* Riga, Latvia: Avots, 1981.

Argenbright, Robert T. "The Russian Railroad System and the Founding of the Communist State, 1917–1922." Ph.D. dissertation, University of California, 1990.

Argudiaeva, Iulia V. *Trud i byt molodezhi BAMa: Nastoiashchee i budushchee.* Moscow: Mysl', 1988.

Armstrong, John A. "The Autonomy of Ethnic Identity: Historic Cleavages and Nationality Relations in the USSR." In Alexander J. Motyl, ed., *Thinking Theoretically about Soviet Nationalities: History and Comparison in the Study of the USSR.* New York: Columbia University Press, 1992, 23–43.

———. *Nations before Nationalism.* Chapel Hill: University of North Carolina Press, 1982.

Aksiutin, Iurii V., ed. *L. I. Brezhnev: Materialy k biografii.* Moscow: Izdatel'stvo politicheskoi literatury, 1991.

Bhabha, Homi K., ed. *Nation and Narration.* London: Routledge, 1990.

Baeten, Elizabeth M. *The Magic Mirror: Myth's Abiding Power.* Albany: State University of New York Press, 1996.

Bagramov, Eduard A. *Natsional'nyi vopros v bor'be idei.* Moscow: Izdatel'stvo politicheskoi literatury, 1982.

Baikal i problema chistoi vody v Sibiri. Kollektivnyi doklad Limnologicheskogo izdatel'stva SO AN SSSR, Gosudarstvennogo universiteta imeni A. A. Zhdanova, kafedry obshchii gigeny Irkutskogo Medinstituta i Baikal'skoi basseinovoi inspektsii po ispol'zovaniiu i okhrane vodnykh resursov. Irkutsk: Akademiia nauk SSSR, Sibirskoe otdelenie, and Limnologicheskii institut, 1968.

Baikalo-Amurskaia magistral'—panorama vsenarodnoi stroiki. 1st through 10th editions. Khabarovsk: Khabarovskoe knizhnoe izdatel'stvo, 1975–84.

Bakhtamov, Rafail B. *Azerbaidzhan na BAMe.* Baku, Azerbaijan: Elm, 1978.

BAM—zemlia komsomol'skaia. Panorama vsenarodnoi stroiki. Vypusk chetvertyi—1977 god. Khabarovsk: Khabarovskoe knizhnoe izdatel'stvo, 1978.

BAM—zemlia komsomol'skaia. Panorama vsenarodnoi stroiki. Vypusk odinnadtsatyi—1983 god. Blagoveshchensk: Khabarovskoe knizhnoe izdatel'stvo, Amurskoe otdelenie, 1984.

Baranskaia, Natalia. *A Week Like Any Other.* Translated by Pieta Monks. Seattle: Seal Press, 1989.

Barr, Brenton M. "Forest and Fishing Industries." In Allan Rodgers, ed., *The Soviet Far East: Geographic Perspectives on Development.* London: Routledge, 1990, 114–62.

Belkin, Evgenii V., and Frants E. Sheregi. *Formirovanie naseleniia v zone BAM.* Moscow: Mysl', 1985.

Berman, Marshall. *All That Is Solid Melts into Air: The Experience of Modernity.* New York: Simon and Schuster, 1982.

Bialer, Seweryn, and Thane Gustafson, eds. *Russia at the Crossroads: The Twenty-sixth Congress of the CPSU.* London: Allen and Unwin, 1982.

Bilshai, Vera L. *Reshenie zhenskogo voprosa v SSSR.* 2d edition. Moscow: Gosudarstvennoe izdatel'stvo politicheskoi literatury, 1959.

Bogatko, Sergei. *BAM—Road to New Possibilities.* Moscow: Novosti Press Agency Publishing House, 1981.

———. *Vtoroi put' k okeanu.* Moscow: Molodaia gvardiia, 1975.

Boiko, Vladimir I. "Osobennosti sotsial'nogo upravleniia razvitiem narodov Severa v sviazi so stroitel'stvom BAMa." In *Sotsial'nye problemy stroitel'stva BAMa.* Novosibirsk: Institut istorii, filologii i filosofii SO AN SSSR, 1977, 45–68.

———. *Sotsial'noe razvitie narodov Nizhnego Amura.* Novosibirsk: Nauka, 1977.

———, S. N. Eremin, and V. N. Beloshapkin. *BAM i narody Severa.* Novosibirsk: Nauka, 1979.

Borisov, A. G., and O. K. Mamontova. *Baikalo-Amurskaia zheleznaia doroga imeni Leninskogo komsomola.* Blagoveshchensk: Khabarovskoe knizhnoe izdatel'stvo, Amurskoe otdelenie, 1987.

Bovin, Aleksandr. "Kurs na stabil'nost' porodil zastoi." In Aksiutin, *L. I. Brezhnev,* 92–102.

Brass, Paul R. "Language and National Identity in the Soviet Union and India." In Motyl, *Thinking Theoretically about Soviet Nationalities,* 99–128.

Breuilly, John. *Nationalism and the State.* 2nd edition. Manchester, England: Manchester University Press, 1993.

Brezhnev, Leonid I. *Leonid Ilyich Brezhnev: A Short Biography by the Institute of Marxism-Leninism, CPSU Central Committee.* Oxford: Pergamon Press, 1977.

———. *Pages from His Life.* Oxford: Pergamon Press, 1982.

Brick, Philip D., and R. McGreggor Cawley, eds. *A Wolf in the Garden: The Land Rights Movement and the New Environmental Debate.* Lanham, Md.: Rowman & Littlefield, 1996.

Bridger, Sue. "Young Women and Perestroika." In Linda Edmondson, ed., *Women and Society in Russia and the Soviet Union.* Cambridge: Cambridge University Press, 1992, 178–201.

Brooks, Jeffrey. *Thank You, Comrade Stalin!: Soviet Public Culture from Revolution to Cold War.* Princeton, N.J.: Princeton University Press, 2000.

———. *When Russia Learned to Read: Literacy and Popular Culture, 1861–1917.* Princeton, N.J.: Princeton University Press, 1985.

Brown, Kate. *A Biography of No Place: From Ethnic Borderland to Soviet Heartland.* Cambridge: Harvard University Press, 2004.

Bubiakin, D., ed. *Idut poezda v Iakutiiu: Baikalo-Amurskaia magistral'. Sbornik.* Iakutsk: Knizhnoe izdatel'stvo, 1977.

Buckley, Mary. "Soviet Interpretations of the Woman Question." In Barbara Holland, ed., *Soviet Sisterhood: British Feminists on Women in the USSR.* London: Fourth Estate, 1985, 24–53.

Bushnell, John. *Moscow Graffiti: Language and Subculture.* Boston: Unwin Hyman, 1990.

Byrnes, Robert F., ed. *After Brezhnev: Sources of Soviet Conduct in the 1980s.* Bloomington: Indiana University Press, 1983.

Carrère d'Encausse, Hélène. *Decline of an Empire: The Soviet Socialist Republics in Revolt.* Translated by Martin Sokolinsky and Henry A. La Farge. New York: Newsweek Books, 1980.

———. *The End of the Soviet Empire: The Triumph of Nations.* Translated by Franklin Philip. New York: BasicBooks, 1993.

———. *The Nationality Question in the Soviet Union and Russia.* Oslo, Norway: Scandinavian University Press, 1995.

Ceausescu, Florea. *Baikalo-Amurskaia magistral'.* Moscow: Progress, 1988.

Chalidze, Valery. *Criminal Russia: Essays on Crime in the Soviet Union.* Translated by P. S. Falla. New York: Random House, 1977.

Chase, William J. *Workers, Society, and the Soviet State: Labor and Life in Moscow, 1918–1929.* Urbana: University of Illinois Press, 1987.

Chernenko, Konstantin U. *Speeches and Writings.* Oxford: Pergamon Press, 1984.

Clark, Katerina. *Petersburg, Crucible of Cultural Revolution.* Cambridge: Harvard University Press, 1995.

———. *The Soviet Novel: History as Ritual.* 3rd edition. Bloomington: Indiana University Press, 2000.

Cohen, Stephen F. *Rethinking the Soviet Experience: Politics and History since 1917.* New York: Oxford University Press, 1985.

———, ed., *An End to Silence: Uncensored Opinion in the Soviet Union from Roy Medvedev's Underground Magazine Political Diary.* New York: Norton, 1982.

Colton, Timothy J. *The Dilemma of Reform in the Soviet Union.* 2d edition. New York: Council on Foreign Relations, 1986.

Connor, Walter D. *Deviance in Soviet Society: Crime, Delinquency, and Alcoholism.* New York: Columbia University Press, 1972.

Conn, Phyllis. "Cooperation in Space: The Soviet Space Program and International Science, 1957–1972." Ph.D. dissertation, Indiana University, 1994.

Cottam, Kazimiera J., ed. and trans. *Defending Leningrad: Women behind Enemy Lines.* Revised edition. Nepean, Canada: New Military Publishing, 1998.

———. *On the Road to Stalingrad: Memoirs of a Woman Machine Gunner.* Revised edition. Nepean, Canada: New Military Publishing, 1997.

Cushman, Thomas O. "Ritual and the Sacrilization of the Secular: Social Sources of Conformity and Order in Soviet Society." Ph.D. dissertation, University of Virginia, 1987.

Dadvadze, Bondo I. *Baikalo-Amurskaia magistral': Komsomol Gruzii na BAMe.* Tbilisi, Georgia: Metsniereba, 1977.

Danilova, Ekaterina Z., et al. *Sovetskie zhenshchiny: Nekotorye aspekty polozheniia zhenshchin v SSSR.* Moscow: Progress, 1975.

Davidow, Mike. *The Third Soviet Generation.* Moscow: Progress, 1983.

Denber, Rachel, ed. *The Soviet Nationality Reader: The Disintegration in Context.* Boulder, Colo.: Westview Press, 1992.

"A Deported Nation Appeals to President Mikoyan." In Stephen F. Cohen, ed., *An End to Silence: Uncensored Opinion in the Soviet Union from Roy Medvedev's Underground Magazine* Political Diary. New York: Norton, 1982, 240–44.

Derevianko, A. P., ed. *BAM: Problemy, perspektivy.* Moscow: Molodaia gvardiia, 1976.

Deutsch, Karl W. *Nationalism and Social Communication: An Inquiry into the Foundations of Nationality.* Cambridge: Technology Press of the Massachusetts Institute of Technology, 1953.

———, and William J. Foltz, eds. *Nation-Building.* New York: Atherton Press, 1963.

Dienes, Leslie. "Economic and Strategic Position of the Soviet Far East: Development and Prospect." In Rodgers, *Soviet Far East,* 269–301.

Dobrenko, E. A., ed. *Izbavlenie ot mirazhei: Sotsrealizm segodnia.* Moscow: Sovetskii pisatel', 1990.

Dobrovolskii, G. P., A. A. Koshelev, and V. A. Khanaev, eds. *Toplivno-energeticheskii kompleks zony BAMa.* Irkutsk: Sibirskii energeticheskii institut SO AN SSSR, 1981.

Donaldson, Robert H, ed. *The Soviet Union in the Third World: Successes and Failures.* Boulder, Colo.: Westview Press, 1981.

Druzenko, Anatolii, ed. *Trassa: Ot vyezdnoi redaktsii "Izvestii" na BAMe.* Moscow: *Izvestiia,* 1985.

Edwards, Laura F. *Gendered Strife and Confusion: The Political Culture of Reconstruction.* Urbana: University of Illinois Press, 1997.

Egorov, Nikolai P. *Zori na BAMe.* Ioshkar-Ola: Mariiskoe knizhnoe izdatel'stvo, 1980.

Elantseva, Olga P. "BAM: Nauchno-tekhnicheskoe obespechenie stroitel'stva v 30-e gody." In L. M. Goriushkin, ed., *Rol' nauki v osvoenii vostochnikh raionov strany: Tezisy dokladov i soobshchenii vserossiiskoi nauchnoi konferentsii (17–19 noiabria 1992 g.).* Novosibirsk: Rossiiskaia akademiia nauk, Sibirskoe otdelenie, 1992, 225–27.

———. "Mesto foto-kinodokumentov v osveshchenii istorii stroitel'stva BAMa." In V. P. Bondarenko, ed., *Arkhivy Dal'nego Vostoka Rossii na puti v novoe tysiacheletie: Materialy regional'noi nauchno-praticheskoi konferentsii, posviashchennoi 80-letiiu so dnia prinatiia dekreta Soveta narodnykh komissarov RSFSR "O reorganizatsii i tsentralizatsii arkhivnogo dela v RSFSR."* Vladivostok: Rossiiskii gosudarstvennyi istoricheskii arkhiv Dal'nego Vostoka, 1998, 232–38.

————. *Obrechennaia doroga: BAM, 1932–1941.* Vladivostok: Izdatel'stvo Dal'nevostochnogo universiteta, 1994.

————. *Stroitel'stvo no. 500 NKVD SSSR: Zheleznaia doroga Komsomol'sk-Sovetskaia Gavan' 1930–40e gody.* Vladivostok: Izdatel'stvo Dal'nevostochnogo universiteta, 1995.

Engel, Barbara Alpern, and Anastasia Posadskaya-Vanderbeck. *A Revolution of Their Own: Voices of Women in Soviet History.* Translated by Sona Hoisington. Boulder, Colo.: Westview Press, 1998.

Fadeev, L. *BAM: Zolotoe zveno [Chitinskii uchastok]. Illiustrirovannyi spetsvypusk. Podgotovlen pravleniem Chitinskoi oblastnoi organizatsii Soiuza zhurnalistov SSSR.* Chita: Tipografiia uprpoligrafizdata, 1984.

Fedin, Vasilii M. *BAM—kuznitsa komsomol'skogo kharaktera.* Blagoveshchensk: Khabarovskoe knizhnoe izdatel'stvo, Amurskoe otdelenie, 1977.

————. *Vedushchaia sila BAMa: Partiinoe rukovodstvo stroitel'stvom Baikalo-Amurskoi magistrali.* Khabarovsk: Khabarovskoe knizhnoe izdatel'stvo, 1984.

Feshbach, Murray, and Alfred Friendly. *Ecocide in the USSR: Health and Nature under Siege.* New York: BasicBooks, 1992.

Filtzer, Donald. *Soviet Workers and Stalinist Industrialization: The Formation of Modern Soviet Production Relations, 1928–1941.* Armonk, N.Y.: M. E. Sharpe, 1986.

Foucault, Michel. *Discipline and Punish: The Birth of the Prison.* 2d edition. Translated by Alan Sheridan. New York: Vintage Books, 1995.

Fowkes, Ben. *The Disintegration of the Soviet Union: A Study in the Rise and Triumph of Nationalism.* New York: St. Martin's Press, 1997.

Gelman, Harry. *The Soviet Union in the Third World: A Retrospective Overview and Prognosis.* Santa Monica, Calif.: Rand/UCLA Center for the Study of Soviet International Behavior, 1986.

Glickman, Rose L. *Russian Factory Women: Workplace and Society, 1880–1914.* Berkeley: University of California Press, 1984.

Goldman, Wendy Z. *Women, the State, and Revolution: Soviet Family Policy and Social Life, 1917–1936.* New York: Cambridge University Press, 1993.

Gouré, Leon, and Morris Rothenberg. *Soviet Penetration of Latin America.* Washington, D.C.: Monographs in International Affairs, 1975.

Graham, Loren R. *The Ghost of the Executed Engineer: Technology and the Fall of the Soviet Union.* Cambridge: Harvard University Press, 1993.

Granberg, Aleksandr G., and Valerii V. Kuleshov. *Region BAM: Kontseptsiia razvitiia na novom etape.* Novosibirsk: Institut ekonomiki i organizatsii promyshlennogo proizvodstva, 1996.

Gray, Francine du Plessix. *Soviet Women: Walking the Tightrope.* New York: Anchor Books, 1990.

Grishina, Galina I. *BAM—stroika veka: Rekordnyi obzor literatury.* Moscow: Kniga, 1978.

Gullickson, Gay L. "Commentary: New Labor History from the Perspective of a Women's Historian." In Lenard R. Berlanstein, ed., *Rethinking Labor History.* Urbana: University of Illinois Press, 1993, 200–13.

Hanagan, Michael. "Commentary: For Reconstruction in Labor History." In Berlanstein, *Rethinking Labor History*, 182–99.

Hara, Kimie. *Japanese-Soviet/Russian Relations since 1945: A Difficult Peace.* London: Routledge, 1998.

Helgeson, Ann C. "Population and Labour Force." In Rodgers, *Soviet Far East*, 58–82.

Hobsbawm, Eric. *Primitive Rebels: Studies in Archaic Forms of Social Movement in the Nineteenth and Twentieth Centuries.* 3d edition. Manchester, England: Manchester University Press, 1971.

————. *Uncommon People: Resistance, Rebellion, and Jazz.* New York: New Press, 1998.

————, and Terence Ranger, eds. *The Invention of Tradition.* Cambridge: Cambridge University Press, 1983.

Horowitz, Donald J. "How to Begin Thinking Comparatively about Soviet Ethnic Problems." In Motyl, *Thinking Theoretically about Soviet Nationalities,* 9–22.

Humphrey, Caroline. "Buryats." In Graham Smith, ed., *The Nationalities Question in the Soviet Union.* London: Longman, 1990, 290–303.

Hunt, Lynn, ed. *The New Cultural History.* Berkeley: University of California Press, 1989.

Iakovlev, A. A. *Liudi BAMa: Zhivopis'. Al'bom.* Moscow: Sovetskii khudozhnik, 1986.

Iakovlev, Andrei. *Soprichastnost'.* Leningrad: Khudozhnik RSFSR, 1987.

Iakovleva, M. E. *BAM i Iakutiia. Rekordnyi ukazatel'.* Iakutsk: Iakutknigoizdat, 1977.

Ianitskii, Oleg N. *Ekologicheskoe dvizhenie v Rossii. Kriticheskii analiz.* Moscow: Rossiiskaia Akademia Nauk, Institut sotsiologii, 1996.

————, ed. *Ekologiia, demokratiia, molodezh'. Sbornik.* Moscow: Filosofskoe obshchestvo SSSR, Moskovskoe otdelenie, 1990.

Iliushchenko, Lidiia. *Ot Baikala do Amura: staroe, novoe, vechnoe.* Moscow: Molodaia gvardiia, 1984.

Ivanov, V. N., and P. I. Kapryrin. *Internatsional'naia gordost' narodov sotsialisticheskogo sodruzhestva: Sushchnost', istoki, osnovy.* Moscow: Nauka, 1984.

Johnson, Christopher H. "Lifeworld, System, and Communicative Action: The Habermasian Alternative in Social History." In Berlanstein, *Rethinking Labor History,* 55–89.

Josephson, Paul R. *New Atlantis Revisited: Akademgorodok, The Siberian City of Science.* Princeton, N. J.: Princeton University Press, 1997.

————. *Physics and Politics in Revolutionary Russia.* Berkeley: University of California Press, 1991.

————. *Red Atom: Russia's Nuclear Power Program from Stalin to Today.* New York: W. H. Freeman, 2000.

————. "Science and Technology as Panacea in Gorbachev's Russia." In James P. Scanlan, ed., *Technology, Culture, and Development: The Experience of the Soviet Model.* Armonk: M. E. Sharpe, 1992, 25–61.

————. *Totalitarian Science and Technology.* Atlantic Highlands, N.J.: Humanities Press, 1996.

Kagarlitsky, Boris. *The Thinking Reed: Intellectuals and the Soviet State, 1917 to the Present.* Translated by Brian Pierce. London: Verso, 1988.

Kaminskaia, L. P. *BAM—doroga druzhby: Dokumental'no-khudozhestvennyi sbornik. Zapiski, dnevniki, ocherki o stroitel'stve Baikalo-Amurskoi magistrali.* Irkutsk: Vostochno-Sibirskoe knizhnoe izdatel'stvo, 1984.

Kasischke, Eric S. *NASA Land Use and Land Cover Change Program: Effects of the Develop-ment and Disturbance on Boreal Forest Cover and Carbon Fluxes in Southern Siberia.* 1999.

————. *Environmental Working Group Boreal Forest Study: Effects of the Development of the Baikal-Amur Railway Railroad on Patterns of Boreal Forest Cover and Carbon Fluxes in Southern Siberia.* 1998.

Kavunenko, Oleksandr S. *Chervonyi pozd: Publitsystychna povist'-mozaka.* Kiev, Ukraine: Molod, 1987.

Kenez, Peter. *The Birth of the Propaganda State: Soviet Methods of Mass Mobilization, 1917–1929.* Cambridge: Cambridge University Press, 1985.

Kharchev, A. G., and S. I. Golod. *Professional'naia rabota zhenshchin i sem'ia: Sotsiologich-eskoe issledovanie.* Leningrad: Nauka, 1971.

Khitrov, M. N. *Sotsial'naia aktivnost' molodezhi i kommunisty.* Prague: Mir i sotsializm, 1975.

Khodza, Nison A. *Zvonkoe slovo BAM: Dokumental'nyi rasskaz.* Leningrad: Detskaia liter-atura, 1978.

Khripkova, A. G., and D. V. Kolesov. *Devochka—podrostok—devushka: Posobie dlia uchitelei.* Moscow: Prosveshchenie, 1981.

Kionka, Riina. "Estonians." In Smith, *Nationalities Question in the Soviet Union,* 40–53.

Klinghoffer, Arthur J. "The Soviet Union and Angola." In Donaldson, *Soviet Union in the Third World,* 97–124.

Klots, O. I., ed. *Regional'nye problemy bor'by s prestupnost'iu v period sovershenstvovaniia za-konodatel'stva: Mezhvuzovskii sbornik nauchnykh trudov.* Tyumen: Tiumenskii gosu-darstvennyi universitet, 1992.

Knabe, B. *Aktivitäten im Gebiet Baikal-See-Amur-Eisenbahn.* Cologne, Germany: Berichte des Bundesinstituts für ostwissenschaftlichte und internationale Studien, 1977.

Koenker, Diane. *Moscow Workers and the 1917 Revolution.* Princeton, N.J.: Princeton Uni-versity Press, 1981.

Kogatko, G. I. "Mify i real'nost'." In G. I. Kogatko, ed. *Doroga, kotoruiu ne vybirali.* Moscow: Izdatel'skii tsentr ROSS, 1993, 5–12.

————, ed. *Doroga, kotoruiu ne vybirali.* Moscow: Izdatel'skii tsentr ROSS, 1993.

Kolesov, L. I., and N. A. Ripinen, eds. *Edinaia transportnaia sistema zony BAM i problemy ekspluatatsii Baikalo-Amurskoi zheleznodorozhnoi magistrali.* Novosibirsk: Akademiia nauk SSSR, Sibirskoe otdelenie. Institut ekonomiki i organizatsii promyshlennogo proizvodstva, 1981.

Kolesova, S. "Magistral' druzhby." In *BAM—zemlia komsomol'skaia. Panorama vsenarodnoi stroiki. Vypusk chetvertyi—1977 god.* Khabarovsk: Khabarovskoe knizhnoe izdatel'stvo, 1978, 61–64.

Komarov, Boris [Zeev Wolfson]. *Unichtozhenie prirody: Obostrenie ekologicheskogo krizisa v SSSR.* Frankfurt: Possev-Verlag, 1978.

Komogortsev, I. I. *K istorii stroitelstva Baikalo-Amurskoi magistrali: Tezisy dokladov Vs-esoiuznoi nauchnoi konferentsii "Istoriia stroitelstva Baikalo-Amurskoi magistrali," 20–22 iiunia 1984 g.* Novosibirsk: Akademiia nauk SSSR. Sibirskoe otdelenie. Institut istorii, filologii i filosofii, 1984.

Koptyug, Valentin A., and Martin Uppenbrink, eds. *Sustainable Development of the Lake Baikal Region: A Model Territory for the World.* Berlin: Springer-Verlag, 1996.

Kostiuk, Vsevolod G., Magniia M. Traskunova, and David L. Konstantinovskii. *Molodezh' Sibiri: Obrazovanie i vybor professii.* Novosibirsk: Nauka, 1980.

Kotkin, Stephen. *Armageddon Averted: The Soviet Collapse, 1970–2000.* Oxford: Oxford University Press, 2001.

———. *Magnetic Mountain: Stalinism as Civilization.* Berkeley: University of California Press, 1995.

Krivoborskaia, Anna I., and Bairon Ishmuratov. *Prirodno-ekonomicheskii potentsial zony BAM: Geograficheskie aspekty.* Novosibirsk: Nauka, 1987.

Krylova, Z. P., et al., eds. *Sovetskaia zhenshchina—trud, materinstvo, sem'ia.* Moscow: Profizdat, 1987.

Kudriavtsev, V. N., ed. *Kriminal'naia motivatsiia.* Moscow: Nauka, 1986.

———. *Preduprezhdenie prestupnosti nesovershennoletnykh.* Moscow: Iuridicheskaia literatura, 1965.

Kuebart, Friedrich. "The Political Socialisation of Schoolchildren." In Jim Riordan, ed., *Soviet Youth Culture.* Bloomington: Indiana University Press, 1989, 103–21.

Kuznetsova, N. F. *Prestuplenie i prestupnost'.* Moscow: Izdatel'stvo Moskovskogo universiteta, 1969.

Lapidus, Gail W. *Women in Soviet Society: Equality, Development, and Social Change.* Berkeley: University of California Press, 1978.

———, ed. *Women, Work, and Family in the Soviet Union.* Translated by Vladimir Talmy. Armonk, N. Y.: M.E. Sharpe, 1982.

Lenoe, Matthew E. *Agitation, Propaganda, and the "Stalinization" of the Soviet Press, 1922–1930.* Pittsburgh: University of Pittsburgh Press, 1998.

———. *Closer to the Masses: Stalinist Culture, Social Revolution, and Soviet Newspapers.* Cambridge: Harvard University Press, 2004.

Levashov, Viktor, ed. *Zolotoe zveno: BAM, ot nulevogo kilometra do nashikh dnei. Rasskazy stroitelei.* Moscow: Molodaia gvardiia, 1982.

Lewin, Moshe. *The Gorbachev Phenomenon: A Historical Interpretation.* Berkeley: University of California Press, 1991.

Liubarskii, Anatolii V. *Rozhdenie velikogo soiuza: Dokumental'noe povestvovanie.* Moscow: Izdatel'stvo politicheskoi literatury, 1982.

Mandrinina, Liudmila A., Antonina A. Tikhoglasova, and A. A. Kin, eds. *Baikalo-Amurskaia magistral': Ukazatel' literatury, 1925–1974 gg.* Novosibirsk: Akademiianauk SSSR, Sibirskoe otdelenie, Gosudarstvennaia publichnnaia nauchno-tekhnicheskaia biblioteka, 1986.

Mankovskii, Viktor S. *BAM stroiat molodye.* Leningrad: Lenizdat, 1984.

Marks, Steven G. *Road to Power: The Trans-Siberian Railroad and the Colonization of Asian Russia, 1850–1917.* Ithaca, N. Y.: Cornell University Press, 1991.

Marx, Leo. *The Machine in the Garden: Technology and the Pastoral Ideal in America.* New York: Oxford University Press, 1964.

Massey Stewart, John. "Air and Water Problems beyond the Urals." In John Massey Stewart, ed., *The Soviet Environment: Problems, Policies, and Politics.* Cambridge: Cambridge University Press, 1992, 223–37.

McReynolds, Louise. *The News under Russia's Old Regime: The Development of a Mass-Circulation Press.* Princeton, N. J.: Princeton University Press, 1991.

Medvedeva, Liudmila M. *Trudovaia i politicheskaia aktivnost' stroitelei Baikalo-Amurskoi zheleznodorozhnoi magistrali, 1974–1984 gg.* Moscow: Nauka, 1988.

Meney, Patrick. *La Kleptocratie: La délinquance en URSS.* Paris: Éditions de Table Ronde, 1982.

Menon, Rajan. *Soviet Power and the Third World.* New Haven, Conn.: Yale University Press, 1986.

Mickiewicz, Ellen Propper. *Split Signals: Television and Politics in the Soviet Union.* New York: Oxford University Press, 1988.

Miller, Nicola. *Soviet Relations with Latin America, 1959–1987.* Cambridge: Cambridge University Press, 1989.

Minakir, Pavel A. *The Russian Far East: An Economic Handbook.* Translated by Gregory L. Freeze. Armonk, N. Y.: M. E. Sharpe, 1994.

Minogue, Kenneth, and Beryl Williams. "Ethnic Conflict in the Soviet Union: The Revenge of Particularism." In Motyl, *Thinking Theoretically about Soviet Nationalities,* 225–42.

Moshenko, O. A., ed. *BAM—budushchee Rossii.* Moscow: Rossiiskie zheleznye dorogi, 1999.

Mote, Victor L. *The Baikal-Amur Railway and Its Implications for the Pacific Basin.* Washington, D.C.: Association of American Geographers, 1980.

———. "BAM after the Fanfare: The Unbearable Ecumene." In Stewart, *Soviet Environment,* 40–56.

———. "The Baykal-Amur Railway: Catalyst for the Development of Pacific Siberia." In Theodore Shabad and Victor L. Mote, eds., *Gateway to Siberian Resources (The BAM).* New York: Scripta, 1977, 63–115.

———. *Case Study of the BAM and East Siberian Transport Capacity Problems.* Philadelphia: Wharton Econometric Forecasting Associates, 1982.

———. *Siberia: Worlds Apart.* Boulder, Colo.: Westview Press, 1998.

———. "The South Yakutian Territorial Production Complex." In Rodgers, *Soviet Far East,* 163–84.

Motyl, Alexander J. *Sovietology, Rationality, Nationality: Coming to Grips with Nationalism in the USSR.* New York: Columbia University Press, 1990.

Mukonin, V. I. "VKSh-BAM: doroga moei zhizni." In I. M. Il'inskii, ed., *Nash strazh i svetoch: K 30-letiiu Vysshei komsomol'skoi shkoly-Instituta molodezhi 1969–1999.* Moscow: Institut molodezhi, 1999, 209–25.

Nazarov, Viktor A. *Vertolety na Baikalo-Amurskoi magistrali.* Moscow: Transport, 1975.

Nedeshev, Aleksei A., et al., eds. *BAM i osvoenie Zabaikalia.* Novosibirsk: Nauka, 1979.

Neuberger, Joan. *Hooliganism: Crime, Culture, and Power in St. Petersburg, 1900–1914.* Berkeley: University of California Press, 1993.

Nogee, Joseph L., and Robert H. Donaldson. *Soviet Foreign Policy since World War II.* 4th edition. New York: Macmillan Publishing Company, 1992.

Novikova, E. E. *Zhenshchina v razvitom sotsialisticheskom obshchestve.* Moscow: Mysl', 1985.

Orlov, Valerii. *Druz'ia moi, tonnel'shchiki.* Ulan-Ude: Buriatskoe knizhnoe izdatel'stvo, 1983.

Pavlishin, G., and V. Sungorkin. *Navstrechu vremeni: Ot Baikala do Amura. Khudozhnik G. Pavlishin i zhurnalist V. Sungorkin o stroitel'stve BAMa.* Moscow: Sovetskaia Rossiia, 1985.

Pavlov, Mikhail. *The BAM Zone: Permanent Residents.* East Siberian Documentary Film Studio, 18 minutes, 1987.

Payne, Matthew J. *Stalin's Railroad: Turksib and the Building of Socialism.* Pittsburgh: University of Pittsburgh Press, 2001.

———. "Turksib: The Building of the Turkestano-Siberian Railroad and the Politics of Production during the Cultural Revolution, 1926–1931." Ph.D. dissertation, University of Chicago, 1995.

Pecheniuk, Iosif L., ed. *BAM, doroga sozidaniia*. Moscow: Sovetskaia Rossiia, 1983.

Peterson, D. J. *Troubled Lands: The Legacy of Soviet Environmental Destruction*. Santa Monica, Calif.: RAND Center for Russia and Eurasia, 1993.

Pike, Douglas. "The USSR and Vietnam." In Donaldson, *Soviet Union in the Third World*, 251–66.

Pilkington, Hilary, ed. *Gender, Generation, and Identity in Contemporary Russia*. London: Routledge, 1996.

———. "Russia and the Former Soviet Republics. Behind the Mask of Soviet Unity: Realities of Women's Lives." In Chris Corrin, ed., *Superwomen and the Double Burden: Women's Experience of Change in Central and Eastern Europe and the Former Soviet Union*. Toronto: Second Story Press, 1992, 180–235.

———. *Russia's Youth and Its Culture: A Nation's Constructors and Constructed*. London: Routledge, 1994.

Pohl, Michaela. "The Virgin Lands between Memory and Forgetting: People and Transformation in the Soviet Union, 1954–1960." Ph.D. dissertation, Indiana University, 1999.

Pozdyshev, S. I., et al., eds. *Muzei zheleznodorozhnykh voisk: Putevoditel'*. Moscow: Voennoe izdatel'stvo MO SSSR, 1980.

Prokhorov, A. "Konflikt svoego i chuzhogo v sovetskoi kul'ture 70-kh godov (na primere vizual'nykh reprezentatsii zhenshchin v zhurnale 'Ogonek')." In Valerii Tishkov, ed., *Sem'ia, gender, kul'tura: Materialy mezhdunarodnykh konferentsii 1994 i 1995 gg*. Moscow: Institut etnologii i antropologii RAN, 1997, 375–81.

Pryde, Philip R. and Victor L. Mote. "Environmental Constraints and Biosphere Protection in the Soviet Far East." In Rodgers, *Soviet Far East*, 36–57.

Raksha, Irina E. *An Unusual Journey*. Translated by Jan Butler. Moscow: Progress, 1980.

Raskin, Iosif. *Entsiklopediia khuliganstvuiushchego ortodoksa*. Moscow: Stook, 1997.

Rassweiler, Anne D. *The Generation of Power: The History of Dneprostroi*. New York: Oxford University Press, 1988.

Reichman, Henry. *Railwaymen and Revolution: Russia, 1905*. Berkeley: University of California Press, 1987.

Remnek, Richard B. "Soviet Policy in the Horn of Africa: The Decision to Intervene." In Donaldson, *Soviet Union in the Third World*, 125–49.

Rezun, Miron. *Science, Technology, and Ecopolitics in the USSR*. Westport, Conn.: Praeger, 1996.

Riordan, Jim. "The Komsomol." In Riordan, *Soviet Youth Culture*. Bloomington: Indiana University Press, 1989, 16–44.

Rubinstein, Alvin Z., ed. *Soviet and Chinese Influence in the Third World*. New York: Praeger, 1975.

Sanchez, James J. *The Baykal-Amur Railway: Soviet Power and the Opening of Trans-Baykalia to Regional Economic Development. An Annotated Bibliography*. Monticello, Ill.: Vance Bibliographies, 1986.

Scanlan, James P. *Marxism in the USSR: A Critical Survey of Current Soviet Thought*. Ithaca, N.Y.: Cornell University Press, 1985.

———, ed. *Russian Thought after Communism: The Recovery of a Philosophical Heritage*. Armonk, N.Y.: M. E. Sharpe, 1994.

———, ed. *Technology, Culture, and Development: The Experience of the Soviet Model*. Armonk, N.Y.: M. E. Sharpe, 1992.

Scott, James C. *Seeing Like a State: How Certain Schemes to Improve the Human Condition Have Failed.* New Haven, Conn.: Yale University Press, 1998.

Scott, Joan W. "On Gender, Language, and Working-Class History." In Joan W. Scott, ed., *Gender and the Politics of History.* New York: Columbia University Press, 1988, 53– 67.

Scott, John. *Behind the Urals: An American Worker in Russia's City of Steel.* Enlarged edition. Bloomington: Indiana University Press, 1989.

Sergeyev, Victor M. *The Wild East: Crime and Lawlessness in Post-Communist Russia.* Armonk, N.Y.: M. E. Sharpe, 1998.

Sewell, William H. "Toward a Post-Materialist Rhetoric for Labor History." In Berlanstein, *Rethinking Labor History,* 15–38.

Shabad, Theodore. "Siberia and the Soviet Far East Exploitation Policies in Energy and Raw Materials Sectors: A Commercial Assessment." In *Regional Development in the USSR: Trends and Prospects, Colloquium 25–27 April 1979, Brussels.* Newtonville, Mass.: Oriental Research Partners, 1979, 141–59.

Shinkarev, Leonid. *Vtoroi Transsib: Novyi etap osvoeniia vostochnykh raionov SSSR.* 2d edition. Moscow: Politizdat, 1979.

Shlapentokh, Vladimir. *Love, Marriage, and Friendship in the Soviet Union: Ideals and Practices.* New York: Praeger, 1984.

Siegelbaum, Lewis H. *Stakhanovism and the Politics of Productivity in the USSR, 1935–1941.* Cambridge: Cambridge University Press, 1988.

Slezkine, Yuri. *Arctic Mirrors: Russia and the Small Peoples of the North.* Ithaca, N.Y.: Cornell University Press, 1994.

Smith, Anthony D. "Ethnic Identity and Territorial Nationalism in Comparative Perspective." In Motyl, *Thinking Theoretically about Soviet Nationalities,* 45–65.

———. *Myths and Memories of the Nation.* Oxford: Oxford University Press, 1999.

———. *National Identity.* Reno: University of Nevada Press, 1991.

Smith, Graham. "Latvians." In Smith, *Nationalities Question in the Soviet Union,* 54–71.

———. "Nationalities Policy from Lenin to Gorbachev." In Smith, *Nationalities Question in the Soviet Union,* 1–20.

Sobolev, Iurii A. *Zona Baikalo-Amurskoi magistrali: Puti ekonomicheskogo razvitiia.* Moscow: Mysl', 1979.

Soktoeva, Inessa I., and Margarita V. Khabarova. *BAM postroen: Po materialam Vserossiiskoi khudozhestvennoi vystavki "Khudozhniki Sovetskoi Rossii—BAMu."* Leningrad: Khudozhnik RSFSR, 1987.

Starin, Boris S. *Sotsialisticheskoe sorevnovanie stroitelei BAMa, 1974–1984 gg.* Novosibirsk: Nauka, 1987.

Stephan, John. *The Russian Far East: A History.* Stanford, Calif.: Stanford University Press, 1994.

Stites, Richard. "World Outlook and Inner Fears in Soviet Science Fiction." In Loren R. Graham, ed., *Science and the Soviet Social Order.* Cambridge: Harvard University Press, 1990, 299–324.

Sukhanov, N. V. "BAM stroit vsia strana." In A. G. Aganbegian and A. A. Kin, eds., *BAM: Pervoe desiatiletie.* 2nd edition. Novosibirsk: Nauka, 1985, 44–62.

Suny, Ronald G. *The Revenge of the Past: Nationalism, Revolution, and the Collapse of the Soviet Union.* Stanford, Calif.: Stanford University Press, 1993.

Sushchevich, Valentin A. "Trudovaia i obshchestvenno-politicheskaia aktivnost' stroitelei

Baikalo-Amurskoi zheleznodorozhnoi magistrali, 1974–1984 gg." Candidate dissertation, Institute of History, Archeology, and Ethnography of the Peoples of the Far East, 1986.

———, and I. Ordzhonikidze, eds. *BAM: Fotoal'bom.* Moscow: Planeta, 1984.

Sverchkov, Vasilii I. *Internatsionalizm sibiriakov: Opyt i problemy (60-e-nachalo 80-kh gg.).* Irkutsk: Izdatel'stvo Irkutskogo universiteta, 1992.

Tanasevich, V. G., ed. *Preduprezhdenie khishchenii sotsialisticheskogo imushchestva. Deiatel'nost' sledovatelia, prokurora i suda.* Moscow: Iuridicheskaia literatura, 1969.

Ten, Valentin S. *Rukovodstvo KPSS protsessom sblizheniia natsii v usloviiakh razvitogo sotsializma (1959–1975 gg.).* Tashkent, Uzbekistan: Uzbekistan, 1981.

Thakur, Ramesh, and Carlyle A. Thayer. *Soviet Relations with India and Vietnam.* New York: St. Martin's Press, 1992.

Thompson, E. P. *Whigs and Hunters: The Origins of the Black Act.* London: Pantheon Books, 1975.

Thurston, Robert W. *Liberal City, Conservative State: Moscow and Russia's Urban Crisis, 1906–1914.* New York: Oxford University Press, 1987.

Tilly, Louise A., and Joan W. Scott. *Women, Work, and Family.* New York: Methuen, 1987.

Tirado, Isabel A. *Young Guard! The Communist Youth League, Petrograd, 1917–1920.* New York: Greenwood Press, 1988.

Tishkin, G. A. *Zhenskii vopros v Rossii (50—60-e gody XIX v.).* Leningrad: Izdatel'stvo Leningradskogo universiteta, 1984.

Tishkov, Valerii. *Ethnicity, Nationalism, and Conflict in and after the Soviet Union: The Mind Aflame.* London: Sage, 1997.

Tomina, Tatiana. "Pesnia—Tozhe oruzhie." In *BAM—zemlia komsomol'skaia. Panorama vsenarodnoi stroiki. Vypusk odinnadtsatyi—1983 god.* Blagoveshchensk: Khabarovskoe knizhnoe izdatel'stvo, Amurskoe otdelenie, 1984, 265–67.

———. "Vladek snova edet na BAM." In *BAM—zemlia komsomol'skaia,* 263–65.

Transchel, Kate. *Under the Influence: Drinking, Temperance, and Cultural Revolution in Russia, 1900–1932.* Pittsburgh: University of Pittsburgh Press, 2006.

Tsamerian, Ivan P. *Natsional'nye otnosheniia v SSSR.* Moscow: Nauka, 1987.

———. *Teoreticheskie problemy obrazovaniia i razvitiia sovetskogo mnogonatsional'nogo gosudarstva.* Moscow: Nauka, 1973.

Tsyrendorzhiev, S. S., ed. *Ot Baikala do Amura—sbornik.* Moscow: Sovremennik, 1986.

Tumarkin, Nina. *Lenin Lives! The Lenin Cult in Soviet Russia.* Cambridge: Harvard University Press, 1983.

———. *The Living and the Dead: The Rise and Fall of the Cult of World War II in Russia.* New York: BasicBooks, 1994.

United States-Russian Environmental Working Group. *EWG Forestry Project: Biryusa River Basin, Russia Test Site.* 1998.

———. *EWG Forestry Study—Biryusa River Basin, Usolsk Forest Study Site. Study 4—Analysis of Long-term Change.* 1998.

———. *EWG Forestry Study—Biryusa River Basin, Usolsk Forest Study Site. Study 5—Monitoring of Forest Health.* 1998.

University of Texas at Austin. "China-USSR Border: Eastern Sector." *Perry-Castañeda Library Map Collection. Russia and the Former Soviet Republics Maps.* 2001. Courtesy of the General Libraries, University of Texas at Austin. Available online at http://www.lib .utexas.edu/maps/middle_east_and_asia/china_ussr_e_88.jpg. Accessed on July 10, 2007.

————. "Japan-USSR Border: Northern Territories." *Perry-Castañeda Library Map Collection. Japan Maps.* 2001. Courtesy of the General Libraries, University of Texas at Austin. Available online at http://www.lib.utexas.edu/maps/middle_east_and_asia/japan_ussr_rel88.jpg. Accessed on July 10, 2007.

————. "Russia." *Perry-Castañeda Library Map Collection. Russia and the Former Soviet Republics Maps.* 2001. Courtesy of the General Libraries, University of Texas at Austin. Available online at http://www.lib.utexas.edu/maps/commonwealth/russia_autonomous92.jpg. Accessed on July 19, 2007.

Vardys, V. Stanley. "Lithuanians." In Smith, *Nationalities Question in the Soviet Union,* 54–71.

Vasilev, Mikhail I. *Turistskie marshruty Zapadnogo BAMa.* Moscow: Fizkul'tura i sport, 1984.

"Viewpoints on the Possibility of a Soviet-Chinese War." In Cohen, *An End to Silence,* 235–39.

Vikulov, Valerian E. *BAM i mineral'nye resursy severa Buriatii.* Ulan-Ude: Buriatskoe knizhnoe izdatel'stvo, 1976.

Volkov, V. O., and V. A. Savin. "Mezhdunarodnoe sotrudnichestvo v sozdanii Ust'-Ilimskogo lesopromyshlennogo kompleksa." In Aganbegian and Kin, *BAM: Pervoe desiatiletie,* 163–69.

Walkowitz, Judith R. *Prostitution and Victorian Society: Women, Class, and the State.* Cambridge: Cambridge University Press, 1980.

Ward, Chris. *Russia's Cotton Workers and the New Economic Policy: Shop-Floor Culture and State Policy, 1921–1929.* Cambridge: Cambridge University Press, 1990.

Weiner, Douglas R. *A Little Corner of Freedom: Russian Nature Protection from Stalin to Gorbachev.* Berkeley: University of California Press, 1999.

————. *Models of Nature: Ecology, Conservation, and Cultural Revolution in Soviet Russia.* Bloomington: Indiana University Press, 1988.

Whiting, Allen S. *Siberian Development and East Asia: Threat or Promise?* Stanford, Calif.: Stanford University Press, 1981.

Wolf, William K. "Russia's Revolutionary Underground: The Construction of the Moscow Subway, 1931–1935." Ph.D. dissertation, Ohio State University, 1994.

Wood, Elizabeth A. *The Baba and the Comrade: Gender and Politics in Revolutionary Russia.* Bloomington: Indiana University Press, 1997.

XIX s"ezd Vsesoiuznogo Leninskogo Kommunisticheskogo Soiuza Molodezhi, 18–21 maia 1982 goda. Stenograficheskii otchet. Volume 1. Moscow: Molodaia gvardiia, 1982.

XVII s"ezd Vsesoiuznogo Leninskogo Kommunisticheskogo Soiuza Molodezhi, 23–27 aprelia 1974 goda. Stenograficheskii otchet. Volume 1. Moscow: Molodaia gvardiia, 1975.

XXII s"ezd Kommunisticheskoi Partii Sovetskogo Soiuza. Stenograficheskii otchet. Moscow: Izdatel'stvo politicheskoi literatury, 1961.

Yates, Athol. *Siberian BAM Railway Guide: The Second Trans-Siberian Railway.* Hindhead, U.K.: Trailblazer Publications, 1995.

Zarubezhnye molodezhnye organizatsii. Moscow: Molodaia gvardiia, 1985.

Zelenchuk, Valentin S., and M. N. Guboglo. *Natsional'noe i internatsional'noe v sovetskom obraze zhizni.* Chisinau, Moldova: Shtiintsa, 1979.

Zhelezko, Sergei N. *Sotsial'no-demograficheskie problemy v zone BAMa.* Moscow: Statistika, 1980.

Zhitov, K. E., et al., eds. *Velikaia sila druzhby narodov. Sbornik statei.* Tashkent, Uzbekistan: Uzbekistan, 1973.

Zhuravlev, Vladimir. *Reportazh o BAMe.* Moscow: Mysl', 1976.

———. *Skazanie o BAMe.* Moscow: Mysl', 1976.

ZumBrunnen, Craig. "The Lake Baikal Controversy: A Serious Water Pollution Threat or a Turning Point in Soviet Environmental Consciousness?" In Ivan Volgyes, ed., *Environmental Deterioration in the Soviet Union and Eastern Europe.* New York: Praeger, 1974, 80–122.

INDEX

Bulgaria, 126, 147; Bulgarians, 144, 147
Bureau of International Youth Tourism, 126, 129–30
Buriat Autonomous Region. *See* Buriat Autonomous Soviet Socialist Republic
Buriat Autonomous Soviet Socialist Republic, 5, 17, 27, 29, 31–32, 89; authorities in, 22; Council of Ministers of, 21; female population of, 90; Komsomol organization in, 115–17; tunneling brigades in, 78; VOOP members in, 32
Buriat BAM Segment, 19, 22; Komsomol headquarters in, 31
Buriats, 37, 101, 114, 163nn103–4

cafeterias, 76, 88–89, 91, 113
capitalism, 42, 45, 71–72, 76, 102
Caribbean, 130, 135
Castro, Fidel, 130, 136–37
Caucasians, 108, 111, 113, 120, 123–24
Caucasus, 105, 107, 111, 115; BAM participants from, 108, 111, 116, 118, 122; ethnic groups in, 108; multi-nationalism among residents of, 111; national consciousness in, 104; population of, 102; shock brigades from, 116; states of, 101
Central Asia, 4, 101–2, 106–7, 111, 114–16, 122; Central Asians, 108, 111, 120
Central BAM Segment, 19, 36, 48, 117
Central Committee. *See* CPSU Central Committee
Chechens, 110, 118
Chernobyl, 38
childcare, 71–74, 88, 90, 92
children, 33, 43, 50, 64, 79, 88, 90, 96, 155; of BAMers, 43; and families, 64, 72; female, 79; militias of, 49; multiple births of, 71; newspapers for, 51; patriarchal policies and, 71–72; positive image of BAM among, 79; of prominent individuals, 44; relationship with the Komsomol, 50; in Tynda, 33. *See also druzhiny*; schoolchildren
Chile, 135, 138–39, 144; Chileans, 138–40, 142
China. *See* People's Republic of China
Chinese, 5–6, 80, 127, 148–49, 153
Chita, 36–37
Chita Oblast, 16–17
Chudnovskii, O., 81–82
Churaeva, Liubov, 77–78, 80
class, 100–101, 122. *See also* laboring classes
clubs, 15, 47, 54–56, 91. *See also* leisure
collectives, 48, 64, 112, 139, 153
collectivization of agriculture, 72, 102

command-administrative system, 2, 7
Commission to Combat Drunkenness and Alcoholism. *See* Anti-Drunkenness and Alcoholism Commission
Communism, 10, 133; attainment of, 10, 153; BAM as path to, 28, 43, 46; BAM as promised land of, 9; BAMer women as shock troops of, 76; building of, 80, 109, 152; Khrushchev's declaration of attainment by 1980, 10; *sliianie* and, 102; young people as constructors of, 68
Communists: in Cuba, 136; in Japan, 133; in West Germany, 65
"Communist morality," 28, 42, 44–48, 67, 83
Communist Party of the Soviet Union (CPSU), 4, 8, 13, 38, 150, 152; Amur Oblast council of, 79; "environmental discipline" and, 32; Great Purges and, 4; Josef Stalin and, 102; membership in, 93; officials within, 11; organization of, 159n1; outlawing of, 23; Prometheanism in publications of, 15; reports of criminal activity by, 47; swearing of oaths to, 75; upper echelons of, 5; Verbitskii affair and, 65; Women's Bureau of, 71
"Comrade Afanaseva," 85–86
conservationism, 12; conservationists, 14, 19, 41; official rejection of, 41
corruption, 47, 62, 64, 66–67, 128
Cossacks, 76
cotton, 4, 123
Council of Ministers. *See* USSR Council of Ministers
CPSU. *See* Communist Party of the Soviet Union
CPSU Central Committee, 19, 20–22, 33; archives of, 23; *nomenklatura* and, 103; resolutions of, 33, 35
criminal activity, 3, 43–47, 54, 68, 132, 152; fencing (sale of stolen property), 62–63; petty crimes, 3, 47, 49, 51–52, 55, 61, 118; theft, 3, 45, 51–52, 58, 60–63, 67, 116
criminals, 45, 52, 67, 116
criminology, 44–45, 49
Cuba, 9, 77, 92, 126, 130–32, 135–36; Cubans, 130–32, 136–37, 140
Czechoslovakia, 9–10, 126; Czechoslovak Communist Party, 140; Czechoslovaks, 140–42, 144, 147; Soviet invasion of, 103

Dagestan, 115, 118, 123
Danilova, Vladilena, 76
Davidow, Mike, 64

Davydchik, Tamara, 57
Denisova, Tatiana, 92–96
Department for Combating Theft of Socialist
    Property (OBKhSS), 62–63
"developed socialism," 10, 73, 103, 150, 153
deviancy, 43, 45–46, 53, 59, 67–68
"discipline days," 49, 55
divorce, 73, 77, 155
Dneprostroi hydroelectric dam, 4, 14, 154, 158n13
dormitories, 54, 77; assaults in, 91; BAMers in,
    53; construction of, 66, 81, 111, 129, 131, 140,
    143; criminal activities in, 54; fires in, 57; sale
    of stolen goods in, 63; sexual harassment in,
    57; in Shimanovsk, 56; in Tynda, 80; women
    in, 59, 91. See also living conditions
Doronin, 89
Dresden, 129, 146
Druzhba (organization), 92, 126, 128, 130–31, 133
drunkenness. See intoxication
druzhiny (volunteer patrollers), 32, 49–52, 57
Dymova, M., 82
Dzerzhinskii, Feliks Edmundovich, 50–51
Dzerzhinskiites. See Young Dzerzhinskiite
    Youth Movement

Eastern BAM Segment, 19, 28, 148
Eastern Europe, 11, 45
Eastern Siberia, 12, 122; BAMers from, 116;
    building of Communism in, 152; ecology
    of, 13; Far East and, 6; forests in, 19; riches
    of, 11, 16; Soviet military and economic
    might in, 148; taiga of, 43; topographical
    and geological conditions of, 149
East Germany, 9, 92, 126, 129, 132, 135, 140–41;
    East Germans, 127, 129, 140–42, 144, 146
ecology: of Amur Oblast, 80; of the BAM
    Zone, 12, 37, 39, 152; of Eastern Siberia, 13;
    ecologists, 41; of Lake Baikal, 20, 156; of the
    Soviet Far East, 13
education, 41, 100, 109–10, 144; ecology and, 39;
    environment and, 24–25, 35, 38; foreigners
    and, 145, 149; ideology and, 45; low levels
    of among Armenian BAMers, 106, 110;
    native languages and, 101; reform of, 71;
    Russification in, 103; science and, 10;
    under-representation of non-Slavs in, 104,
    106; use of propaganda in, 15; vocational
    training and, 134, 145; women and, 78, 82
Efimov, E. A., 62
Eighteenth Komsomol Congress Pacesetting
    Brigade, 55, 89
electricity, 16, 43, 65; and electrocution, 54, 112;
    and electronics, 11, 60, 62, 133, 145

environmental consciousness, 13–14, 20, 23, 26, 31
environmentalism, 3, 18, 23, 30, 34–35, 41
environmentalists, 13–15, 18, 30, 34, 41
"environmental propaganda," 22, 26, 34
environmental protection group (EPG), 30–31
Eremenko, Olga, 39–40
Ermolaev, P., 35
Esquina, José, 136–37
Estonia. See Estonian Soviet Socialist Republic
Estonians, 106, 108
Estonian Soviet Socialist Republic, 9, 63, 89,
    102, 105–8, 115
Ethiopia, 144, 175n5
Eurasia, 11, 127
Europe, 100, 102
European USSR, 81; and BAM as link from
    and to the east, 6, 153–54; deportation of
    nationalities from, 102; industries of, 59,
    67; journalists and officials based in, 11, 18;
    trade with Pacific Rim, 127
Evenk, 37, 163n103

Fadeev, L., 110–11
Family Code of 1918, 71
Far East. See Russian Far East
fauna, 25–26, 82; damage to, 35; danger to,
    posed by BAM construction, 18; fate of
    along BAM route, 13; green zones and, 28;
    protection of, 39; USSR as defender of, 23
Fedina, S., 113
feminism, 71
Filippov, Dmitrii, 65, 115, 121
film, 24, 48, 131
flora, 13, 18, 25, 39, 82
forest fires, 19–20, 28, 31
former Soviet Union (USSR). See Russian
    Federation
"For Participation in BAM Construction"
    award, 91, 113–14
Friendship Brigade. See International Student
    Construction Brigade

Gaeva, Z., 35
Galmakov, Iurii V.: accidental worker deaths
    and, 54; anti-drunkenness efforts and, 56;
    apology for behavior of BAMers in East
    Germany, 129; Buriat BAM Segment and,
    31; campaign against absenteeism and apa-
    thy, 63; criticism of Ivan Rekhlov, 131; in-
    vestigation of automobile thefts and, 61;
    investigation of forest fires and, 31
gender, 73–74, 88, 100; division of *druzhiny* by,
    51; dynamic of during Brezhnev years, 70;

Iran, 104, 113
Irkutsk, 18–19, 26, 36–38, 66–67
Irkutsk Oblast, 5, 20, 111, 123; Komsomol organization in, 25, 67
Islam, 103–104, 108, 113
Izvestiia (newspaper), 15–17, 110–11, 113, 135

Japan, 5, 60, 62, 65, 127, 132–34; Japanese, 5, 133–34, 149; Japanese Communist Party, 133
Jewish Autonomous Oblast, 113–14
Jews, 113–14
jokes. *See* humor
journalists, 2, 18, 39, 91, 112, 140, 144; *Amurskii Komsomolets* and, 23; in BAM Zone, 14, 23, 112; Buriat Autonomous Soviet Socialist Republic and, 17; characterizations of BAMers as trailblazers and, 16; Denisova Affair and, 94–95; ecological issues and, 23; environmental debate and, 13–14; from foreign countries, 135; Gudok and, 111; indigenous groups and, 37; *Izvestiia* and, 16; newspaper *BAM* and, 113; portrayal of women by, 75–77, 81–82; *Pravda* and, 16; Prometheanism and, 16–18; promotion of BAM as a multinational endeavor, 112; and promotion of BAM as savior of the Soviet economy, 156; and promoters of BAM's virtue, 7; and promotion of life in Siberia, 145; recruitment of women by, 80; scientific–technical revolution and, 11; unification theme and, 110; VOOP and, 26; as witnesses of environmental destruction, 18

Kaminskaia, L. P., 122
Karamyshev, A. A., 46
Karpikov, Aleksandr V., 18, 22
Kashirskii, A. N., 54–55
Kaskapov, Khamat, 110
Kasischke, Eric, 19
Kazakhstan, 4, 9, 80, 106, 115
Kazakov, E., 60–61
Keler, Franz, 135
KGB (*Komitet gosudarstvennoi bezopastnosti*) (Committee for State Security), 50, 104
Khabarovsk, 19, 37–38, 56
Khabarovsk Krai, 5, 24; CPSU organization in, 85, 133; LOVD organization in, 53
Khakhanov, G., 53
Khrushchev era, 4, 103
Khrushchev, Nikita S., 4, 10, 72, 103, 151
Kichera, 55, 64
Kishinev, 141
Kniazev, A. D., 142–43

Kokhan, E., 83
Kolesnikov, Aleksandr, 52
Kollontai, Aleksandra, 71
Komarov, Boris (pseudonym). *See* Wolfson, Zeev
Komarova, Larisa, 78
Komsomol (All-Union Leninist Communist Youth League), 58, 88, 115, 131–32, 143, 152, 158n23; ages of members, 74, 133; agitational-propaganda trains and, 128, 142; announcement of BAM construction by, 6; archives of, 29, 36, 61, 85, 111, 120, 123, 133, 142, 159n1; Armenia and, 106, 117, 123; Azerbaijan and, 117, 123; BAMstroiput and, 48; BAM Zone organizations of, 38, 55, 62–63, 84; Belorussia and, 120; Bulgaria and, 147; bureaucracy of, 31, 55, 67–68, 74, 89, 95, 104, 114, 116, 125, 131–32, 134; Buriat ASSR and, 115–16; Central Committee of, 24, 27, 35, 38, 42, 48, 61, 65, 113, 120–21, 126, 146; Central Committee BAM Construction Headquarters of, 20, 23, 25, 27, 30, 32, 41, 48–49, 61–62, 64, 85–86, 89, 92, 94–95, 98–99, 106, 118, 120, 125, 128–29, 131, 136, 139, 142, 147; chaperones within, 130; Chile and, 138–39; conservationism within, 18, 38; criminal activity by members, 46–47, 52, 63–64, 123; criteria for membership, 44, 115; criticism by, 116; criticism of, 38–39; cruises abroad organized by, 131; Cuba and, 136; Czechoslovakia and, 147; deficiencies of, 44, 48, 90, 149–50; Denisova Affair and, 92–96; *druzhiny* and, 49–52; elite formations within, 89, 105–6, 108; "environmental discipline" and, 32; environmentalism within, 13, 36; ethnic composition of, 104, 106; expulsion from, 61, 64–65, 93, 123; former members of, 83, 94, 116, 118, 120; Georgia and, 122; "I Am the Master of the Project" campaign and, 132; labor organization and, 10, 63; Latvia and, 107, 119; leadership of, 46, 85; loyalty to, 75; members as percentage of BAMers, 8; members of in VOOP, 24; Moldavia and, 117; Moscow and, 120, 141; national minorities and, 109–10; newspapers of, 79, 113, 142, 145; non-Slavs within, 115, 119; petitioning of, 59, 85; policing activities of, 47–49; promotion of BAM abroad by, 133–34; propaganda use by, 42–43, 78, 94; recruitment efforts by, 59–60, 119–20, 149; rehabilitation efforts by, 49; responsibilities of, 8, 43–44; RSFSR and, 120–21; self-regulation

Molodaia gvardiia (publishing house), 84, 137–38

Mongolia, 127, 141; Mongolians, 141, 144

Monina, Valentina, 79

morality, 31–32, 46, 48, 50–51, 67

Moroz, V., 104–5

Morozov, N., 33–34. *See also* VOOP

Moscow, 56, 81, 95, 153; administrators in, 13, 66, 77, 99, 104–5, 109, 113–14, 129,156; BAM's distance from, 2, 124; BAM supporters in, 124–25, 153; brigades from, 121, 129; bureaucracy in, 41; Bureau of International Youth Tourism and, 129; CPSU Central Committee in, 103; directives from, 22; Japan and, 133; journalists in, 17, 25, 93, 156; Komsomol Central Committee in, 48, 61, 146; Komsomol headquarters in, 24, 54, 65–66, 85–86, 95, 106, 125, 141; lack of awareness in, 145; Lake Baikal Environmental Committee and, 22–23; metro system, 4, 157n12; MVD headquarters in, 47; officials in, 11, 13, 17–18, 25, 38; Patrice Lumumba Peoples' Friendship University in, 143–44; Prometheanism and, 23; Seventeenth Komsomol Congress in, 16; Seventeenth Komsomol Congress Brigade and, 107; tension between other regions and, 105; Trans-Siberian Railway and, 5; travel to, 64; visit of Kakuei Tanaka to, 133; visit of Salvador Allende to, 138; VOOP and, 24

Moscow News (newspaper), 1, 152

Mosgidrotrans. *See* bridges; USSR Ministry of Transportation

Moskovskii komsomolets (newspaper), 142, 145

Mostostroi-9. *See* bridges

Mostransstroi. *See* bridges; USSR Ministry of Transportation

motorcycles, 62

Mozambique, 9, 175n5

Mukonin, Vladimir, 136–37

Murashova, Liubov, 81–82

Musalitin, Boris, 75–76

Muslims, 103, 110, 115. *See also* Islam

murder, 3, 39, 51, 123

MVD (*Ministerstvo vnutrennikh del*). *See* USSR Ministry of Internal Affairs

MZhK (*molodezhnie zhilie kompleksy*). *See* dormitories

Nasrullaev, Nikolai, 109

NATO (North Atlantic Treaty Organization), 21, 135

Nazis, 102, 105

Neriungri, 40, 122–23

Nesterova, Nina, 78

newspapers, 8, 38–39, 51, 89, 109–110, 141

Nicaragua, 135, 138

Nigeria, 144

Niia, 111, 118

Nikitin, Nikolai V., 18, 20, 23, 47, 62, 89, 127

Nineteenth Komsomol Congress BAM Construction Brigade, 107–8, 118

Nizhneangarsk, 63–64, 66

Nizhneangarsktransstroi, 63–64, 66, 115, 145. *See also* USSR Ministry of Transportation

nomenklatura (high-level officials), 103

North Korea, 65, 131

North Muisk Tunnel, 22, 57, 61, 84, 156

North Muya Tunnel. *See* North Muisk Tunnel

North Ossetia, 114, 119

NOT (*nauchnaia organizatsiia truda*). *See* "scientific organization of labor"

Novaya Zemlya, 38

Novosibirsk, 36

oil, 21–22, 29, 36, 57

Olekma River, 7, 36

omul (fish species), 26

Order of Lenin, 89–90, 120

Osokina, Natalia, 93–95

Pacific Ocean, 7, 11

Pacific Rim, 11, 67, 127

panacea, 2, 7, 11, 41, 67, 152

Panchenko, Galina, 84

The Party. *See* Communist Party of the Soviet Union (CPSU)

"Path to the Future" (*Put k budushchemu*): Armenians and, 113; BAMers and, 43; Brezhnev's conception of, 10; deficiencies of, 150; fate of, 156; portrayal of BAM as, 6, 151; Slavs and, 99; Soviet will to build, 153; women and, 96; young people and, 33

patriarchy, 70–73, 86, 97

Patrice Lumumba Peoples' Friendship University, 143–44, 178n67

People's Republic of China: attack on Vietnam by, 176n20; construction of BAM to impress, 126; ideological rivalry between Soviet Union and, 135, 144; relations between Soviet Union and, 80, 135, 144, 147–49; Russian border with, 7

permafrost: battle with nature and, 17; building methods and, 118; destruction of, 41; difficulties of rail-laying on, 37; ecology of, 13, 26, 35; melting of, 156; taiga and, 159n27

petroleum, 11, 18, 26, 36, 40

Petruk, Iurii, 144–45
Philippines, 65, 131
Pobozhii, A., 76
Poland, 9, 102, 105, 127, 132, 170n76; Poles, 142, 144
Poleshak, Vladimir, 42, 64
Politburo, 19–20
pollution, 20–22, 26, 29–30, 34, 39, 154. *See also* soil; water pollution
Popov, V., 140–41, 142
Postnikov, D. G., 50, 52
post-Soviet period, 3, 8, 68, 100, 156
Pravda (newspaper), 15–17, 113
Prikhodko, Valentin, 121
Privalov, K., 142, 145
"Project of the Century" (*Stroika veka*), 27, 44, 135, 151–52; conception of BAM as, 4; exclusion of Chinese youth from, 127; official portrayal of BAM as, 6; promotion of, 99; women and, 70
Prokhorov, B., 16–17
Prometheanism: adherence to, 15; BAM as vanguard of, 12; environmental propaganda and, 22; expression of in post-Stalin era, 2, 7; language of, 16–18, 24; propaganda and, 22; qualities of in BAM, 13; rejection of, 3; rhetoric of, 23; state use of, 15, 18, 23, 40; theme of, 41; triumph of over nature, 76, 141
propaganda: common themes of, 10; development of, 15; disparity between reality and, 3; goals of, 138; history of, 157n6; Komsomol and, 38, 42, 46, 99; multinationalism and, 134; official campaign of, 2–3, 46, 69, 150, 152–55; as officially generated apparatus, 12; purpose of, 15; stagnation of, 155; system of, 2, 69, 98, 126; Tynda and, 20; women and, 78, 80, 83, 86. *See also* "environmental propaganda"
propagandists: utopianism and, 2, 16–17, 75–76, 82, 148
prostitution, 59–60, 71
"punished peoples," 102

quotas, 61; building, 14; construction, 29, 40, 116, 118, 129; earth-moving, 118; exceeding, 55; production, 128, 131; recruitment, 114, 121

radio, 38, 64, 85, 110
Radtke, Kirsten, 146
Railway Construction Directorate. See USSR Ministry of Transportation.

railway workers, 8, 35, 108. *See also* Union of Professional Railway Workers
rape, 58–60; attempted, 55; BAMer participation in, 3; frequency of, 45, 51, 67; high rates of, 47; nature and, 41; threats of, 57, 91; unreported cases of, 58
Raspopova, Nina, 78
rehabilitation, 45, 49
religion, 104–5, 108, 113, 125
Romania, 127
romanticism, 42, 81
Rostovshchikova, Liudmila, 91
RSFSR. *See* Russian Soviet Federated Socialist Republic
RSFSR Council of Ministers, 19, 24, 54
RSFSR Ministry of Forestry, 19–20, 33–34
Russian Civil War, 3, 17
Russian Empire, 3–5, 101–2
Russian Far East, 1, 12, 109; Eastern Siberia and, 6; economic integration of, 76, 152; forest cover in, 19; interest in BAM in, 156; opening of, 153; rivers of, 7; RSFSR and, 80; taiga of, 43. *See also* Soviet Far East
Russian Federation, 7, 11, 15, 21–23, 156, 158n26
Russian language, 134, 144
Russian nationalism, 99, 102
Russian Republic. *See* Russian Soviet Federated Socialist Republic
Russians, 107; BAM bureaucracy and, 104; BAMer origins of, 8–9; elite units and, 107; multinational brigades and, 117; percentage of in BAM workforce, 8; population reduction of, 103; relations between non-Slavs and, 99; Russification and, 104
Russian Soviet Federated Socialist Republic (RSFSR), 107, 115; administrative regions outside of, 104; BAMers from, 8; cities in, 121; forest fires and, 19–20; Komsomol and, 120–21; ministries of, 38; Muslim regions within, 115; Slavs from outside of, 106; women from, 77, 80, 83
Russification, 103–4
Rwanda, 144–45

Santiago de Cuba, 131, 136–37
Sarkisian, Pavel, 111
Save the Birch campaign, 27–28, 31
schoolchildren, 27, 31–33, 41, 52, 58
"scientific organization of labor," 54
"scientific-technical revolution," 10–11
scientists, 7, 13–15, 23, 37–38
Sechkovskii, Marek, 76
Second World War. *See* World War II

Verbitskii Affair. *See* Verbitskii, Iurii
Videoton electronics factory, 145–46
Vietnam, 65, 127, 131, 176n20
Virgin Lands Campaign, 4, 6–7, 14
Vitiaz (labor detachment), 142–43, 145
vodka, 56–57. *See also* alcoholism
Volga River, 14
volunteerism, 24, 47, 69, 78, 80, 87, 120, 135
volunteers: from Argentina, 138; Armenian, 106, 114; from Azerbaijan, 114; Caucasian and Central Asian, 111; from Cuba, 136; from Dagestan, 115; *druzhiny* as, 32; from East Germany, 140; from Georgia, 114; green patrollers as, 32; Komsomol and, 121; from North Ossetia, 114; Order of Lenin recipients and, 120; recruitment of, 48, 119; RSFSR and, 121; shortages of, 116, 146; from Turkmenistan, 115; from Uzbekistan, 115; Western BAM Segment and, 119; women, 69, 78, 80–81, 87
VOOP (*Vserossiiskoe obshchestvo okhrany prirody*) (All-Russian Society for the Protection of Nature), 24, 41; Amur Oblast, 24, 33; blue patrols and, 31, 33; Buriat ASSR, 32; Central Council of, 38; environmentalism and, 26, 33; green patrols and, 31, 33; N. Morozov and, 33–34; North Baikal and, 33–34; Russian Federation, 38; Tynda, 32–33
Vorobeva, Lidiia, 83
Voronezh, 55, 109
vouchers: apartment, 9; automobile, 9, 48, 60, 62, 64 119, 122, 127, 154–55
Vozin, V., 40

Waganda, Michael, 144
Warsaw Pact, 9, 135, 140, 142, 149
water pollution, 26, 39
watersheds, 6, 21
Weiner, Douglas, 14–15, 24
Western BAM Segment, 19, 27, 66, 119, 129
Western Europe, 3, 45, 71, 127
Western Siberia, 18, 85
West Germany, 17, 65, 135
Wolfson, Zeev (pseudonym Boris Komarov), 17–19
"women's question," 69–74
working conditions, 86, 91, 141, 147
World Festival of Youth and Students, 136–37
World War II, 44, 69, 71, 78, 102, 121

Yakutsk. *See* Iakutsk
Yevtushenko, Yevgeny, 7. See also *Bratsk Station*
Young Dzerzhinskiite Youth Movement, 50–52
youth housing projects. *See* dormitories

Zaichek, Vladek, 140–41
zastoi (stagnation), 3, 155, 157n7
Zbrueva, Anna, 77
Zeia River, 7, 16
Zhenbao (Damanskii) Island, 148. *See also* Sino-Soviet split
Zhuravlev, Vladimir, 112–13
Znanie (All-Union Knowledge Society), 32, 148
Zolotinka, 81, 117
Zueva, Nina, 85
ZumBrunnen, Craig, 20–21
Zvezdnyi (agitational train), 128–29
Zvezdnyi (settlement), 17, 30, 54, 76, 111, 141

Made in the USA
Columbia, SC
11 January 2019